The Backpacker who sold h*is* Supercar

A road map to achieving your dream life

PATRICK HAMILTON WALSH

Order this book online at www.trafford.com
or email orders@trafford.com

Most Trafford titles are also available at major online book retailers.

Printed in the United States of America.

ISBN: 978-1-4907-1779-1 (sc)
ISBN: 978-1-4907-1778-4 (e)

Trafford rev. 11/25/2013

 www.trafford.com

North America & international
toll-free: 1 888 232 4444 (USA & Canada)
fax: 812 355 4082

Table of Contents

S ociety tells me that I am a white 33-year-old Catholic male from a working class family in Northern Ireland. What society does not know about me is that I live the life of my dreams.

The nice people that I meet on a daily basis often wonder how I came to live this life. They often ask me *"Did you win the lottery?"* *"Do you have rich parents?"* *"Did a rich uncle leave you a big inheritance?"* and many other questions to that affect. To be able to answer *"Yes"* to any of these questions would be nice, but the fact is I was not born with a silver spoon in my mouth and no one handed me this life on a plate. Quite the contrary.

In fact, I am a child of *"The Troubles,"* a period from 1969 to 1998 when Northern Ireland became embroiled in the worst ethno-political violence in Europe. During this time, bullets and bombs killed a total of 3,524 people in my community. These were pretty grim times but it was all I knew, it was how my world was and I look back on my childhood fondly.

So, how did a boy from the wrong side of the tracks come to design and live the life of his dreams? In this book, I plan to show you the very simple method that I used. To prove that this method works, I will then provide you with an insight into some of the great experiences that I have lived through and what I plan for the future.

However, it must be stressed that this book does not provide a one-size-fits-all short cut to living the life of your dreams. I admit up front that I had to work hard to get into the position where I had the confidence to confront and overcome life's challenges. What I will promise you is that a little bit of focused thought, followed by the determination to achieve your first goal, can lead to the first step on the *Ladder* to a better life.

My desire is that, by following the simple process that I outline and gaining an insight into the resulting life experiences I have been able to live, you will be inspired to take similar steps that will allow you too to escape the rat race and go on to live the life of your dreams.

My outlook is that life is not about finding oneself, but about creating our best self through striving for advancement. I have always held the belief that the people that achieved success did so simply because they chose to be successful, believed they could be and then worked towards it. Therefore, based on this I made the same choice.

To achieve my dream life I decided, at sixteen years of age, that I needed to become more proactive if my dreams were to become a reality. I needed a plan – one that was simple and concise – so I went to my bedroom to consider the best approach. As this was my path in life that I was considering it was no small matter. Nevertheless, no matter the size of the task, once divided into small pieces any task becomes infinitely more manageable. Thus, I thought long and hard before jotting down a three-pronged approach that would later become known as *The Carrot, The Ladder and The Pencil.*

The Carrot

The *Carrot* is a simple tool that I used to help focus my mind on what I really wanted from life. It derives from the parable of the cart driver that hung a carrot from a stick and dangled it in front of a mule to encourage it to move towards the carrot thus drawing the cart forward. It is an idiom that refers to a practice of offering a reward to induce behaviour that helps us move towards our goals. For me personally, the *Carrot* was a single question that I used to narrow my focus.

The *Carrot* question was:

1) *If I could have or do any three things in the world what would they be?*

I specifically kept the *Carrot* to a maximum of three things that I desired. The reason was that I believed that if I were to have too many areas of focus, then I would lose focus by spreading myself too thin and therefore achieve nothing.

The Ladder

Normally ladders can be unpredictable items that take us up into a world of uncertainty. This *Ladder* is different. It only has three steps and it is designed not only to take us up, but up and across. It takes us out from our self-imposed 'Island of Wanting' and over to the 'World of Having'. The *Ladder* is a simple question that helped me to clarify the steps that I had to take in order to reach my goals.

The *Ladder* that I used to reach my goals was:

> 2) *To make my dreams become reality, what do I need to achieve?*

Ultimately, by answering the *Carrot* and *Ladder* questions, the path that would lead me towards living the life of my dreams and experiencing the wonderful things this world has to offer, would become a lot clearer.

To answer the *Carrot* question I had to decide what I considered to be the dream life. This was easy, because I knew exactly what I wanted to experience. At the age of sixteen, this is what I came up with.

I want to:

> - *Own season tickets at Old Trafford*
> - *Own a Porsche before I am thirty*
> - *Explore this great planet – All of it*

Grand dreams indeed for a schoolboy living in an area that was infamously referred to as the "unemployment black spot of Europe." However, I had no doubt in my mind at that time that my dreams would become reality if I was willing to take control and work towards them. I was not going to sit back and wait for fate, luck or destiny to come along and provide me with opportunities. I was going to set out a path that would allow me to achieve my objectives. However, I first had to come up with an answer to the *Ladder* question?

I pondered on my strengths for a while which was not easy, as I did not shine in any particular area. I drew a blank. After much soul searching, I begrudgingly concluded that I was always okay with numbers and analysis in school. The best I could do with this was go on to make it as an accountant.

However, the problem was that I did not know any accountants with whom I could talk to for advice. However, like all non-accountants, I assumed that there was no such thing as a poor accountant, and thus by following this path I believed I would earn enough money to allow me to achieve my dreams. After much thought, I came up with a three-step plan that would answer the *Ladder* question.

I need to:

- *Study hard and finish top of the class in school*
- *Go to University and obtain a Business Degree*
- *Qualify as a char-tered accountant*

Ultimately, I believed that qualifying as a chartered accountant would be the springboard to allowing the dreams on my *Carrot* list to come true. (A typical package for an Irish chartered accountant with approximately five years experience post qualification was €76,000 in 2011).

The Pencil

With my *Carrot* and *Ladder* clarified in my mind, I took out a *Pencil* and a single piece of paper and wrote down the three dreams from my *Carrot* list at the top, with the three steps on my *Ladder* below them. I stuck this list to my wardrobe door where I would see it first thing every morning and last thing at night.

I did not know it as a sixteen year old, but the *Pencil* is a mighty tool and to write down my life goals was a very powerful thing to do. I would later discover that this was a simple tactic to which some of the world's most successful people directly attribute their success. Apparently, writing down our goals sets off a trigger in our brain, causing it to push these objectives into the 'Must Do' section. It creates a challenge and our brain functions operate in a way that supports us to overcome this challenge and achieve the objective.

The power of committing goals to paper comes from the fact that it brings what is a mere idea from the mental to the physical. All of the advancements that we have made as humans have derived from a simple thought. Someone had to act on that thought for it to manifest in our physical world.

Personally, I find that committing goals to paper brings clarity and focus. It makes it easier to maintain motivation and self-discipline. Ultimately, it allows me to track my progress and it holds me accountable for my development. One of my bosses once taught me: *"If you don't measure it, you can't control it."* This has been proven to be right time and time again over the years.

The Rocky Path

Once I was clear about the path I wanted to follow I became very excited for the future and more of my time and effort was channelled into making my dreams become a reality. I never held back when it came to sharing my dreams with others.

When a teacher would ask the class: *"Who knows what they are going to do upon leaving school?"* my hand always shot up. I would enthusiastically declare: *"I am going to be an accountant, Miss."* I was so proud. Unfortunately, the responses, from the teachers, to my declarations were seldom positive.

"To qualify as an accountant takes seven and a half years and, in addition to that, the exams have the highest failure rate of all the professions! Are you sure you want to put yourself through that?" is how one teacher responded.

Another, the supposedly 'cool' teacher, put his hand on my shoulder and said, *"Maybe you should contemplate this further, Patrick. I'll tell you this; my most intelligent friend sat those exams many times, but could never pass them. I think it may be wise to consider another career!"*

So, I had chosen a rocky path, one that not everyone could traverse? Good! I was up for the challenge and I wanted to do something that others sensed was difficult. If it was easy, then everyone would be able to become a chartered accountant and it would then lose its value. It was the value that I chased. What these teachers had failed to realise was that through the power of the *Pencil* I had already committed my dreams to paper and all the 'advice' in the world could not change that.

What I learned from my experiences with these naysayers was that a strong sense of self-belief would be required if I was to be the creator of my dream life. Ultimately, in the long run, the opinion of every other person means nothing if I truly believe in myself. I am fully responsible for the path that I have chosen.

When I finally left school, I had met my first objective through hard work: I had finished top of the class. The awards I received further affirmed my belief that I could achieve anything with the correct attitude and approach to life. I did not celebrate this achievement, as it was too early for that.

Instead, I concluded that my mother was right all along. She would tell me repeatedly, *"You can have brains to burn but you won't achieve anything without hard work.*" I would have to work increasingly harder and smarter when studying for my University and Professional exams, if I was going to succeed in ticking the three items off my *Carrot* list.

Awareness

When I tell people of these events now, they seem horrified that some teachers offered such discouragement to my dreams. However, I see discouragement all around. The more new things I try, the more discouragement I encounter. As we mature, so does the discouragement. It becomes more subtle and discreet and often occurs without the instigator even realising.

I find that discouragement is often hidden behind jokes and one-liners, designed to plant the seed that grows into the tree of self-doubt. It is not rejection. Rejection is when another party dismisses your inspiration out right. Discouragement is when you slowly dismiss your own inspiration through letting the seed of doubt grow inside your mind.

To live the life of my dreams I had to figure out how to protect myself from discouragement. I find that seeing the discouragement as an obstacle on the rocky path to achieving the *Carrots* is the best reaction. Obstacles are not there to prevent us from reaching the *Carrots*. They are there simply to make sure that we want them bad enough.

Likewise, everyone that we know wants to see us live the life of our dreams, the jokes and one-liners are just a reflection of their own insecurities. Remember, that given the choice we would all prefer to be surrounded by happy and successful people. Everyone wants to see their family and friends succeed, despite their best attempts to show otherwise.

They are proud of us and what we achieve, they just do not want to show it. It is best summed up in the old Irish saying; *a friend would travel kilometres in the wind and rain to attend your funeral but would be reluctant to cross the road to offer congratulations.*

Of course, along this rocky path that has taken me towards living the life of my dreams I have had to go through many valleys and peaks. Life has its ups and downs and discouragement can make it harder to get to the next destination. The great Dale Carnegie best summed it up when he stated, *"Develop success from failures. Discouragement and failure are two of the surest stepping stones to success."* Obtaining our objectives may be tough, but it is certainly not impossible. Success is not achieved through never falling but through getting back up after each tumble.

Today and Tomorrow

I am always mindful of the seeds I allow to be planted in my mind each day, as they will determine the crop that I harvest in the future. I source the seeds of joy and abundance whilst researching the fantastic experiences that this world has to offer. I find that this act can bring me as much joy today as living that moment when it comes tomorrow.

I constantly remind myself to be grateful for what I have when I am living through a great experience. Through these experiences, I always end up meeting the most fascinating people. In conversation, I often learn about the great adventures that these like-minded people have experienced whilst travelling throughout the world. Of course, then I just have to add to my list the experiences that my newfound friends have relayed to me.

As a result, my humble three-item *Carrot* list has grown into what has become a book of what I consider to be life's great objectives. The objectives, like my life, are constantly evolving. As I progress through life, the level of importance attached to individual dreams continually changes. During the various stages of my life, I will have the opportunity to focus more on some areas than others.

Looking back now, I have a lot to thank that initial three-item *Carrot* list for. Three very different dreams that have culminated in this book and allowed me to live what I consider to be the life of *my* dreams. It was the *Ladder* list that helped focus my mind on what I needed to do to achieve these dreams, with the power to succeed derived from the *Pencil*.

Through staying positive and focused, I was able to feel the intangible, see the invisible and achieve the impossible on the path to achieving my dreams. Now, I welcome you to take a look into my life, both past and future.

The objectives that I have reached and achieved, I have ticked off ☑

Those objectives that I am still to accomplish remain unticked ☐

It is my desire that what you see and learn may inspire you to decide to finally do that one thing that you have been putting off until tomorrow. It is my hope that you will use the *Pencil* to help you aim for your own *Carrots* and consider the appropriate steps on the *Ladder* that will lead you towards your dream life.

This is my dream life and I am living it...

"Our deepest fear is not that we are inadequate. Our deepest fear is that we are powerful beyond measure. It is our light, not our darkness that most frightens us. We ask ourselves, 'Who am I to be brilliant, gorgeous, talented, fabulous?' Actually, who are you not to be? You are a child of God. Your playing small does not serve the world.

There is nothing enlightened about shrinking so that other people won't feel insecure around you. We are all meant to shine, as children do. We were born to make manifest the glory of God that is within us. It's not just in some of us, it's in everyone. And as we let our own light shine, we unconsciously give other people permission to do the same. As we are liberated from our own fear, our presence automatically liberates others."

Marianne Williamson (Author and international lecturer)

I

Family is
the only thing that really matters

We are all on a journey despite our level of active involvement. As we walk our path, we are all looking for one thing or another. This could be true love, additional wealth, improved health or even a simple purpose in life. As we make our way through this 'rat-race' world, we often become so busy concentrating on the path itself that we lose touch with what really matters. We concentrate on things like our career, the seasonal fashions, the size of our house and the latest gadgets.

For some it is a family tragedy that forces them to take stock, but for most others it is usually when we get close to the end of our journey that we begin to realise that we neglect that which we cherish most: the members of our family and the memories of the times we have spent together. I find this to be particularly evident when I enter the home of an elderly person. Framed photographs of members of their wider family are hanging on every wall and sitting on every surface.

Recently I visited an elderly relative of a friend and as I sat in the background observing, I noticed that as the family members chatted, the elderly lady sat smiling silently. She had no interest in chitchat and only got involved in the conversation to answer a question aimed directly at her. However, when I went over to have a closer look at the many photographs and inquire as to whom the people were, the elderly lady bounced up from her chair and enthusiastically talked to me in detail about the people in each photograph.

She was so happy just to have her family members around to visit. She thrived on the energy they brought into her home. It was obvious that she understood what really mattered in life. Maybe in the past, her focus was on accumulating material wealth and possessions, but not any more.

What I have learned from elderly people is that, in the end, there is no place for materialism. What we value most is the family around us, the friends that have stuck by us and the experiences and memories shared. The most precious things are the little things, the things that cannot be priced.

In our last days, none of us will be sat at home surrounded by copies of our bank statements or versions of our curriculum vitae. Neither will we have photographs of the fancy house, the Porsche or the diamond jewellery hanging on our walls. The things that will surround us will have deep meaning and be of real importance.

As you will see, I am as guilty as anyone else when it comes to focusing on material goods. However, thankfully as I become more experienced in life, I now make a conscious effort to spend more time with the people that I care about; doing the things we enjoy.

I wish to enjoy life, love and friendship with those closest to me, spending more time creating new memories, sharing our mutual interests and laughing at the jokes that only we can understand. I want to plan for my future family, providing for them so that their journey gets off to the best possible start. We are all on a journey and I want to ensure that my journey is a great one and that I have my family close by as I take each step.

F a m i l y

For me, happiness in my family life is the most important thing that there is. I believe that marrying the right person will directly determine how happy I will be throughout life. If I am happy at home, with a great family life built on solid foundations then this will provide me with a strong base from which to achieve great things in other areas of my life.

"There is no doubt that it is around the family and the home that all the greatest virtues, the most dominating virtues of human society, are created, strengthened and maintained."
~ Winston Churchill (Writer and former British Prime Minister)

☑ **Find the woman of my dreams.** *We all know the attributes that we want the man or woman of our dreams to possess. It is not about how they look, it is more to do with who they are as a person. Surely, looks do come into it, although they are not the most important thing. We are all different and we are all looking for different things in our perfect partner. The best way that I can describe the love of my life is that she ticked all the boxes on my imaginary list, but she increasingly reveals other amazing attributes that I had not considered. In short,* she is more than the woman of my dreams.

When I first met her, it was love at first sight. I would not even try to explain this to my mates, but it was not the fact that she was a tall, blonde Swedish girl with a beautiful face and a perfect body. It was her energy. She just seemed to radiate in light as everything around her went blurry. It was almost like a comedy sketch in a movie, but this was real. I was never one to go and look for love, I just knew that it would come to me when the time was right. I feel privileged that I have found my perfect girl. Our relationship started out well and with every passing day it gets better and better.

☑ **Get engaged. Surprise her.** *I was nervous about this, which surprised me, as I already knew that she wanted to marry me and I could not even imagine another woman as my wife. However, I still wanted to be romantic and surprise her. I pondered on what to do for months before finally coming up with a plan. This is what I came up with.*

I would buy her 'a ring', not 'thee ring', and I would ask her to marry me without her suspecting anything. The reason for this is because I wanted her to have the perfect ring and as she has her own unique style, I wanted her to design it herself according to her own tastes. So, armed with a not-very-expensive ring in my pocket we ventured out to The Hill of Tara, the mystical location that has been Ireland's spiritual heart for thousands of years. I chose this location because, in addition to it being Ireland's heart, it is also possible to view half of the counties of the country from there.

Quite bizarrely, neither of us had ever been there before and did not really know where the centre of this, now green field, site was. When we arrived at the site, there were many people mingling around despite it being a very overcast winters day. With all the people around and the threat of rain, I was having my doubts as I nervously shuffled the boxed ring around in my coat pocket. As we walked around the site, I was trying to hide my nerves and keep myself from acting too strange as my eyes scanned the site for the perfect, quiet spot.

As we got to the summit of the gentle sloped hill, I noticed a standing stone that seemed to indicate the centre of the site. As we stood there looking over half the counties of Ireland, I beckoned my girl to come over and stand in close to me, as she so often does on cold days. As we both stood facing the same direction looking out on the beauty that unfolded, I was trembling, not with cold, but with nerves. However, as I looked around the site, the grey clouds had parted, the sun was shining directly down on us and it seemed as if everyone had disappeared. The entire site was now empty.

I have no idea what I was saying as we stood on the summit of The Hill

of Tara, but I can only assume I was trying to set the scene. Sensing the time was right I dropped my leather gloves on the muddy grass, so that I could have a dry spot to kneel on, then, with a lump in my throat and a dry mouth, I dropped down on one knee and pulled the ring out of my pocket.

I had planned to ask her to marry me in Swedish, her native tongue, but as I looked up at her my mind went blank, so in a broken tone I nervously stammered out the hardest four words I have ever had to say: "Will you marry me?"

When she did not say anything in response for what may have been only a few seconds, but seemed like hours, my stomach sank! She just stood there looking down at me and I have never felt as vulnerable before or since. Then as a tear ran down her face from her left eye she accepted my proposal with words that I cannot remember. I then clumsily put the ring on her finger and jumped to my feet and held my new fiancé in my arms. We squeezed each other tight as the sun shone down on us on that fresh February morning.

I would later learn that the part of the hill that we stood on was known as Ráith na Ríogh (the Fort of the Kings). The most prominent earthwork within the enclosure is known as Forradh (The Royal Seat). In the middle of the Forradh, at the spot where I proposed, is the standing stone that is believed to be the Lia Fáil (Stone of Destiny) which served as the coronation stone for the High Kings of Ireland. As I walked down the hill from the Lia Fáil hand in hand with my beautiful new fiancé, I certainly felt like the High King of Ireland.

☐ **Get married and have a fantastic wedding.**

☐ **Go on the honeymoon of our dreams.**

☐ **Raise healthy and happy children and be present at the significant moments of their lives.**

☐ **Create a home that has a relaxed, inviting, comfortable and joy-filled atmosphere.**

☐ **Welcome a pet dog in to our family (one that does not sleep on our bed).**

☐ **Pass on stories of the places I have visited and the people I have met to our children.**

☐ **Take my family to the places I have visited and on the journeys I have completed.**

☐ **Celebrate our 30th Wedding Anniversary in Sydney, Australia, where we met.**

☐ **Spoil my grandchildren.**

II

Education and Business is what encourages us to think

We all make our living working for only one person: ourselves. This is the case whether we are employed, self-employed or in education. Initially we invest time, money and effort in obtaining our training and education to enhance our saleable skills. After this focused commitment in perfecting our skills we then put our skills up for rent in the market place. The market then determines the value on what it deems our skills to be worth. We trade the skills we have developed at a rate of one hour of our time for a predetermined monetary rate.

This is the same for everyone from football players and musicians to accountants and street cleaners. For some people this value is zero. The value placed on our skills is zero when we complete a project and the results are not what the market values at that time. Thus, the market, as a collective, places low or no value on these skills. In more simple terms, we are not hired.

Unfortunately, in today's world, the success or failure of a project is defined by the amount of money that it creates. It is for this reason that many of us are reluctant to put ourselves forward and work on a project that may be rejected by the market. We are afraid to make a mistake, as we do not want to let ourselves down in public.

I used to think like this, but now I see it differently. Now I believe that the success of a project is determined by how much is learned in the performance of the tasks. Thus, mistakes are a significant part of our development, as they teach us essential lessons and take us one step closer to our ultimate goal. When we take a risk and put ourselves out there, we learn the most about our capabilities. No matter the monetary outcome, the process that starts with an initial thought and develops into something material provides us with an invaluable learning experience. Thus, it is a success.

Everything begins with a simple thought and perhaps the timing is correct for that thought to become a worldwide success. Maybe someone else has already put the wheels in motion. Maybe the world is not ready for it yet. The most important thing is that we act on our ideas, think them through and give the market the opportunity to decide whether the time is right.

The people that make mistakes are the ones that are taking the risks. It is because of the risk takers that the human race has achieved such magnificent feats. Experience is what we get when we do not get what we want at the first attempt. Nevertheless, we must persist. Ex-President of the United States, Calvin Coolidge put it better than I ever could when he said:

"Nothing in the world can take the place of persistence. Talent will not; nothing is more common than unsuccessful men with talent. Genius will not; unrewarded genius is almost a proverb. Education will not; the world is full of educated derelicts. Persistence and determination alone are omnipotent. The slogan, 'Press on' has solved and always will solve the problems of the human race."

Not achieving all we dream of at our first attempt is nothing to be ashamed of.

Failure on one project should not be a cause of heartache. Ultimately, the failure that will cause the most heartache is deciding to do nothing, simply out of the fear of making a mistake.

Press on.

E d u c a t i o n

All education is self-education. Whether I am hiking in Patagonia or attending a lecture on International Accounting Standards, I am educating myself on subjects that are of interest to me. My self-education is all the information that I open myself to. I only learn what I wish to learn. We all put in time and effort obtaining knowledge on various subjects ranging from our favourite pop star to quantum physics, but it is through our interests that we earn our real education in this world.

We are all the product of continuous self-education. Most of the knowledge that I have gained as a person has come through my interests. Through travelling the world, surfing the web, reading books and talking to friends and strangers, I have amassed more information than a lifetime in formal education. It is difficult to quantify and list all the areas that attract my interest, thus what I have listed below are my objectives in life as far as my formal education and languages are concerned.

"Formal education will make you a living. Self education will make you a fortune."
~ Jim Rohn (Speaker and author)

☑ **Study hard and finish top of the class in school.**

☑ **Receive a Bachelor of Arts Honours Degree in Business Studies.**

☑ **Complete a Diploma of Higher Education in Accounting.**

☑ **Qualify as a CAI chartered accountant, passing all exams at first attempt.**

☑ **Complete all Irish Taxation Institute exams in one year, passing all at first attempt.**

☑ **Complete all Qualified Financial Advisor exams, passing all at first attempt.**

☑ **Be awarded the Chartered Tax Advisor accreditation.**

These achievements have left me in a situation where I now have more letters after my name that I have in it.

Patrick Hamilton Walsh ACA, AITI, CTA, QFA, BA (Honours), Dip HE.

If nothing else, it makes my parents proud.

☐ **Complete the IIPM Certificate in Pensions, Investments and Insurance.**

☐ **Study Digital Marketing.**

☐ **Become fluent in Swedish.**

☐ **Be able to hold a conversation in Spanish.**

☐ **Know enough Mandarin to get through a business meeting.**

☑ **Learn to say "Thanks" in more than 25 languages.**

Afrikaans: Dankie; Arabic: Shukran; Chinese (Mandarin): xièxie; Croatian: Hvala; Czech: Díky; Danish: Tak; Dutch: Dank U; English: Thanks; Estonian: Aitäh; Faroese: Takk; Finnish: Kiitos; French: Merci; German: Danke; Greek: Efharistó; Hebrew: Toda; Icelandic: Takk; Indonesian: Terima kasih ya; Irish (Gaelic): Go raibh maith agat; Italian: Grazie; Japanese: arigatō; Latvian: Paldies; Lithuanian: Ačiū; Lao: khàwp jaI; Maltese: Grazzi; Mongolian: Bayarlalaa; Norwegien: Takk; Polish: Dziekuje; Portugese: Obrigado; Romanian: Mersi; Russian: Spasiba; Serbian: Hvala; Spanish: Gracias; Swahili: Asante sana; Swedish: Tack; Ukrainian: Diakuju; Vietnamese: Cảm ơn.

Did you see what I did there? I casually listed a number of formal qualifications that I have achieved, ticked them off, made it sound easy and moved on to what I hope to achieve in the future. The truth is that it was anything but easy and climbing to each new step on the *Ladder* required immense effort.

To obtain the B.A. Honours Degree in Business Studies, in addition to all the exams, I had to complete a dissertation that required me to spend late nights and weekends researching the topic *'Corporate Reporting on the internet by Irish Companies'*. The hard work that went in to the completion of this project provided me with a glance into how my life would unfurl over the following few years. However, the hard work paid off and when I graduated with my class mates it was such a big deal for me due to the fact that it marked the achievement of the second step on my initial three-step *Ladder*.

In 2001, after graduation, I moved to Dublin to begin my professional training as a chartered accountant, signing up to work for Grant Thornton as an Auditor. The standard working week was 36.25 hours, but in reality, a 60-hour working week was not uncommon. In addition to this, I had to complete exams at Professional Two, Professional Three and FAE (Final Admitting Exam) level in order to qualify as a chartered accountant.

This meant that I had to attend class in the evenings after work from 6:30pm to 9:30pm and from 9:30am to 5:00pm most weekends. A day off from work, class and study was a rare commodity. However, all the hard work and determination paid off and within the timeframe of my training contract I had passed all the examinations at the first attempt to qualify as a chartered accountant in May 2005.

This marked the completion of the third and final step on the three-step *Ladder* that I had drafted as a 16-year-old and it was a very proud day for me, my family and even my community. It was the culmination of ten years of focused determination and hard work. Attending the graduation ceremony and collecting my certificate of membership was the final proof that the very simple path to success that I had designed as a 16-year-old was an effective one. This saw me complete the final objective on my initial *Ladder*.

However, in the intervening years I had added new steps on to my *Ladder*, as I desired to climb higher. Thus, I was far from finished with my formal education as I developed the desire to complete the Irish Taxation Institute exams and the newly introduced Qualified Financial Advisor exams.

It was at this stage that I stopped to consider the path that I was about to go down. Looking at the education that I still desired to complete, I would be studying for at least another five years, if I passed all exams at the first attempt. This was just too much and I could not justify giving up such a big portion of my youth to further study when, at the age of 26, I had already given up so much.

I did my research and learned that if I was willing to double up on the courses then I could just about squeeze the full courses and all of the exams for both qualifications into a period of just over 20 months. It would mean that I would disappear into a mountain of books and a life of work-class-study-work-class-study for the entirety of the 20 months. Nonetheless, I felt that it was worth it as, if I was successful, I would be left with a few years to enjoy my twenties as I travelled the world.

I knew that I could do it. I was in the zone when it came to exams. I knew 'how to' pass them; I knew the phrases and structures that would help me to clock up the marks to get the pass rates I required in the exams. All I needed was the knowledge base. This I would get from attending every single class and studying hard in my spare time.

I would begin these studies in May 2005 and my objective was to be on a flight out of Dublin by May 2007 with the Taxation and Qualified Financial Advisor exams completed and the letters 'AITI' and 'QFA' placed firmly after my name, along side 'ACA'.

What I needed to do was to double up on the exams and complete two levels at a time. First up was Level One and Two of the QFA exams. Classes started in June with the first exams in September. I was forbidden from attempting Level Two until Level One was completed. To get around this, I simply submitted two separate application forms, one for each level, and I was delighted when I was accepted on each course and went on to pass both exams.

Next up were the Irish Taxation Institute exams. The exam sittings were in May and September following the completion of the course with an attendance requirement of not below 80 percent. My plan was to sit Part Two in May and Part Three in September, but attend all classes during the term from September to April. I made the choice that I would study Part Two and attend the classes for it in the evenings during the week and I would study and attend classes for Part Three at the weekends. I did my old trick of submitting two separate application forms and, once again, I was accepted on both courses.

This was the toughest year of them all. It was relentless. I never got a break and that year just seems like a blur to me now. What made it all the more difficult was that it was all legislation based. The course was all about tax law. I sat the Part Two exams in May 2006 and the results came out in July 2006 stating that I had passed. The good news was that I could now sit the Part Three exams in September 2006. The bad news was that I only had six weeks to prepare.

By the time the results had come out for the Part Three tax exams, I was delighted to learn that I had passed, but by that stage I was already well into the classes for the final two parts of the 'QFA' exams. It was in January of 2007 that I sat these exams and thankfully, having studied hard again and

attended all classes religiously, I had passed. I was now finished with exams.

I had put myself through the grind to get to that point. In truth, I had probably pushed myself too hard, but now it was all over and it was worth it. I was to be best man at my best friends wedding on the last Saturday in May 2007 and the following Monday morning I would fly out of Dublin airport to New York with just over 24 months experience in PricewaterhouseCoopers completed on top of 42 months experience in Grant Thornton.

In that time, I had become a chartered accountant, a taxation consultant and a Qualified Financial Advisor. It was not easy, but now the world was my oyster and I was free to live the life that I had always dreamed of. From where I would go after New York, I did not know and every day from then on would be determined on a whim. It was not an easy road to go down but it certainly was worth it. As you will see in the following pages, the three steps that I listed on that initial *Ladder* are directly responsible for taking me up to the life of my dreams.

Career

In our careers, I believe that at the most basic level there are only two forms of exchange: time and money. For me personally, time is the more valuable of the two simply because once it is spent, it is gone, it cannot be earned or topped up.

When we are in employment, we sell our lives to our employers at a rate of one hour of our life for a predetermined monetary rate (the associated portion of our earnings). It does not matter how highly skilled we are, or how much we are paid for our time, we will reach a point when we have no more time to give and our earnings will eventually level out. We simply run out of time. For this reason, it is my desire to move away from employment as a way of earning money.

Instead, I aim to concentrate the majority of my working time and effort on generating passive income. When I was a taxation consultant to Ireland's rich and famous, I always admired their ability to generate passive income. Passive income, for those that are not aware of the term, is an income that can be earned over a long period, with little effort required to maintain it after the performance of the initial task.

Some examples of passive income are rent from property, dividends from stocks and bonds and royalties from publishing a book or licensing a patent. To generate passive income, I wish to spend the majority of the time I allocate to work creating new products and services that enhance lives, of which I can place a monetary value on. I believe that this will simultaneously increase my cash flow whilst saving me time to do the things that I like with the people I love.

For me, the true assessment of success is having spare time and the freedom to do as I choose with it. Work should be more fun than fun. If I am not working towards building my own dreams, then I am working towards helping someone else build theirs. Ultimately I do not want to spend the best days of my life fulfilling the dreams of another person, as I grow old. I want to create work that I and everyone else will enjoy and want to be a part of because ultimately, the most important question to ask on the job is not *'What am I getting?'* but rather *'What am I becoming?'*

"Your time is limited, so don't waste it living someone else's life. Don't be trapped by dogma – which is living with the results of other people's thinking. Don't let the noise of other's opinions drown out your own inner voice. And most important, have the courage to follow your heart and intuition. They somehow already know what you truly want to become. Everything else is secondary."
~ Steve Jobs (Businessman and inventor)

☑ **Gain experience as a chartered accountant in many business sectors.** *When most people think about accountants two words automatically pop into their mind: "Boring" and "Numbers". Then the first thing they will say to me, after they ask what I work as, is "You don't look like an accountant." That always makes me laugh, as I am never sure whether or not to take that as a compliment. I can only assume that I "don't look like" the kind of guy that is good with numbers, but I have not bored them yet! The truth about accounting is that it is the most wide-ranging of all the professions and as a result it attracts a wide range of people.*

The spread of people that I have worked with is as wide-ranging as the work that is on offer. What I have come to realise is that every one of us is passionate, determined and willing to work hard to better ourselves, whilst at the same time being a total geek at heart. Some of the funniest and craziest people I have ever met have been within the profession. During my time, I have worked with everyone from Olympic athletes to a guy that suffered from Bananaphobia (a fear of bananas)!

I have only worked as an accountant for a few years and already I have gained experience working for Grant Thornton, Hewlett Packard, PricewaterhouseCoopers, a shipping company, Allco Finance Group, Brookfield Multiplex, Chartered Accountants Ireland and Trinity College Dublin. In addition to that, I have turned down opportunities to work for Google and Yahoo for one reason or another. Since beginning work as an accountant I have come to realise that this qualification can take me anywhere I want.

As a result, I would suggest the accounting profession to almost any student looking to get into business. Just to clarify this, being good at numbers is not what is required to be an accountant. People that I have worked with have completed their degrees in medicine, science, arts, marketing and nearly everything else. All are welcome in the accounting profession, simply due to the fact that businesses in every sector need an accountant. If an individual has a background in a non-financial subject then that makes them a valuable asset to an accounting firm, as they possess insights that those from a financial background do not have.

Personally, I believe that the greatest value of this qualification is yet to unfold for me. That will be revealed when it comes to running my own businesses. After many years of being in close contact with successful clients and learning about their businesses and what made them successful, I will use the inside knowledge that has made them a success and apply that to my own business. As a result, this has turned out to be a great qualification to have. It has opened so many doors for me and allowed me to travel around the world and work anywhere. The old saying, 'a great qualification is easily carried' has proved to be true.

☑ **Work for a 'Big 4' accounting firm.** *I obtained great work experience during my time in PricewaterhouseCoopers and learned a lot about myself and the world of business. The training I received has been very transferable and has allowed me to work on projects of any kind. (The 'Big 4' are the four largest international professional networks in accounting and professional services. Between them, they complete the audits for the majority of publicly traded and large privately owned companies).*

☑ **Work as a chartered accountant in a foreign country.** *I worked for several international companies while in Australia, which allowed me to take on positions that may not necessarily have been open to me in Ireland. Working abroad in your chosen career is something that I highly recommend. This is something that I want to experience again, but next time I want it to be in a non-English speaking country, preferably in Asia.*

☑ **Release 'Life is' audios on iTunes, Amazon and Spotify to motivate and inspire.** *I believe that it is our thoughts that create our reality, so the motivation behind this range of products is to allow people to empower themselves through listening to these audios. They are designed to allow people that live busy lifestyles to create positivity in their lives in relation* to the subject matter of the audio. The first 'Life is' audio to be released was 'Life is: Wealth' and deals with helping people to attract more wealth and cash flow into their lives.

The other 'Life is' audios that are due for release are; 'Life is: Health', 'Life is: Beauty' (separate audios for men and women), 'Life is: Examinations' (designed to empower people facing difficult examinations) and 'Life is: Running' to name but a few. These audios can be accessed and downloaded on iTunes, Amazon, Spotify, RouteNote, Rdio, eMusic, Deezer or through links on www. theisbook.com

☐ **Travel the world taking unique 'phoneographs' that I can sell.** *This is the combination of two of my great passions, so it is my desire to make a career out of these. 'Phoneographs' are photographs captured on a mobile phone. I always use Nokia devices due to the high quality photos that they allow me to capture. Nokia devices also possess an astonishingly good battery life and are easily hidden whilst not in use, which is a massive benefit considering some of the locations I travel to. When I am about to set off on a long backpacking journey, I always weigh up the 'pros and cons' of the kit that will best meet the requirements of my trip and for the last five years the answer has always been a Nokia device.*

As it stands, I now have thousands of 'phoneographs' that I captured as

I travelled the world. Out of those I would have around 100 really good images, which would make people stop and ask, "Was that really captured on a mobile phone?" To get this project started I have posted some of the images I have taken from across the seven continents on www. vimeo.com/ThePhoneographer in order to obtain some feedback from around the world. In addition, I have set up the Facebook page 'The Phoneographer' where people from all over the world can get involved and share the images that they have captured using their iPhone, Samsung, Sony, Nokia or whatever camera phone they use.

The ultimate plan for this project is that I will release books of the images I have captured giving people the option to come to www.thephoneographer.org and purchase the images that they like, either singularly or as a collage, in a size of their liking, with the images delivered directly to their door. In addition I hope to further develop this website to the point that phoneographers from around the world can then use the medium of the site to sell their own images and make some money from their art. So, if this is something that you would be interested in, then please get in touch.

☐ **Release a range of clothing aimed directly at backpackers.** I find it astonishing that this massive market with a requirement for specific clothing still remains untapped. Due to the nature of our lives as backpackers, we require clothing that is light, hardwearing, trendy and distinctive. It must be distinctive in a manner that it sets us apart from the locals just enough for other backpackers to recognise what we are, but without the locals noticing.

During my many bus, train and airplane journeys I have put significant thought into this to the

Travel the world taking unique phoneographs

point that I have a name for the range and I have even drafted designs. This is something that I would like to bring to the market quite quickly, but I feel that I would need the backing of one of the large clothing brands such as Nike, Adidas, Berghaus, Haglöfs, Helly Hansen, The North Face or one similar.

☐ **Complete and release 'Only Footprints'.** I have always had a deep appreciation for Mother Earth and the contrasting beauty that exists on her. With this in mind, I have always supported those that have done all that they can to protect the Earth from destruction through the greed and ignorance of individuals, corporations and governments.

Therefore, as I travelled the world I have taken a phoneograph of my foot on every unique surface that I have come across. On one surface will be a picture of my left foot, on the next surface it will be a picture of my right, then my left, then my right and so on as I have made my way across the seven continents of this planet. When the phoneographs are laid out, they will depict a person walking across this beautiful planet and appreciating the natural beauty of Mother Earth before moving on and leaving only footprints, with the environment as they found it, still intact.

I have two more phoneographs to take to bring this project to a completion and then I hope that I can use the finished product to help one of the large organisations, which are focused on saving the planet and highlighting the importance of our actions, in raising awareness.

☐ **Help a 'start-up' to flourish.** A 'start-up' is a business that has been newly founded with a focus on high growth. The beauty of a start-up is the constant chaos that exists that forces the team members to think on their feet at all times. Everything is new and exciting and in today's ever-changing world, the projects that start-ups are working on can be groundbreaking. It is work that no one has ever undertaken before. There is no reference manual. Most start-ups fail within a year, but the ones that do make it, can make it big and that is what appeals to me.

☐ **Sell my original artwork.** What a compliment it would be for someone to purchase something that I have produced and hang it on the wall of their home where they see it everyday. The closest I have got to this was when I was involved in my first photographic exhibition. I had shown seven photographs that I had captured on my Nokia, one from each continent. They hung on the wall for one week and when I went to collect my prints at the end of the week, the organisers were deeply apologetic, as one of my prints had been stolen from the wall.

As the organisers stood apologising, all I could think was that someone so admired my work that they were willing to steal it. All I wanted to do was determine which print had made such an impact. I soon determined that it was the photograph that I had chosen to represent Europe, that I had captured in Auschwitz one autumn evening as the sun set between the barbed wire and watch towers. As I gathered up my six remaining prints, I felt so proud and happy that a person appreciated my work so much they were willing to steal it. Whoever you are, thank you.

☐ **Set up a business that allows young artists to bring their work to the world.** *This is an idea that I really should have brought to fruition a few years ago as part of the 'is' brand. The idea behind it is to help young artists from all over the world to monetise their work whilst lighting up peoples homes with their skills. In addition, a percentage of the profits will go into a fund that enables artists from difficult backgrounds to obtain the tools that they need to earn a living from their gift.*

I want this project to be one strand of the overall 'is' brand. Ultimately it is my dream to light up the London skyline with 'is'. This may seem very specific to you, but I believe that what happens in London today ripples across the world tomorrow. Thus, if I can light up the London skyline, then I can light up the world. I want to get to the point that I have developed 'is' into such a success that it appears when people throughout the world type the letter 'i' into Google and Bing.

☐ **Release 'ThisisMe@3'.** *If I am totally honest, I am not really sure what I should do with this project in order to bring it to a completion in a way that it can be packaged and sold. So to give you a bit of information into this, it all started when I was at a street art exhibition in Gothenburg, Sweden a few years ago. There were so many fascinating and interesting works of art being developed in the streets all over the city that I felt inspired to create something on a large scale.*

I have no idea why, but the idea that flashed into my mind was that I would take one phoneograph of myself at 3:00pm every day for a year. This project suited me because I would always have my Nokia in my pocket, with the alarm set to ring at 3:00pm to remind me to take the phoneograph.

The reason why I chose to take the phoneograph at 3:00pm everyday was that I feel that whatever I am doing and wherever I am at this time defines my day. If I am at home writing, walking through a city, sitting on a bus, chilling on a sofa or lying in bed sick at 3:00pm then that says a lot about how I spent that day in my life. I believed that it would be a way in which to show the world how I live my life with the main point of interest being what was right behind me at 3:00pm each day. That was the plan.

However, as I get close to the 900th day of 'ThisisMe@3' this project has turned into something much bigger.

It has provided me with an insight into my soul. This project has shown me a part of my life that I did not really know existed. I always feel happy and energetic but through these phoneographs I have noticed long periods of time where I have not been smiling at 3:00pm, were I have rolled out of bed and into the same old hoody to begin a day in front of my laptop, away from the eyes of the world.

The life of an artist can be a lonely and repetitive one. The life of a backpacker can be a fun-filled, action packed and ever-changing existence. The life of an accountant can be a mixture of both. This project has provided me with an insight into the contrasting life's that I live and how each affects me.

Maybe I will come up with a way of turning these daily insights into an interesting book, maybe Nokia may want to use them as part of a marketing campaign or maybe they will be printed to adorn the walls of a gallery somewhere in this world. Whatever happens to this project, it has provided me with a great insight into my life. I may keep on taking my 'ThisisMe@3' phoneographs on my trusty Nokia until someone shows interest in the project. I may continue until I get to 1,000 continuous days or I may stop tomorrow, but either way, the result has surprised even me.

Writing

When people ask me for advice, I always tell them the same thing: to follow their heart. To many it seems like a throwaway comment and at times people think that I am trying to palm them off with an overused cliché. That could not be further from the truth. Every moment of every day, I try to listen to my heart and follow what I 'feel' to be right. Many times it will feel as if what my heart is telling me is the opposite of what I should do, until I just go along with it anyway only to find that the result was better than anything I could have imagined.

Sometimes it almost seems as if there are two paths; one is brightly lit with flowers and fruits hanging from the trees. The other is dark, unpaved and overgrown and not very appealing. I have to choose a path and the obvious path to choose is the one that is brightly lit. However, my heart is telling me something different. It is urging me to go down the unpaved pathway. Therefore, what I do in this situation is simply follow my heart.

Down the unpaved pathway I go, taking care not to stumble, only to find that just out of sight, around the corner, is a land of abundance and exactly what I was looking for. As I bask in this paradise without a care, I later learn that the brightly lit path got its light from a setting sun and was soon bathed in darkness, offering nothing more than false dawns.

Ultimately, what I am trying to say is that when we follow the noise in our heads we can end up lost. On the contrary, the heart will lead us to where we want to be, if we follow it to the very end. Therefore, it was by listening to my heart that I came up with the idea to write my first book.

The desire to write came to me as I lay on the beach in Bali and from every fibre of my being it seemed like the right thing to do. So that is what I did – I started writing. That simple idea has changed my entire life and opened up numerous possibilities for me. As my heart was urging me on, my head was telling me *"You are not a writer," "Accountants don't write," "No one wants to read your story"* and so on. Thankfully, I ignored that.

Now, when I wake up in the morning I bounce up out of bed, as I love to start work. I love the challenge of getting the right words to flow from my heart and onto a page in the correct order. I love how everyday I progress and get better at what I do. My first attempt was a book based on using 140 characters to give an insight into our world but my dream is to go on to write a novel that wins the Man Booker Prize.

Right now I have no idea how I am going to get to that level but as the late, great Steve Jobs once said, *"You can't connect the dots looking forward; you can only connect them looking backwards. So, you have to trust that the dots will somehow connect in your future. You have to trust in something – your gut, destiny, life, karma, whatever. This approach has never let me down, and it has made all the difference in my life."* I trust in something, and that something is my heart. I will leave the dot connecting until my final days.

"And by the way, everything in life is writable about if you have the outgoing guts to do it, and the imagination to improvise. The worst enemy to creativity is self-doubt."
~ Sylvia Plath (Poet, novelist and short story writer)

☑ **Write and publish a unique book.** *In October 2007, I was lying on Kuta beach in Bali not really thinking about much, when out of nowhere, the idea to write a book came into my mind. Writing a book was something I had never considered. The idea was for a book that would present an insight into everyday life in the 21st century. The original slant was that the book would present this insight through the medium of Facebook status updates and Twitter tweets. I wanted to highlight the joys and pressures of today's world with a 'warts and all' collection of status updates and tweets that covered every area of life in Western society,* within 140 characters, with each telling an individual story.

As I continued on my travels, I made a point of noting down interesting insights that I picked up during conversation, or overheard people talking about. As a way of storing and accessing them I would email the status updates and tweets to myself as I travelled around the world. Eventually I had enough witty, poignant, weird, wonderful, laugh-out-loud, crude and downright rude status updates and tweets to fill a book. I pulled them all together under various headings, added a simple introduction whilst sitting in an Internet cafe and sent the document off to a publisher. From there, I went off on my travels again.

A few months later, just as I had come off the boat from Antarctica I received an email from the publisher stating that my book was now for sale around the world at 22,000 online retailers and many bookstores. It addition to that, the book was also available for sale in electronic format through Kindle Direct Publishing. It was as easy as that. I now welcome you to go and invest in my book, 'is: The Phenomenon of the Facebook Status' as 100 percent of the proceeds are donated to charities and good causes and always will be. It is a great read for a lazy day. On the other hand, as one reviewer remarked, it is "the perfect sit-on-the-toilet-and-laugh" book. I suppose that is a compliment.

☑ **Publish an article about my travels.** *Accountancy Ireland Magazine, April 2011.*

☐ **Write and publish a book that inspires people to make the most of their life.** *I hope that this is that book. However, I will not tick this off the list until someone that I have never met contacts me to tell me that this book has inspired them. Only then can I be sure that it has achieved its objective.*

☐ **Write and publish a book of fiction.** *I have quite a few ideas on what this book would be about, however, I would need to put in a lot of practice writing short stories before I would even consider attempting this project. It would be awesome if I could write a book that makes it to #1 on the New York Times Best Sellers List, but a bigger indicator of success for me would be writing a book that is translated into another language.*

☐ **Complete 'This is Nokia'.** *This is an idea that I have had in my mind for quite a while and one that I hope to work on with Nokia once I have this book published. I am not going to let you know what it consists of just yet though, but if you never hear this mentioned again, then they did not like the idea.*

☐ **Write and publish a children's book.** *They say that you should only write about what you know. The question that I have been asking myself is what area of my life should I focus on, that would be*

most beneficial to the development of children?

☐ **Write and publish a textbook for students.** *I intend that this book will give students a greater insight into examinations and what the people that correct exams are looking for. I am ideally placed to provide this information, as I have been involved in the correcting of the Final Admitting Exams for Chartered Accountants Ireland for numerous years. This book will provide advice that will allow students to achieve greater results, through focused study practices and examination techniques.*

☐ **Publish an article in National Geographic Magazine.** *For me to achieve this would be a great honour, as I am a big fan of National Geographic. I already have the 'phoneographs' organised for a number of articles that I have in mind. However, I am not sure what collection would lead to the best article, or even if it would be good enough to make it into the National Geographic. I suppose there is only one way to find out.*

☐ **Publish a book of the 'Phoneographs' from my travels.** *I have captured thousands of images from all over the world to date and, as it stands, I just need to finalise the images for each of the books that I have planned. My initial thoughts are to publish a series of books based on specific subject matters. I have already gathered together the images under* the headings; 'The Cars of Havana', 'African People', 'The Doors of our World', 'The Seven Continents' and 'The Girl in the Red Dress' amongst many others. These books should be following soon after the release of this book.

The images that I have included in this book have been captured on my various Nokia devices over the years. What really interests me about this is that I can see a clear pattern in how my skills have been enhanced over time as the cameras and the apps within the Nokia devices have become consistently better. As this is not my 'phoneography' book, I have not felt under pressure to include my best images. Instead, I have chosen the images that fit the flow of the various chapters of the book and give the reader some respite from my ramblings, with each, hopefully, contributing the proverbial 1,000 words.

Recognition

When I told the people on my street that I wanted to own a Porsche before I was thirty, they laughed at me. The entire world may laugh when they read of my desire to become a Billionaire and be awarded a Nobel Prize. To be honest, I have no idea what I would need to do at this stage of my life to win such an award. What I do know is that fortune favours the brave. This world is full of opportunities and I believe that every one of us is capable of remarkable feats.

"It is not the critic who counts; not the man who points out how the strong man stumbled or where the doer of deeds could have done better. The credit belongs to the man who actually is in the arena; whose face is marred by dust and sweat and blood; who strives valiantly; who errs and comes short again and again; who knows the great enthusiasms, the great devotions, and spends himself in a worthy cause; who, at the best, knows the triumph of high achievement; and who, at the worst, if he fails, at least falls while daring so that his place shall never be with those cold and timid souls who knew neither victory nor defeat"
~ Theodore Roosevelt (President of the United States)

☑ **Business Studies Student of the Year.** *I received the Bank of Ireland award for excellence in Business Studies in my final year at school, which made me very proud. In addition to this, I was the runner up in a UK wide CIMA Marketing competition. This was very exciting at the time, as I was flown to London to collect my award in a ceremony at the Lloyds of London building. That was a great experience and one that I look back on fondly because it proved to me that I was on the right track. It was the completion of the first step on my Ladder and it further energised me to go on and aim for bigger and brighter things.*

☑ **Be commissioned to exhibit my photographs in a gallery.** *I was privileged enough to be asked to provide some of my work for*

Be commissioned to exhibit in a gallery

the 'Pixel This 2011' exhibition in London. *Thanks to the organiser, Dan Shearman of CreateHive, the phoneographs I captured on my Nokia, shared the exhibition space with entries from a host of celebrities including Ruby Wax and Stephen Fry. I was delighted to be involved in this great project, as all the images on show at the exhibition were made available for purchase, with the top entries auctioned to raise money for the Kids Company charity.*

☑ **Be featured on the front page of a magazine.** *I was interviewed by Accountancy Ireland magazine in relation to my travels and how my accounting qualification has enabled me to obtain work abroad. I was asked to provide some of the phoneographs from my travels for the piece and I was quite surprised when they asked if they could use a phoneograph I had captured on my Nokia on the front cover of the magazine. Of course, I was honoured that they would even consider it. As an accountant that is as good as it gets. That is the first step on the road to the cover of Time magazine.*

☐ **Receive an Honorary Masters from Trinity College Dublin, Ireland.** *Formally known as the "College of the Holy and Undivided Trinity of Queen Elizabeth near Dublin", the college was founded in 1592 and is continually ranked as one of the best universities in the world.*

☐ **Receive an Honorary PhD from the University of Ulster, Magee College.** *This great University is where I first started my third level education and for that reason it will always remain close to my heart.*

☐ **Receive a Fellowship from Chartered Accountants Ireland.**

☐ **Win the Man Booker Prize.** *This is a literary prize awarded each year for the best original full-length novel, written in the English language, by a citizen of the Commonwealth of Nations, Ireland or Zimbabwe. It is a very prestigious award and I want to be the first person born in Northern Ireland to win this. I had better raise my game.*

☐ **Receive a Knighthood.**

☐ **Become a Nobel Prize winning Laureate.** *Every time I am in Stockholm I like to go over and spend time just hanging around the Stockholm Concert Hall (where the ceremony is held) and Stockholm City Hall (where the banquet follows immediately after) just imagining how splendid it would be to be a recipient of a Nobel Prize.*

☐ **Have lunch with the President of the United States in the White House.**

☐ **Be made a Freeman of Dublin.**

☐ **Be internationally recognized as the person leading the way in 'Phoneography' (photography using a mobile phone).**

□ **Have a street named after me.** *Whilst working as a Tax Advisor to a large Australian construction company in Sydney I got very close to having a street in Western Australian named after me. The company had given the support staff in the office the opportunity to name the streets in a new housing estate they were building. Of course, we all came up with names that incorporated our own names, with me opting for "Walsh Way". Unfortunately, I left that position before construction was completed and never received the honour.*

Financial Objectives

From a financial perspective, I think that our lives should be split into thirds. The first third of our lives should be concerned only with obtaining enough money to allow us to have enough fun to enjoy our youth, without going too crazy. The middle third of our life should be concerned with making as much money as we possibly can so that we can provide all that our family and friends desire, within reason. Finally, if we have reached the objectives that we set in the middle third, then the final third of our life should be about having fun as we distribute many millions in the support of worthy causes.

I do not believe the old cliché that says obtaining vast sums of money changes people. I think that money is simply the great magnifying glass. It takes whatever the person's core characteristics are and magnifies them. If a person is generous when they were poor then they may become a great philanthropist, if they are flashy then they may become more flamboyant and so on. Money allows people to be a bigger version of what they already are. Whether that is good or bad depends on the individual. I do agree that money does not buy happiness, but I believe that there is nothing better at picking locks and opening doors.

"It is good to have money and the things that money can buy, but it's good too, to check up once in a while and make sure you haven't lost the things money can't buy."

~ George Lorimer (Editor and writer)

☑ **Become a 'Thousandaire'.** The first time I ever received a four-digit cheque was when I was at university and my student grant came through. It was for a grand total of £1,300. As I stood looking down at the cheque with a big smile on my face someone behind me, who had also just received his cheque, shouted out "I am now a thousandaire!" and we all burst out laughing. Walking out of there with those cheques in our hands and our heads held high, we all felt so proud to be 'thousandaires'.

☐ **Obtain that first €1 million.** They say that the first million is the hardest to get. As we all know, this is correct and the reason is simply because you are starting from nothing. However, to earn a million you do not need to be a financial whizz-kid. Calculations prove that if you invest €16,000 per annum (say, €1,333 per month) and gain a return of 10 percent on that money then it would take 20 years to earn the first €1 million. However, this is where it gets interesting.

If you continued to invest this amount, it is calculated to take only another six years to reach €2 million, with €3 million being reached within another four years. How, you may ask? Well, this is simply due to compound interest. Interest on interest. For most people this saving amount and return on investment is totally unrealistic, however, as an example, it just goes to prove that money begets money and that the first million is indeed the hardest to get.

☐ **Have a net worth of €111 million.** A million is not what it used to be and it will not buy as much as it once did. In fact, in most European cities right now it would be very difficult to get a proper house with a decent size garden in a nice area for €1 million. This is the reality of it, unfortunately. Therefore, I want to aim big and €111,000,000 has always been the

Become a Billionaire

number that I have been working towards. You may think that a boy that grew up in the "unemployment black spot of Europe" is crazy if he thinks that he can achieve nine-digit wealth. Well if you do, then you may really start to worry about me when you learn that I plan to achieve this wealth by giving my money away – simply because I believe that what you give out, you get back.

☐ **Become a Billionaire.** *I have not ticked this one off, despite the fact that it could be argued that I am a Billionaire. In fact, I may even be a Trillionaire. Let me explain. When I was in Zimbabwe, I was able to pick up quite a few notes that contained many zeros after the 'one'. The largest note I purchased when I was down there was the One Hundred Trillion Dollar note. That is a 'one' with fourteen 'zeros' after it and looks like this: $100,000,000,000,000. I keep it on my desk in front of me, just to remind me that I am a Trillionaire, at least in one part of the world.*

☐ **Create enough passive income so that I can choose not to work another day in my life.**

☐ **Own a portfolio of properties in prime locations that generate rental income.** *A successful property portfolio can turn into a nice little nest egg that provides financial independence within a few years. This can then be developed into providing for a very comfortable retirement. Right now, with the world economy going* through economic hardship, is the perfect time to be purchasing properties and land, which is exactly what many of the worlds rich are currently doing, after selling off their holdings at the top of the boom. It is at times like this when the rich get richer. The one piece of advice that has always stuck in my mind when it comes to developing a property portfolio is something that I learned as a teenager and it was this: 'When there is blood on the street, buy property'.

☐ **Leave a decent inheritance to my children.** *It is my desire to leave my children enough money so that they are able to do something, but not so much that they are able to do nothing.*

III

The Journey is more important than the destination

My approach to travel has always been more about focusing on the journey than on the destination. All my trips start with the same act: I will take out a globe and look at the areas that I have never explored. From there, I will pick two points on the globe with the objective of starting at one and finishing at the other. I do not plan a specific route or a time frame. I do not have any accommodation booked in advance for any stage of the trip and I have no inclination as to the means of transport that I will use to get to my final destination. I just let go and allow my heart to guide me.

Whilst looking at the globe recently, I noticed that I had never properly explored Scandinavia nor been into the Arctic. Other glaring omissions from my travels were the traditional Communist countries of Russia, Mongolia, China and Vietnam. Thailand and Malaysia were the only countries in South East Asia that I had experienced properly.

Based on this, I decided that it would be nice for me to set off on a journey that would take me through this entire area of the world. My starting point was to be the small town of Narvik, nestled within the Arctic Circle on the north west coast of Norway. My destination would be Singapore, at the lower end of South East Asia. By running my finger over Russia, Mongolia and China on the globe, my route was roughly planned but the stops I would make and areas I would explore would all be determined en route.

When 'on the road', I acquire the information that I need from locals and other travellers that I meet. Apart from that, I just follow my heart. Of course, there are places that I wish to visit in every country, and I will make a good effort to visit them, but if an adventure takes me on a different path then so be it. I can always come back at a later date.

There is so much to be gained from this approach to travel. When I travel like this, I am afforded the opportunity to gain a true understanding of the outside world. As I have no time constraints or set plans, I am allowed to stop and stay and talk and play as my heart desires. This allows me to get a feel for a country and its people and break through the prejudices that the Western media instils in us.

In the early days of my travels, I found it extraordinary how different places turned out to be when I visited them. The scare stories of various regions fed through the media are always so wide of the mark. The reality is usually smiles and invitations to dinner. Most people in the world have exactly the same desires, which is to be happy and healthy and create a better life for themselves and a better future for their children.

As a rule of thumb, I have found that the more negatively a region of the world is portrayed by the Western media, then the more kind, generous and warm the people are. This was particularly the case when I recently travelled through the Middle East. Travel is full of pleasant surprises.

Ever since I first set out alone to travel to Germany in 1997, I have always been excited about the journeys ahead, as I get to experience the most magnificent sights this world has to offer. I also get to learn more about who I am and what my purpose is in life. My desire is to see the world, but ultimately when I travel, it is a journey within myself.

At times, I find myself in the middle of nowhere. At times, in the middle of nowhere I find myself.

J o u r n e y s : R o a d

Being able to set out on long journeys comes down to two things: time and money. We need both to be able to set out into the world without knowing where our next meal will come from, where we will sleep that night or how we will get to the next destination. To be able to live like this, there must not be major time constraints and there must be access to funding to allow us to meet our challenges.

With this in mind, I believe that the optimum period of life for setting out on long journeys is between the ages of 25 and 35, and after retirement. This is a total generalisation, but for most people in their teens and early twenties they have an abundance of free time, but not so much disposable income.

On the other hand, people in their late thirties, forties and fifties are bringing up families and building their careers. These people are close to the top of their earning potential, but they have a limit on their spare time, which prevents prolonged travel of a year or more.

Therefore, I have noticed that retirees and people between the ages of 25 and 35, as long as they do not have a dependant family, are the ideal candidates to set off on journeys of prolonged travel. The people within the 25 – 35 age group and those over 60 that

I meet travelling have usually completed their education, from which they have been able to gain employment and earn a fair bit of disposable income.

Then, if their heart is willing, it does not take much for them to gather up the funds, leave their job and set off to live the life of their dreams. That is exactly what I did and what follows are some of the journeys that interested me.

"If you do not change direction, you may end up where you are heading."
~ Lao Tzu (Philosopher of ancient China)

☑ **North Atlantic Ocean – North Pacific Ocean:** *New York – Los Angeles, via Texas.* *When I thought of America before this trip I automatically thought of either New York or Los Angeles due to those cities obtaining the most coverage in movies. However, after a few months touring through the centre of this illustrious country I gained a fine appreciation for the greatness of this land. With such a variety of landscapes on offer, the USA can offer nearly every travel experience. It was from this trip that I grew to understand why passport possession in the United States had remained relatively low with only 38% of Americans owning a passport (according to State Department statistics as at January 2012) – America has everything.*

☑ **North Atlantic Ocean – North Pacific Ocean: *Narvik, Norway – Beijing, China.*** It was my intention to travel from coast to coast on both the major landmasses of the Northern Hemisphere, thus the reason why I planned such a trip. However, despite my initial plan being to complete this as a road journey, the majority of this journey was completed by train, as detailed in that section.

☑ **South Pacific Ocean – South Atlantic Ocean: *Lima, Peru – Rio de Janeiro, Brazil.*** This journey consisted of visiting Machu Picchu, Colca Canyon, The Sacred Valley, Lake Titicaca, Salar de Uyuní, The Pantanal, The Amazon Rainforest, Iguaçu Falls and Paraty to name a few of the highlights. This was one of the great road trips.

☑ **South Atlantic Ocean – Indian Ocean: *Skeleton Coast, Namibia – Dar es Salaam, Tanzania.*** I was fortunate enough to complete this route as part of a larger journey that carried me from Cape Town, South Africa – Kigali, Rwanda. The countries that I was privileged to visit during this tour included South Africa, Namibia, Botswana, Zimbabwe, Zambia, Malawi, Tanzania, Kenya, Uganda and Rwanda. When I am driving through the centre of Africa, I am in paradise.

☑ **Mexico City, Mexico – Panama City, Panama.** I had always wanted to experience an overland journey as part of a tour group, as I always believed that it was a great way to see many fantastic sites in a short amount of time. Therefore, when I found myself with a two-month window to do a stint of travel I really wanted to complete the Mexico to Panama trip. However, I knew that if I were to complete this journey alone I would need maybe four or five months, as I really like to settle in and get a good feel for the places I find. I decided to look online for tour groups that would be going on a similar route and I was surprised to learn that there were quite a few. It seems that for any route you want to complete, the tour groups will have a tour available, no matter how long or short the journey is.

After much research into the various trips on offer by the various tour operators, I settled on Tucan Travel. For me, they were the operator that seemed to have the perfect balance between what was included in the price and the optional excursions. Some operators include too many excursions, which I would have been forced to pay for upfront, whether I was interested in going or not. Other operators were very cheap and as a result offered a very basic tour. For me, Tucan Travel seemed to have it right, so I signed up for the 37-day tour from Cancun to Panama City. The dates fell perfect for me, as they afforded me the chance to spend some time exploring the region between Mexico City and Cancun as a solo traveller before joining the group.

This was an overland adventure tour that consisted of us using public transport as much as possible, which is what I normally do anyway. However, we had the benefit of being led by a guide that had the bus tickets organised prior and escorted us straight to the buses without us having to worry about the language barrier or the transport being overbooked. I really liked this because it allowed me to gain exposure to the local way of life, which is the most important part of any trip. In addition, we had the benefit of an experienced guide to make life easy, through pre-booking accommodation and providing inside-knowledge of the region.

Another great benefit of this type of travel is that I was exposed to a wider range of travellers. Normally in hostels, the age group of people I predominantly meet would range between 20 – 35 years old. However, on that tour, I travelled within a much wider age range. The youngest person on the tour was a 19-year-old Asian girl travelling solo, with the oldest being a retired English couple in their sixties. The remainder of the group were born during every decade in between. It was fascinating to be able to talk to such a great bunch of people of all different age groups, on the same wave length and all geared up for the experience of a lifetime.

These overland expeditions offer a fun, economical, exciting and more relaxed manner in which to gain genuine insights into the people and culture of the region. For anyone that wants to see the world, but does not want to set out on their own, these type of tours offer a great way of uniting adventure seekers from all over the world with those that have similar interests and passions. I would definitely choose this as a travel option again.

☑ **London, England – Sydney, Australia.** *Many find this hard to believe, but it is possible to travel overland from the UK to Australia, when a few short boat crossings are included. When I tell people of this it often leaves them with their eyebrows raised, so I will explain in summary format (as this experience could be a book in itself). We departed from Cleopatra's Needle in London and drove to Dover, from where we got the ferry to France. Now, if you go and look at your atlas you will discover that there is a solid landmass stretching from France all the way to Malaysia. We drove across that.*

The route we chose, for those that are interested, was via Iran and Pakistan. We then entered India and climbed the Himalayas into Nepal before driving down through South East Asia, into Malaysia. To get from Malaysia to Australia, we boarded a ferry in Malaysia, sailing to the Indonesian island of Sumatra. We then drove to the other side of the island, boarded another boat there to the island of Java and then onto Bali and so on, until we got to Darwin in the 'Land Down Under.'

Drive around Australia

From Darwin it was a few weeks drive through the red centre of Australia until we arrived in beautiful Sydney. This was a great trip, but my only regret is that we did not take more time to complete the journey and ended up rushing it in some parts. I recommend setting aside a year to complete this, as the longer you take the greater the experience will be.

☑ **Valparaiso, Chile – Antarctica.** The route through this isolated region of the world started off good and got better and better with each passing day. The fact that it led me through Patagonia is enough to make me want to do this again. The route that I ended up travelling was as follows: Valparaiso – Viña del Mar – Santiago – Osorno – Puerto Montt – San Carlos de Bariloche – Perito Moreno – El Chalten – El Calafate – Puerto Natales – Torres del Paine – Punta Arenas – Ushuaia. If Ushuaia was not isolated enough for me, it was from here that I was able to board a ship and set sail to Antarctica.

☐ **Drive around Australia.** As Australia is such a massive country, I attempted to complete this objective in many different sections over the course of a year. My initial journey went from the scorched tropics of Darwin in the north to the cooler climes of Adelaide in the south. This journey allowed me to get a close look at the hot and dusty heart of Australia, taking in such wonders as Uluru, Kings Canyon and Coober

Pedy, offering an experience that no other part of this planet can provide.

Leaving Adelaide my objective was to make my way up the east coast of Australia to the luscious Cape Tribulation; one of the great backpacker journeys. Travelling along the Great Ocean Road offered views unlike anything I had ever imagined. The views of the terrain as the road wound along the edge of this southern coast of Australia were stunning. There were also several prominent landmarks along the route including the significant 'Twelve Apostles'. Despite offering beautiful vistas, it was the naming of the limestone stacks that humoured me. At the time of changing the name from 'The Sow and Piglets', to the biblical 'Twelve Apostles' there were only nine stacks. When I visited, there were eight.

At the end of the Great Ocean Road, I ended up in the thriving cosmopolitan city of Melbourne and the all night parties in St. Kilda. From here, I moved on to the centre of government in Canberra and the nations capital, if only in name. Canberra has a reputation for being quite a boring town, which is wholly unfair. It cannot be compared to any of the other major Australian cities but it has its touristy draws. I enjoyed my time there. From Canberra, I moved on to glorious Sydney, spending a lot of time on the lazy beaches that the city is famous for. I then began my assault of the east coast with a stop off at bohemian Byron Bay and the hippy hideaway of Nimbin.

Carrying on up the coast, I partied in Surfers Paradise before stopping in Brisbane to meet up with some friends. Noosa was the next stop on the itinerary as this is where I learned to surf. Before I reached the backpacker Mecca of Cairns, I had further stops in Rainbow Beach, Bundaberg, Townsville and Mission Beach. Port Douglas was my last port of call before Cape Tribulation, my tropical paradise destination. What a trip. I visited thriving cities, experienced mind-blowing sights, chilled out in rural beach retreats and shared many laughs with the new friends I picked up en route.

After completing the well-trodden east coast, I worked in Sydney for a few months, before setting out to complete my drive around this continent island once again. This time the objective was to tour the rugged west coast of Australia, travelling from Perth to Broome. This is the lesser-travelled route in Australia for reasons that I cannot comprehend, as the west coast left me feeling as if I was experiencing the 'real Australia'. On offer was the famous Monkey Mia dolphins of Shark Bay and the spectacular tranquil freshwater swimming holes in Karijini National Park, to name some of the highlights.

Despite the great experiences that I had, I believe that the west coast is a superior trip to travelling up the east coast of Australia, regardless of the fact that it may be a little bit more expensive. If you have limited time in Australia, I would recommend the west coast as the journey to take. I would like to say that I had completed my drive around Australia, but it is my intention to travel from the South Pacific Ocean at Sydney to the Indian Ocean at Perth, hitchhiking across the Nullabor Desert. The fact that I have to go back to do this is not such a bad thing.

☐ **Europe: *Tromsø, Norway – Athens, Greece.*** The planned route on this trip is: Norway – Sweden – Finland – Estonia – Latvia – Lithuania – Belarus – Poland – Czech Republic – Slovakia – Hungary – Croatia – Bosnia and Herzegovina – Serbia – Montenegro – Kosovo – FYR Macedonia – Albania – Greece.

☐ **The Icelandic Ring Road.** This is 1,350 kilometres of glaciers, geysers and greyness as Highway One circles the island of Iceland. The plan is to take a week to complete this journey in the middle of June so that I can experience 168 hours of uninterrupted day light as I drive through some of the most awe inspiring scenery available anywhere.

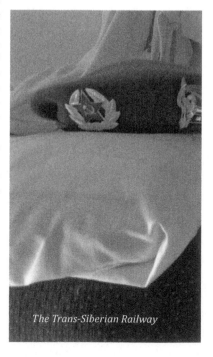

The Trans-Siberian Railway

Journeys: Rail

"Travel is fatal to prejudice, bigotry, and narrow-mindedness, and many of our people need it sorely on these accounts. Broad, wholesome, charitable views of men and things cannot be acquired by vegetating in one little corner of the earth all one's lifetime."

~ Mark Twain (Author and adventurer)

☑ **The Trans-Siberian Railway: Moscow to Beijing, through the Eastern Russian provinces and Mongolia.** *Most people with an interest in travel will be fully aware of what this magnificent route* consists of. However, I will say that the experience itself is even better than you can imagine. We specifically had no plans made before leaving (don't tell the Russian authorities), as we were confident we would be able to organise (blag) every part of this journey as we went along with the help of friendly locals.

We wanted to avoid having to deal with the organised tours, which we expected would dilute the vast experience to be gained on this trip. One major reason for this was that the organised tour groups always book second-class compartments, which meant that we would have been locked in a 'four person carriage' with other Western tourists. Our desire was to travel third-class, where the

train was completely open and we could wander around and talk to the locals, share food and vodka and sing along to old Russian military songs.

For me, this is what the Trans-Siberian is all about. It is not about sitting down in the restaurant carriage day after day with a group of Western tourists drinking overpriced beers and hoping a local person wanders in, so I can have my 'local-experience story' to relay when I get home. I would seriously recommend booking this trip on your own as you go, as this is a great part of the experience and it is too good to be missed by joining a tour group.

Despite their stern exteriors, I found the Russian people to be among some of the friendliest and most helpful in the world. Tour companies vastly inflate their prices because they say that this journey is nearly impossible to organise on an individual basis. This is incorrect. The local people will go out of their way to ensure you have a great trip and have fun getting to your destination, from my experiences.

I would recommend doing this trip sooner rather than later, as the trains are becoming more modern and I can only imagine that they are just a few years away from having wifi installed in them. This is a trip that is better done before that time. You can complete this trip all in one go, over seven days without ever getting off the train, or you can break it up over a month

or two, getting off to explore each of the towns along the route for a few days. Either way, you will find this trip so rewarding in so many ways. This is one of the great travel experiences.

☑ **Vietnam: *Han Oi – Ho Chi Minh City.*** *Vietnam is such a famous country due to the war that it is better known for. However, for anyone that has spent any amount of time travelling through it, the image that remains the most vividly etched on the memory is that of the motorcycle. Since the war ended the motorcycle has overtaken the bicycle as the main mode of transport. The motorcycle is to the Vietnamese, what the horse was to Genghis Khan and his armies.*

Not only do the Vietnamese use their motorcycle to transport people but also to transport every imaginable and unimaginable object, produce and service. Can you imagine what 200 chickens strapped to a motorcycle looks like? How about a cow with its head chopped off laying over the lap of a moped driver? How about bags filled with water containing Goldfish piled high around the driver?

The major reason for this, which may seem like madness to outsiders, lies in the Vietnamese fixation with having fresh ingredients for every meal. Such importance is attached to eating there that frozen meat is just not acceptable. There is a demand to obtain their foodstuffs directly from the farmer and from the boats, thus the preference to have the food delivered alive, if not freshly butchered. Thus, the reason why motorcycles are used as the preferred mode of transport is because there is no need to transport large quantities at one time, instead many relatively small loads are distributed to each region throughout the day.

Just getting to witness what the local people stack on the back of their motorcycles is worth the trip, alone. To get any idea of what I am talking about it may be worth checking out the book "Bikes of Burden" by Hans Kemp. We are all aware of the increasing pace of change throughout the world, but despite developments, it is still the motorcycle that puts the food in the stomachs of Vietnamese people and keeps their economy growing.

☑ **The Fjords of Norway.** *Train travel provides the most relaxing and hassle free way in which to meander through the best scenery Norway has to offer. With my eyes constantly on the fjords and mountain scenery outside, I was afforded some of the most beautiful vistas imaginable as I completed this trip at the peak of summer. However, I have a sneaking intuition that this trip may be even better at the end of a harsh winter.*

☑ **Europe: *Brussels, Belgium – Athens, Greece.*** *This was a trip that I had wanted to complete for a long time. I had travelled to every continent on earth and yet I had not seen half of Europe. Like all my*

previous trips, I found two points on the globe and set out from one with the intention of getting to the other using Europe's great rail infrastructure. The route I chose was as follows: Brussels – Paris – Bordeaux – Bilbao – Madrid – Blanes – Barcelona – Montpellier – Marseille – Cannes – Nice – Monte Carlo – Milan – Rome – Venice – Ljubljana – Zagreb – Belgrade – Sarajevo – Podgorica – Pristina – Tirana – Skopje – Thessaloniki – Athens.

☑ **Arctic – Equator: *Narvik, Norway to Singapore.*** *This was the longest train journey I could find on the Eurasia landmass. A rough outline of the towns and cities that I visited en route are as follows: Narvik – Kiruna – Sveg – Stockholm – Helsinki – St. Petersburg – Moscow – Yekaterinburg – Novosibirsk – Irkutsk – Ulan-Ude – Ulaanbaatar – Beijing – Xi'an – Shanghai – Nanning – Ha Noi – Ho Chi Minh City – Phnom Penh – Vientiane – Bangkok – Kuala Lumpur – Singapore. (Where a train was not available, I made my way by other means). This journey did not disappoint. Just imagine how different a city in Sweden, a town in Siberia and a village in Cambodia are when compared to each other and that will give you a glimpse into how remarkable it was to complete this trip all in one go.*

☐ **The Channel Tunnel: *London, England – Paris, France.*** *French mining engineer Albert Mathieu first proposed the idea for a tunnel under the English Channel that* connected England with France in 1802. His plans consisted of lighting the tunnel using oil lamps as horse-drawn coaches pulled passengers and freight as far as an artificial island mid-Channel, where the horses would be changed. Today a 50.5 kilometre undersea rail tunnel links England with northern France as the high-speed Eurostar passenger train speeds below the English Channel. Since the day this opened, I have wanted to experience this.

□ **The Orient Express.** Once known as "The world's most exclusive train", the two cities most prominently associated with the Orient Express are Istanbul and Paris as they were the original endpoints of the timetabled service. However, in 1977, the Orient Express stopped serving Istanbul, running only to Vienna as an overnight service from Paris. The last Orient Express train to Vienna left from Paris on 8 June 2007 when the route, still called the "Orient Express," was shortened to start from Strasbourg.

Sadly, all good things must come to an end and on 14 December 2009, the Orient Express ceased to operate permanently and the route disappeared from European railway timetables, reportedly a "victim of high-speed trains and cut-rate airlines." Thankfully a private venture has taken over the Orient Express and, using original carriages from the 1920s and 30s, continues to run the trains along the original route from Paris to Istanbul

as well as to other destinations in Europe. Although it will not be quite the same as the original, I am delighted that a private venture has kept this great travel experience alive.

□ **Beijing, China – Lhasa, Tibet.** This journey is 4,064 kilometres long and takes the best part of three days to complete as the train passes through mountains, past lakes and between herds of endangered animals, whilst encountering many diverse ethnic groups. The Qinghai-Tibet section of the Railway is the highest in the world, climbing from 2,829 metres above sea level at Golmud and rising to over 5,000 metres at Tanggula Pass, before dropping back down to 3,641 metres at Lhasa, with much of it built on permafrost. Due to the lack of oxygen at this altitude, all passenger carriages have extra oxygen pumped into them, with oxygen available through tubes if passengers are having issues with altitude sickness.

□ **Canada: *Vancouver, B.C. – Halifax, Nova Scotia.*** Canada is the second largest country on earth after Russia, spanning 9,984,670 kilometres^2 over six time zones. With a population of only 33 million, vast areas of this unique country are either sparsely populated or completely uninhabited. This means that it is possible to travel for days without ever meeting another soul.

With a continuous series of connecting train services running *from the Pacific to the Atlantic, combined with the fact that most Canadians choose to fly between cities means that this trans-continental journey remains one of the greatest railway journeys on the planet. A rough plan of the route, which I plan to complete in around 40 days is as follows: Vancouver, British Columbia – Jasper, Alberta – Edmonton, Alberta – Saskatoon, Saskatchewan – Winnipeg, Manitoba – Toronto, Ontario – Ottawa, Ontario – Montreal, Quebec – Quebec City, Quebec – Halifax, Nova Scotia.*

☐ **India: *New Delhi – Goa.*** *Preferably, I will complete this journey whilst hanging off the side of the train or sitting on the roof with thousands of others. You may think that this is a lazy stereotype of train travel in India and you may be right, as of course, not all journeys are like this. There is the option of taking the superfast and comfortable Goa Express but what would be the point of that? When in India, do as the Indian's do and get the cheapest ticket possible and get in amongst the locals.*

During my last visit to India I travelled through this vast country by bus and I soon came to realise once I had left that the best way to see India is whilst travelling the incredible Indian railway system. In fact, no visit to India is complete without experiencing the bustle of Indian railway stations and a few journeys on an Indian express train.

Journeys: Sail

"Twenty years from now you will be more disappointed by the things you didn't do than by the ones you did do. So throw off the bowlines, sail away from the safe harbour. Catch the trade winds in your sails. Explore. Dream. Discover."

~ Mark Twain (Author and adventurer)

☑ **The Drake Passage:** *Ushuaia, Argentina – Antarctic Peninsula.* *The roughest sea passage in the world left some of my fellow passengers bruised, battered and green with seasickness. Thankfully, I was one of only two people that never felt sick on the crossing, but I will admit that it was challenging. To have any idea of what I am talking about, check out the YouTube clips of this crossing. 'Storm in the Drake Passage' is one that I have posted up on www.theisbook.com/fun-blog that I would recommend watching, whilst trying to imagine how it would feel to be onboard that boat.*

☑ **The Antarctic Peninsula.** *This is a rugged mountain chain averaging more than 2,000 metres high. Sailing through this is an experience that one is not likely to forget very easily, as we were constantly faced with huge walls of ice calving off the cliff faces and into the water around our ship. The area differs from most of the rest of Antarctica because it has a summer melting season, which produces* many isolated snow-free areas. This allowed us to enter the continent quite easily on these areas, which are also breeding grounds for mammals and birds. Sailing along here on the Zodiacs offered a win-win situation.*

☑ **Stockholm, Sweden – Helsinki, Finland via the skärgård.** *I was lucky enough to complete this passage at the peak of summer, so it never really got dark. The sky was bright blue all day as the temperature hit 33 degrees Celsius. Throughout the night, the sky maintained a bright red that emanated from the sun just peaking below the horizon for a short time before coming back up again. It was wonderful to watch as the night sky went from sunset*

Ha Long Bay

and back to sunrise again within an hour. There was nothing left for me to do as we cruised through the 30,000 islands, inlets and skerries but enjoy the view from the Jacuzzi, whilst sipping on champagne and eating Gummy Bears (they were selling huge bags of duty-free candy at the docks and I could not resist).

☑ **Whitsunday Islands, Australia.** *Yes, sailing around this visually stunning part of the world is as good as you can imagine it to be. With names such as Daydream Island, Long Island and Hamilton Island (possibly named after an ancestor of mine?), the 74 tropical islands of the Whitsundays are the very definition of a picture postcard paradise. Sailing around*

the Whitsundays, on the tropical coast off Queensland, is a feast of the senses. Every direction I looked the natural beauty was jumping out at me.

As the other passengers on the boat soon got a bit tired of my excitement of pointing things out, I grabbed a cool drink and went and sat up on the bow on my own. With my feet dangling over the water and the Great Barrier Reef rushing past below I have this vivid memory of the sun setting to my right and the breeze blowing gently as I sat in silence taking it all in.

☑ **Ha Long Bay, Vietnam.** *Admired from inside a traditional junk boat as we departed the Vietnamese coast,*

Ha Long Bay looked like a solid mountain. For nearly 300 million years, the 1,969 stone mushrooms mountains have mesmerised all that visited the region and I have to admit I was seriously impressed by this trip.

☑ **The River Nile:** *Luxor – Alexandria, Egypt.* Well this is a strange one. I have ticked this one off, as although I did start it I did not get to complete it. See what you think.

In December 2010, I was in Egypt just before the revolution kicked off. It was a great time to be in Cairo, as there was a real sense that something was about to happen. However, my lungs and nose really needed some respite from the thick smoggy air of the city. I decided that I needed some time out of this great city for a while, so I jumped on an overnight train and went to Aswan in the south of Egypt, close to the Sudanese border. The plan was to do some exploring in the south and then sail back up the Nile by whatever means possible. Great plan.

I was in Abu Simble when I learned that it is possible to jump on a boat from Luxor that will be sailing north up the Nile. Perfect. I made my way to Luxor, where I organised to join a three-day tour that would take me some of the way on what seemed to be a fantastic boat for a great price. In the late afternoon I was picked up at the rendezvous spot along with a young Japanese girl and some French Hippies, before we sped away on the back of a pick-up towards the 'dock'.

What we found at the riverbank was that our home for the foreseeable future would be a catamaran. Our bags were packed away underneath and we would eat and sleep on the deck, under the sun and the stars for the duration of the journey. This was going to be a great experience.

After much sitting around and chitchatting between the five passengers, we eventually departed out into the middle of the mighty Nile, heading north. Or so it seemed. After a while, we noticed that instead of going up river, we were getting closer to the riverbank opposite from where we departed. Turns out, as we pulled up and docked on the riverbank, that this was to be our destination for the day, as one of the crew climbed up and started untying the sail. The other two crewmembers started clinking pots and pans together, before informing us that dinner would be ready in 45 minutes.

Fantastic. Yet confusing. After dinner, we were told to get comfortable for the night, as "we will set sail during the night." "Maybe the tide was too strong," I thought to myself, but either way I was not too fussed. After the five of us had finished the grand total of three beers that we had brought on board, we eventually all went to sleep on the deck under the stars.

When I awoke at sunrise, I was not that surprised to learn that we were still exactly where we had docked the day before and the sail for the catamaran was still laying in a heap on the bank. A few hours after all the passengers awoke, the crew finally showed up. After some talking among them, the Captain casually strolled up the riverbank, around the corner and out of sight. I then got the feeling that I would never see this man again. The two younger crewmembers started preparing the catamaran for departure.

They eventually got us back to the other side of the river, to where we had started, and began taking our bags off with big smiles. "We are here, I suppose?" I said jokingly as he handed me my possessions. "Yes" he replied as he motioned to be tipped for the great journey we had just been on.

I never got to sail up the River Nile. He did not receive his tip.

☐ **The Pacific Ocean: *Sydney, Australia – Panama City, Panama.*** My desired route is: Sydney – New Caledonia – Vanuatu – Fiji – Tonga – Samoa – American Samoa – Cook Islands – French Polynesia – Pitcairn Islands – Galapagos Islands – Panama.

☐ **The Atlantic Ocean: *The Canary Islands – The Caribbean.*** In Stockholm, Sweden, they have this 'thing', that the only people 'allowed' to wear red trousers are those that have earned the right to do so, by sailing across the Atlantic Ocean. It is a badge of honour, in a way. As my sister has already purchased a nice pair of red chinos for me, I look forward to that sunny Sunday morning when I walk into the Royal Swedish Yacht Club in Stockholm proudly wearing them.

☐ **Sail through the world's great canals.** I have been fortunate enough to visit many canals around the world including the Suez Canal, Egypt and the Panama Canal, Panama. I even got to spend a day at the Miraflores Locks at the Panama Canal observing as the massive ships passed through the continental divide from the Atlantic Ocean to the Pacific Ocean and vice versa. However, instead of quenching my thirst for sailing through the canals, this just further added to my desire to be on board a luxury yacht as it passed through these great landmasses.

☐ **Lake Mälaren, Västerås – Stockholm skärgård, Sweden.** I would like to take at least a week to complete this journey. The perfect manner in which to finish this journey would be to moor the boat at the entrance to a chilled out restaurant on a nice island deep in the Stockholm skärgård. Whilst there, I would bask in the hot summer sun whilst enjoying a cold drink with some of the worlds finest seafood.

IV

Travel is

the best education

The word education comes from the Latin *e-ducere* meaning "to lead out." In ancient Greece, Socrates was of the conviction that education was about opening the students mind and drawing out what was already there. *"I cannot teach anybody anything, I can only make them think"* was his approach to education.

I entered the formal schooling system as a four-year-old and exited as a 28-year-old. I spent just short of 24 years being taught and in all that time, I never had to repeat a year and never had a break. I am truly grateful for the opportunities that I received within the education system. However, my one gripe with the education system is that the man who graduated was more 'closed-minded' than the child that entered.

I believe that as a child, I had a mind that was open to all possibilities. My only limit was my imagination. I would question everything and when the adults around me provided me with an answer, I would then ask "why?"

This was my approach to gaining knowledge when I first attended school. However – when I was treated as a 'trouble-maker' for asking too many questions – I soon learned the realities of how our modern education system works. Socrates' approach has long since died and, as a broad generalisation, the students that excel are the ones that learn to accept what 'authority' dictates, without question. Teachers are now sculptors that mould as apposed to gardeners that encourage natural flowering.

Ultimately what we now have is an education system that has developed into a form of programming. Our minds are programmed to develop the skills necessary to fulfil the characteristics of our chosen careers. Therefore, the further we go in education, the more finely tuned we become to suit our chosen specialism or field of expertise. This is not a bad thing if one's objective in life is to keep one's head down, work hard and climb as far up the corporate ladder as possible before retiring with a gold watch at age 65.

However, I am one of those that like to keep my head up and look people in the eye as I learn from them and I still ask too many questions. My 24 years of structured education offered much; but alas, it did not fulfil my burning desire to be educated in the ways of Socrates. The skills that I acquired in my formal schooling provided me with a passport to the world and as a 28-year-old man with the world as my oyster I fully intended to use that opportunity "to lead out" the person that I truly was.

Harping back to the third *Carrot* on my initial list and my objective of exploring this great planet, I believed that this was the best way to open my mind. Therefore, I packed my bag, sold all that I owned and set out into the world, immersing myself in all that this fabulous planet had to offer. Travel, I believe, is necessary to develop the mind and expand one's knowledge of the world. Through travel, I have been given the opportunity to complete my education and become a more enlightened and well-rounded individual.

In the way that *home-schooling* has become increasingly popular over the years due to the enhanced levels of education on offer, similarly, travelling simply for the sake of curiosity and learning has offered me an education like no other. It is what I like to call *bus-schooling*!

As I have travelled the world, I have been involved in two types of journeys, both offering great education. The more obvious journey is the outer journey. This is the physical experience of travel: the places I have visited, that which I have observed, the individuals I have met and my behaviour whilst there. Then there is the inner journey. This is my *interpretation* of the experience: the understandings I gained, the beliefs I discarded, the insights I acquired and how my perspective on life was irrevocably transformed.

Through travel, I have been able to transform myself as a person, not by becoming a completely new man, but rather by getting back to the individual I truly am. Through peeling back the layers that society had placed on me I have been able to return to that beautiful person I was as a child. It was Rousseau that said, "*Man is born free and everywhere he is in chains.*" It was these chains that I desired to cast off.

It was through travel that I was allowed to abandon the fears and insecurities that I had developed as a teenager and once again allow myself to shine brightly. Through overcoming internal and external challenges, making connections with exceptional people and having prolonged periods alone as I travelled the seven continents, I have been able "to lead out" the person that I truly am. 'The University of Life' continues to offer the best education.

World Experiences

The greatest adventure that we can undertake in our modern world is the one that forces us to fill a backpack with all that we need, sell everything else (including a beloved Porsche) and set out overseas into the unknown. No friends, no family, no tickets, no pre-booked rooms, no plans. Just a sense of adventure and a smile to get by. Many people have done it and many people are packing their bags right now. The author and adventurer, Mark Jenkins did it. Otherwise, his words would not have resonated with so many people for so long:

"Adventure is a path. Real adventure – self-determined, self-motivated, often risky – forces you to have first hand encounters with the world. The world is the way it is, not the way you imagine it. Your body will collide with the earth and you will bear witness. In this way, you will be compelled to grapple with the limitless kindness and bottomless cruelty of humankind – and perhaps realise that you yourself are capable of both. This will change you. Nothing will ever again be black-and-white."

He was right – it will change you, but it will be for your greater good. Trust me, there is nothing holding you back from the greatest adventure of them all. Everything you need can be acquired and accumulated along the path, including money. Your biggest fear right now is that you cannot see the entire path and you have no idea as to where it will lead you or what you will become as you continue along this path. Do not worry about that. You do not need to see the whole path, just have faith and take the first step.

Europe

"France, and the whole of Europe have a great culture and an amazing history. Most important thing though is that people there know how to live! In America, they've forgotten all about it."

~ Johnny Depp (Actor)

☑ **Climb to the Statues of Mount Nemrut, Turkey.** *A group of us awoke in the middle of the night to climb to the top of Mount Nemrut in time for sunrise. It was a tough enough climb considering that I was basically sleep walking the whole way up. Upon arriving at the top, I had to clear my eyes when I was confronted by the huge faces staring back at me. I knew they were going to be big but I did not expect that the heads alone would be up to two metres in height. We had found the 'Easter Island of Turkey'.*

Dating back to the first century B.C., this vast field of gigantic statues surrounded the sanctuary tomb of King Antiochus. These monoliths were huge, measuring up to ten metres in height. As well as statues of the King Antiochus himself, there are eagles, lions, Greek Gods and what looks like a serpent. They were all arranged in seated positions around the burial mound, with the names of the Gods inscribed on them. However, an Earthquake has since scattered them around the site.

☑ **Watch sunset from Calo des Moro bay, Ibiza.** *Despite it being the peak of summer with hundreds of thousands of party people from around the world on the island, the most vivid memory I have of this time, is of sitting down to watch this sunset. As soon as the sun drops behind the sea, everyone claps, a big cheer goes up and the next never-ending party begins in earnest.*

☑ **Explore Venice, Italy by Gondola.** *Venice is idealistically known as La Serenissima, "the most serene one," by those that are least familiar with it. It is a strange place, because as a travel destination it is neither land nor water, managing effortlessly to flicker between both. By standing at the edge of the Grand Canal and studying the city map, I was afforded an insight into the spaghetti-like composition of this unintentional city and decided to do what I do best: I went wandering off the beaten track. Within minutes I was lost in the warren of alleyways and lanes, but it was only then that I got to admire the beauty of Venice: its chaos! The real beauty of this city is to be found there in the back alleyways.*

As the tourists sat out front oblivious, gazing through their oversized sunglasses whilst sipping on their overpriced drinks, I admired the graffiti, got chased by the locals and lifted the veil on the flaky façade of this tourist trap. However, it was not until midnight when the tourists had retired to their hotels and the vendors had counted their cash and gone home, that I got to do what I had came here to do: stop, stand and listen. It was when my ears were free from the hustling tourists and the passing boats that I gained an understanding for the essence of Venice. This is a city that should be heard as well as seen, because despite its chaos, the sound of Venice is the sound of a world without cars.

☑ **Visit Anzac Cove, Gallipoli, Turkey.** *In case you did not know before now, Gallipoli is the spiritual birthplace of both Australia and New Zealand and consists of a beach not more than 600 metres long, were many men died during World War I. Despite everything that happened in this out-of-the way corner of the globe, the tribute from the great Mustafa Kemal Atatürk to the ANZACs (Australian and New Zealand Army Corps) killed at Gallipoli is what sums it up best. It will give an insight into the mutual respect that the two sides now hold for each other following the battle:*

"Heroes who shed their blood and lost their lives, you are now lying in the soil of a friendly country. Therefore, rest in peace. There is no difference between the Johnnies and Mehmets to us where they lie side by side here in this country of ours. You, the mothers, who sent their sons from far away countries, wipe away your tears; your sons are now lying in our bosom and are in peace. After having lost their lives on this land they have become our sons as well."

If you are unaware of the significance of this location then give your mates from 'Down Under' a beer and they will be happy to fill you in on the details.

☑ **Explore the volcanoes of Lanzarote, the Canary Islands.** *There is something magnetic about an erupting volcano. Despite the obvious danger, I have always wanted to be close to a volcano as it erupts and spits lava from the centre of the earth. Laying in the Atlantic Ocean, approximately 125 kilometres off the coast of Africa, Lanzarote owes its landscape entirely to volcanic activity. In September 1730 a fissure eruption started which was to last for six years covering 200 kilometres^2 of land, with lava pouring into the sea along 20 kilometres of coastline. The result is an almost lunar like landscape, which allows for a great day spent exploring the spectacular Timanfaya National Park. Unfortunately, the closest I got to see lava spew, was cooking some chicken over the mouth of the volcano.*

☑ **Discover Middle England.** *England is one of the most visited countries in the world, but most people spend the majority of their visit in the great cities of London, Manchester, Liverpool and Birmingham. Personally, I am quite happy for them to do that. I hope that they continue to go to the cities and buy their 'Union Jack everything' and take enough hilarious photographs of 'Big Ben'* to keep their Facebook friends occupied for a month.

You see I believe that the real value of England is to be found in the villages and small towns far from the Union Jack Hats and flashing cameras. In particular, it is to be found in the Cotswolds and the counties of Gloucestershire, Wiltshire, Bristol, Dorset, Somerset and Oxfordshire. This is what I like to call Middle England (although I really want to call it Middle Earth, despite neither being geographically correct). So with that, I want to let you know that I have pondered on my next statement for the past year and I am yet to find anything that disproves it, so here it goes: On a per kilometre basis there is no better travel destination on the planet than 'Middle England'.

There I said it and I stand by it. This region is simply phenomenal. It seems that around every corner there is a 'stand-on-the-brakes-and-get-out-of-the-car-for-a-better-look-moment'. I was constantly coming across fantastic monuments, castles, landscapes, giants with erections, 100 metre tall horses, 'Banksy's', crop circles, cheese being chased down hills, Tor's and stone formations (including one known as 'Stonehenge').

There is simply so much on offer within such a small area that I have never come across anything like it anywhere on the planet. In addition to that, the people are so open and welcoming and it is based on that

fact that I am reluctant to share this. These nice people do not deserve to be bombarded by any more tourists. So, lets keep this little golden travel nugget to ourselves, shall we?

☑ **Explore Transylvania, Romania.** Lesser known for its beautiful expanse of forests and woodlands, Transylvania is, of course, world famous for its association with vampires. This is primarily due to Bram Stoker's novel Dracula and the many film adaptations. With that in mind I just had to go and visit Bran Castle. It is commonly known as "Dracula's Castle," but unfortunately it is nothing like that depicted in the movies. Today, it seems more like a uniquely shaped large mansion than a castle. Although I am sure that the building fitted the definition of a castle back in 15th century Romania, when it was being redeveloped.

☑ **Unwind in the Blue Lagoon, Grindavik, Iceland.** The warm milky blue waters of this natural geothermal spa are part of a lava formation that the people of Iceland have found many ingenious uses for. First, this hot water is vented from the ground next to a lava flow and is used to generate electricity by running it through turbines. Then after passing through the turbines, the steam and hot water is fed through a heat exchanger that supplies the heat required to warm the public water heating system. Then, the water is used to generate heat and warm water for the local people, before it is filtered into the lagoon at a temperature averaging 37-39 degrees Celsius.

Moreover, it gets better still. As the water in the Blue Lagoon is rich in minerals, not only was it a great place to just chill out, but it also provides medicinal benefits. As it is a natural phenomenon that is exposed to the elements, the temperature of the water can fluctuate. I was quite lucky when I visited, as on a very cold day the water was very hot, which is, of course, the perfect combination. Most people visit the Blue Lagoon on the way to or from the airport, but I set aside a full day for my visit to this natural wonder.

When I arrived, all of the massages had been booked out by those more organised than myself. Nonetheless, buckets of silica mud had been placed around the sides of the lagoon for visitors to smear as much as they liked across their body, which I dutifully took full advantage of. Leaving the Blue Lagoon after a wonderfully relaxing day I felt fully detoxified, I had the hair of Pocahontas, the skin of a newborn and that night I slept like a hibernating bear.

☐ **Participate in La Tomatina food fight in Buñol, Spain.** *La Tomatina is a festival held each year on the last Wednesday of August. Each year up to 40,000 people from all corners of the globe make their way to this small town to fight it out in the streets as more than one hundred metric tons of* over-ripe tomatoes are thrown. What has become known as the "World's Biggest Food Fight" first started in 1945 when, during a parade, a group of lads that wanted to be in the event staged a brawl in the town's Plaza del Pueblo. There was a vegetable stand nearby, so they picked up tomatoes and used them as weapons. This is the most popular of many theories about how La Tomatina started.

Nowadays, the activities begin at 11:00am when the first person attempts to climb to the top of a two-story high, greased-up wooden pole in order to retrieve a coveted ham at the top. This can take quite a long time as it is only when the ham is deemed to be irretrievable, after all attempts, that the festival will start with the firing of water cannons... and so the chaos begins. It is then every man for himself. Exactly one hour after the firing of the water cannons, the fighting ends when the water cannons are fired once more. At this point, no more tomatoes can be thrown, the curtains come down on the festival for another year and the cleaning process begins.

☐ **Explore the Orkney Islands, northern Scotland.** *When asked to think of the exotic the Orkney Islands are not the first thing that comes to mind. For good reason too. This is a harsh and desolate place with a maximum average temperature of twelve degree Celsius, thanks to the constant wind* *coming in from the Atlantic Ocean and the North Sea.*

However, I always see a great beauty in the harsh. I do not spend much time lying on the beach on a hot day, but on a really windy and rainy day when the waves are crashing in, there is nowhere I would rather be than on a beach. I guess that it is because of this bizarre appreciation for nature that the Orkney Islands appeal to me so much. However, the islands have also become known as "the Egypt of the North" due to the large concentration of spectacular archaeological sites there, but I think we should keep that as our little secret.

Middle East

"Palestinian and Israeli leaders finally recover the Road Map to Peace, only to discover that, while they were looking for it, the Lug Nuts of Mutual Interest came off the Front Left Wheel of Accommodation, causing the Sport Utility Vehicle of Progress to crash into the Ditch of Despair."

~ Dave Barry (Author)

☑ **Retrace the steps of Jesus and his twelve stations of the cross through the old city of Jerusalem.** *Pilgrims have retraced the steps that commemorate the torture, sentencing, carrying of the cross, crucifixion, death, burial and resurrection of Jesus to the Church of the Holy Sepulchre since the eighth century. Today the route is well established but this is by tradition rather than archaeological evidence. Known as the route of the Via Dolorosa, it would seem to be less than a kilometre in length, but if even a fraction of the days events are true, then I am sure it felt a lot longer when carrying that cross.*

☑ **Follow the steps of Moses up Mount Sinai to where he received the Ten Commandments.** *This hike up Mount Sinai in the pitch darkness was surreal due to us carefully sharing the small winding path, with less careful camels. Upon reaching the top of Mount Sinai, we unfurled our sleeping bags and camped at St. Catherine's Monastery* *so we could watch the mystical sun, rise over the desert. After daybreak the following morning, I joined a Mass service in the monastery (which was said in South Korean – don't ask!) before setting off back down the other side of the mountain, towards the location where it is said 'The Burning Bush' appeared to Moses.*

This more difficult path combined with sleep deprivation made this a tough and very exhausting descent. A few hours into the hike back towards 'The Burning Bush', I ended up tripping over and falling down the rocks. This resulted in me obtaining a massive scar on my knees and forehead, not to mention ripping every piece of clothing I was wearing. Although I did not really hurt myself too badly, with all my clothing ripped to pieces and blood everywhere, I looked like Rambo as I got to the bottom. Advice: Go slow on the descent. Bizarrely, the authorities had placed a fire extinguisher right beside 'The Burning Bush'. 'Just-in-case', I suppose!

☑ **Relax in chilled-out Dahab, the hippy centre of the Middle East.** *Fewer than 30 Bedouin families apparently inhabited this isolated Egyptian coastal village only 30 years ago. The isolated location and idyllic setting combined with laid-back Bedouin hospitality made it a favourite destination for passers by. It was during the 1980s when hippies discovered Dahab's natural wonders and decided to stay. Like most other hippy hangouts around the world, the backpackers were soon on their trail.*

The combination of the warm waters of the Red Sea and the barrier of the Sinai desert provides Dahab with a 'cubby hole' feel and make it a perfect place to just chill out. However, in recent years it has also become the go to place for world-class windsurfing, rock climbing, scuba diving and, of course, the ever dangerous free diving. Just metres from the dusty track, on the outskirts of the town, is where the world famous 'Blue Hole' is to be found. It offers endless fun for those that like to free dive to over 100 metres whilst holding their breath for up to ten minutes. I did some diving, but generally I just sat back looking across the Red Sea at Saudi Arabia and pondering, as it seemed to be within swimming distance.

☑ **Walk the labyrinth of alleys in Amman, Jordan.** *Amman was little more than a desert town up until 1949 when the population expanded considerably due to clashes between Israeli and Palestinian forces, causing many Palestinians to flee and take refuge in the town. A second wave of refugees arrived following the Six Day War in 1967 with a third wave arriving in 1991 as a result of the first Gulf War. As you can imagine, with so many people flooding into* the area, city planning was not high on the agenda and makeshift housing was built at a rapid pace. In the absence of careful municipal planning, the result is the labyrinth of alleys that climb up the hillsides surrounding the city. This leads to very poor living conditions, but like the favelas of Rio de Janeiro, it makes for a very interesting day of exploring.

☑ **Wander Jaffa Old Town, Tel Aviv-Yafo.** *According to legend, Jaffa was named after Noah's son, Japheth, who built it after the Great Flood. Today it is a vibrant town where Egyptian, Greek, Turkish, French, British, Arab and Jewish history blend into a warren of streets and alleyways providing an incredible sense of history.*

Wandering the maze of narrow streets and alleys provides a sense of a frail ancient city that mixes tiny stores with some of

the best restaurants to be found anywhere, as reflected in the price. I was fascinated by the diversity in materials and people, which seemed to be a world away from central Tel Aviv, who's glass fronted hotels and neon lights shimmered just a few hundred metres, further down the beach, but seem to be from another time.

☑ **Explore Wadi Rum, Jordan.** *I felt very small and insignificant as we explored this valley with the Zalabia Bedouin people. Cut into the sandstone and granite rock, it is known as "The Valley of the Moon", however my main interest was in finding the "Seven Pillars of Wisdom", as named by none other than Lawrence of Arabia. When I eventually found them, I was feeling very much underwhelmed and not very wise at all.*

The lukewarm 'tea' that some nice Bedouin women had given me, after I accidently found them sitting in a

Amman, Jordan

cave, and I drank to be polite had somewhat dulled my enthusiasm. I had spent the 24 hours previous to arriving at these Seven Pillars of Wisdom with fluids screaming out of my every opening as a result of their tea. I could say that I will not let that happen again... but that would go against my whole travelling ethos.

☐ **Visit the crystallized caves of Jeita Grotto, Lebanon.** Laying 18 kilometres north of Beirut, this grotto consists of two (upper and lower) limestone caves, through which a six kilometre long river runs. In the caves, the water has carved the limestone into many magnificent shapes creating cathedral-like vaults that vary in colour, shape and size. Apparently, the resulting stalagmites, stalactites and curtains of rock is like nothing to be found anywhere in the world.

When the New7Wonders of Nature initiative started in 2007, Jeita Grotto was selected as one of the fourteen finalists. It was the only cave to be selected among the nominees. This is not for everyone but I really enjoy venturing into caves. I had planned to visit the caves when I was in the Middle East, but as I had been to Israel before I attempted to enter Lebanon, I was forbidden from entering the country.

☐ **Stroll the alleyways of Damascus Old City, Syria.** Damascus is believed to be the oldest continually inhabited city on the planet. If you have visited an old city anywhere in the Middle East then you will be aware of what makes them very special. I expect Damascus Old City to be no different, with hundreds of merchants in small shops selling crafts, spices, old coins, fabrics, antiques and, of course, carpets.

☐ **Visit the Bu Tinah Shoals, United Arab Emirates.** Bu Tinah is a cluster of low-lying islands and shoals located just off the western shores of Abu Dhabi. What makes this area so special is that it has much to teach mankind about environmental protection and survival. It is a unique natural treasure in that it has been undisturbed by human activity to the point that its thriving ecosystem forms a unique living laboratory that has allowed scientists to place a key significance on research. This distinctive natural habitat consists of shallow waters, seagrass beds and tall mangroves, that are set amid extensive coral reefs whilst playing host to an array of endangered marine life and seabirds. Overall, it is a nature lover's paradise.

☐ **Party until sunrise in Beirut, Lebanon.** Everyone seems to expect Beirut to be more bombs than bars but that is very much wrong. There are literally hundreds of bars in Beirut but Gemmayze is the area where people can bar hop until they can no longer walk. From what I hear, it is Lebanon's version of the Temple Bar, Dublin, the French Quarter, New Orleans or the West

End, Ibiza. *The beautiful people of Beirut party hard and from what I hear, it is one of the great party cities of the world.*

Africa

"I believe there is no sickness of the heart too great it cannot be cured by a dose of Africa. Families must go there to learn why they belong together on this earth, adolescents to discover humility, lovers to plumb old but untried wells of passion, honeymooners to seal marriages with a shared sense of bafflement, those shop-worn with life to find a tonic for futility, the aged to recognise a symmetry to twilight. I know this all sounds a bit much, but if I have ever seen magic, it has been in Africa."

~ John Heminway (Filmmaker and author)

☑ **Explore The Maasai Mara National Reserve, Kenya.** *Three Maasai warriors stood guard. They had taken full responsibility for our safety no matter where we camped on their land. Throughout the night, they would ensure that two warriors, complete with spears and blades, stood guard in the middle of our tents, whilst another warrior patrolled the area to ensure no big cats or herds included our tents in their nightly hunt. "Always check around your area before moving" they warned. "Be aware of the snakes in the trees and use your torches to look for red eyes in the long grass" they explained. They were serious. They take their responsibility for visitors to 'The Mara' very seriously.*

The Maasai Mara is one of the great travel destinations on the planet, but it can be a dangerous place to sleep with only a tent as protection. Travellers tend to measure the risk associated with coming to The Maasai Mara and believe that the experience outweighs the risks. We put our faith in the local tribe to protect us through the night so we lived to see its beauty once the sun rose again. When people from such a modest background are willing to put their lives on the line to protect you, it is a real humbling experience.

☑ **Watch the moon rise over Cape Town, South Africa, from on top of Table Mountain.** *I was sitting up on Lions Head, the mountain peak above Cape Town, admiring the sunset with the locals and as I had just flown in from Buenos Aires that day, I did not even realise that it was full moon time. It was an unexpected dream come true to watch as the moon burned like an inferno behind the hills (I genuinely believed that a massive bush fire had started on the hills in the distance). Then to watch as the moon rose up over Cape Town, to light up the entire city, was a remarkable sight and it astounded me. To see the moon so big and burning so brightly is unforgettable.*

☑ **Visit the Troglodytes in Tunisia.** *In southern Tunisia, the local Berber people live underground in traditional "troglodyte" structures. The troglodytes are created by digging out a large pit and then digging artificial caves out of the* perimeter of the pit. The Berbers use these as rooms to sleep in at night and as shade from the hot midday sun. It was one of those times when I truly believed that I was really getting to experience how life had been in the area for thousands of years, until I went inside one of the troglodytes only to find a television. Spoiled it.

☑ **Navigate a Mokoro through the Okavango Delta, Botswana.** *The Kalahari Desert, (meaning "the great thirst") is one of the world's largest uninterrupted stretches of sand and within it lays one of the world's great contradictions: water in a desert. Within this great desert is the magnificent Okavango Delta, an extensive maze of lagoons, lakes, waterways and islands that are teeming with wildlife.*

Covering 18,000 kilometres^2 and located 1,300 kilometres from the Atlantic Ocean and 1,600 kilometres from the Indian Ocean, the Okavango Delta is Africa's most picturesque oasis. The River Okavango, which is fed from the Angolan rains, never reaches the sea; instead, its waters quench the insatiable thirst of the Kalahari Desert, with most of the water disappearing here, mainly lost to transpiration and evaporation. Within the delta the water flows so slow that it appears to the naked eye to have stopped, which seems to fit the chilled out psyche around there.

The vast expanse of the Okavango Delta proves no barrier to the five ethnic groups of the area who have mastered the art of navigating their way through its tiny, winding channels. Mokoros, which are no more than hollowed out tree trucks that sit just above the water, are the only transportation within the delta. As I pushed myself along using a large pole whilst standing at the back, my main objective, apart from avoiding dangerous hippos, was maintaining my balance. The locals made it look easy, but I was struggling to stay on my feet as I attempted to steer my Mokoro between the reeds of this great delta.

The Okavango Delta

The water in the delta was unusually pure and contaminant-free simply because on its journey from Angola to the Kalahari Desert the route it follows is through very sparsely populated areas. It is so clean that it was acceptable for us to drink straight from the Delta using nothing but our hand to lap the water up into our mouths. What was not so acceptable was the number of times that I was tipped into the water.

☑ **Witness sunrise over Fish River Canyon, Namibia.** *It is the second largest canyon in the world and the largest in Africa, but for some reason it just did not possess the same magic that I experienced at the Grand Canyon in the USA. However, it is still worth a visit. Carved out of the Earth by the Fish River, the result is an enormous canyon, running for 160 kilometres inland. In some parts, the canyon is over 500 metres deep and can be up to 27 kilometres wide. Again, what struck me most about the sunrise here was the total silence of the canyon, as if it acted like a noise vacuum.*

☑ **Stand at the mouth of the Great Rift Valley as it winds its way up through Africa.** *I felt small as I stood at the mouth of this continuous geographic trench that runs approximately 6,000 kilometres from southeast Africa to northern Syria. As I looked north I knew that I was standing in a place where the earth's tectonic forces would pull against each other so violently that they would one day rip the continent of Africa in two. To know what Mother Nature is capable of makes this quite an overwhelming experience.*

☑ **Camp in the Sahara Desert.** *There is something very alluring and attractive about deserts in general. When I am travelling and I am even remotely close to a desert, I will always take a detour and make some time for exploring the desert. I have no idea what draws me to the dessert. Maybe it is the total silence or the crispy clean air. Maybe it is the constant movement of the sands or the array of colours that they project. In theory, all hot deserts are the same and it should be a case of 'seen one, seen them all.' Nevertheless, it is not like that for me. Every desert stands alone, very different from the others, very different from yesterday.*

The Sahara captured my imagination so long ago that I cannot even remember why. Spanning an area as large as China, the Sahara is the world's largest hot desert and the second largest desert overall, after Antarctica. The most distinct memory that I have from my time in the Sahara was not the heat, but the extreme cold there at night. I have never been as cold as I was when I spent the night in "The Great Desert." When you visit a cold region you know what you are getting and prepare accordingly, but nothing had prepared me for the extreme drop in temperature that was to follow when the sun went down. The Sahara Desert at night is the one place that left me the coldest I have ever been. In this harsh and very dangerous climate, even my bones seemed to be shaking due to the cold.

☑ **Explore Ngorongoro Crater, Tanzania.** *Believed to have formed about 2.5 million years ago, it is not really a crater at all, but a collapsed volcano of the once highest mountain in Africa. Thus, it is a caldera by definition. This massive,* unbroken, unflooded volcanic caldera is one of the finest places on the planet for watching game. Its floor covers 260 kilometres², the bottom is flat with very few trees, it has many small creeks and lakes and with steep sides measuring 610 metres high, it is considered to be a natural enclosure with the animals effectively locked in.

As a result, Ngorongoro crater is crawling with game. The crater plays host to almost every individual species of wildlife in East Africa, with an estimated 25,000 animals within the crater. So as well as containing the "big five" of buffalo, elephant, leopard, lion and rhinoceros, it also hosts magnificent herds of gazelle, wildebeest and zebra and many monkeys and birds, including ostrich, call it home. During my visit, it was a case of "Look over there! Look over there! Look over there!" the entire time, as there was such an abundance of wildlife. It was a magnificent adventure. If wildlife is your thing, then Ngorongoro is the only place to be.

☑ **Travel freely around Egypt avoiding all organized tour groups.** In 2004, I went on a package holiday to Egypt, staying in a fantastic complex in Sharm el Sheik, visiting the Pyramids as well as many of the countries great treasures. In spite of this, at my very core, I felt that this trip was a total farce. I never got a feel for the country at all and apart from the hotel staff, I never met a single local person.

The organised tour guides had created a 'them and us' situation. We even had armed guards on our bus as we travelled throughout the country, to keep us 'safe' from the supposedly dangerous locals. I pledged at the end of that holiday that I would return to Egypt on my own and travel freely, mixing with the locals and accepting their hospitality, in order to get a feel for them and their great culture.

Egypt is world renowned for its archaeological treasures, natural beauty and warm hospitality. Upon returning to this great land, I immersed myself in it all. I revered at the magnificent Pyramids and their guardian Sphinx. I explored the colossal statues at Abu Simbel including the majestic Sun Temple of Ramses II. I enjoyed the splendour of the vast desert landscapes as I travelled by train throughout this ancient land. I say, skip the package and do it yourself. It is much cheaper that way too.

☐ **Climb Mount Kilimanjaro, Tanzania.** Kilimanjaro is loosely translated to mean "White Mountain." It is the name of the highest mountain in Africa and it is among the tallest freestanding mountains in the world. The summit of this great mountain (5,895 metres) can be reached without any technical difficulty, which is one of the reasons why it is so appealing to me. When I drove past this majestic beauty a few years ago, I developed a yearning to return and climb this beautiful mass of land. The *beauty of this climb is that it starts with rainforest and then enters the plateau region before the final stretch leads through the snow and glaciers to the top. How good does that sound?*

Asia

"Asia is not going to be civilized after the methods of the West. There is too much Asia and she is too old."
~ Rudyard Kipling (Poet and novelist)

☑ **Listen to Vietnam War stories... from the Vietnamese.** *It is very interesting to hear the other side of the story. Known to them as 'The American War', obviously.*

☑ **Camp in a Ger with Mongolian Nomads.** *Ger in Mongolian simply means "home" and they are as much a part of the Mongolian national identity as horses. Gers are best described as circular shaped felt tents that can easily be taken down and relocated, thus the reason they were widely used by Genghis Khan and his armies when furthering the Mongolian empire.*

However, these are not an antique display from a time gone by, as even today a large share of Mongolia's population live in Gers, even in Ulaanbaatar, the capital city. Whilst staying in a Ger camp deep in the Mongolian Steepes, I was not at all surprised to see a flatscreen TV and a modern stereo when I peaked my head inside the Ger of the camp owner. The tentacles of technology are now far reaching.

☑ **Wander around Akihabara, Tokyo's electronics district, Japan.** *This is heaven for gadget* geeks like myself. Overflowing with pop-culture collectibles and other nerd attractions, the area is full of shops selling videogames, gadgets, toys and anime/manga movies. In addition, there are the "maid cafes," where girls in cosplay outfits serve drinks and snacks to nerd shoppers. What started out as Tokyo's historic electronics district has well and truly morphed into geek paradise. What struck me most about the area was the 'No Smoking' signs on the streets. Here you must smoke inside!

☑ **Ride a bicycle amongst the locals in Beijing, China.** *The infrastructure of this 'bicycle kingdom' is specifically set up for cycling. All major streets have bike lanes and the entire city is flat, with barely an incline to be found anywhere. Biking there is great fun and it is usually the fastest way of travelling due to the increasing congestion in the motorised traffic lanes, resulting from an estimated 1,200 additional cars hitting the streets in Beijing every day.*

☑ **Scale Mount Bromo, Java, Indonesia.** *Desolate beauty. If ever there was a landscape that demonstrated the meaning of this phrase, then this is surely it. Rugged, grey, gravel plains with barren volcanic peaks and an expanse of sand. This is a description that may suit the surface of the moon, but this description is of Mount Bromo and its surrounding area. Although not the highest, Mount Bromo is the most famous peak inside the*

Tengger Caldera on the Island of Java. This picturesque volcano with belching white sulphurous smoke and edges tinged with sulphur is a view to behold and a climb worth the effort.

☑ **Party in Vang Vieng, Laos.** *It is said that Laos does not have a nightlife and as far as backpackers are concerned, this may be somewhat correct. Vang Vieng, the three street, one river town in the middle of the countryside may be the reason for this. Most people leaving here are looking for the first bus to Vietnam to spend a few days recovering by the beach. The reason is because this little town in the middle of nowhere is home to the infamous 'Laos tubing'.*

Most backpackers that come to Laos make their way straight to Vang Vieng and spend the following days floating down the river on an old tractor tube whilst drinking themselves sick. The majority of people cannot handle more than a weekend, some push it to a week, whilst I have heard of a few that were trying to do 100 days in a row. This is where the problems start.

Buckets filled with cheap alcohol and combined with an array of drugs consumed whilst floating down a murky river on a tube, unfortunately equates to danger. In the days before I arrived a young Australian lad had died on the river and it was not an isolated incident. It was reported that an average of one tourist per month dies while tubing or jumping into the river.

I was there during the rainy season and the river was seriously swollen and running very fast. As a result, there were many dislodged trees and sharp rocks not visible to the eye just under the murky water in many places along the river. This resulted in quite a few accidents were backpackers required hospital treatment. I am not sure what it is like outside of rainy season, but when I was there everyone came back with some sort of injury, ranging from a scraped leg to a broken bone.

However, all this madness on the river means that this three street town has been set up simply to allow the injured and the weary to recover from the relentless drinking games and drug-fuelled debauchery. Backpackers can be found sprawled out in the many beanbag-filled cafes and restaurants as they enjoy some much needed food and watch re-runs of the US sitcom, 'Friends' over and over. Only 'Friends'. In every single establishment, they only had 'Friends' on repeat. To make this town even more bizarre some of the restaurants had many drugs, ranging from cannabis to heroin, for sale and listed at the front of the food menu. Vang Vieng is a crazy location, thus, I believe, it is the reason why the rest of the country does not have a nightlife.

☐ **Explore the "beautiful jungle" of Sundarbans, Bangladesh.** The name Sundarban is literally translated as "beautiful jungle" in the Bengali language and derives from the Sundari trees that populate the area. The Sundarbans, laying in the vast delta on the Bay of Bengal, is unique in that it is the largest single area of tidal salt tolerant mangrove forest in the world. This "beautiful jungle" is estimated to cover an area of about 4,110 kilometres^2, of which about 1,700 kilometres^2 of this complex ecosystem is intersected by a network of tidal waterways, small islands of mangrove forests and mudflats, making boat access imperative.

As well as being home to numerous species of birds, spotted deer, crocodiles and snakes, this is also the home of up to 200 endangered Royal Bengal Tigers. The resident tigers get around the Sundarbans by swimming from island to island in the saline waters. There is no doubt that all who enjoy the wonders of nature at its best will appreciate this great location.

☐ **Participate in Songkran, the world's biggest water fight, in Thailand.** Derived from the Sanskrit word meaning, "to move into," Songkran marks the start of Thailand's new year, with water symbolising the cleansing away of bad luck and the splash of a new beginning. Historically it was a ritual of sprinkling scented water from silver bowls onto a Buddha statue to cleanse the statue. This water would then be collected and sprinkled on to the shoulders of others as a sign of good luck.

Over the years, this sprinkling of water has evolved into the world's biggest water fight as people from around the world come face-to-face with the local people throughout the country armed with everything from tiny water pistols to hoses, to wage a liquid war. The celebrations, which run for around three days, usually begin on 13 April each year, which is the start of the New Year on many Asian calendars and coincidentally also happens to be the hottest part of the year.

☐ **Rave all night at a Full Moon Party, Ko Pha Ngan, Thailand.** *No, I still have not attended a Full Moon Party. Poor timing is to blame. The first ever Full Moon Party was an improvised disco not far from Haad Rin beach in 1985 consisting of around 30 backpackers. This party then became a monthly event and quickly gained notoriety through word of mouth, to the point that the event now draws a crowd of over 20,000 people every full moon evening.*

☐ **Discover Tibet.** *I have had two opportunities to visit Tibet so far on my travels. The first was whilst driving from London to Sydney. Some of our group set off the morning after arriving in Kathmandu and I decided not to join them. This was the mid point of our journey and I just felt that it was an ideal time to have a few days rest,*

instead of battling the elements over the infamous Friendship Highway.

The second occasion was when I was travelling around China and I was adamant I would visit Tibet this time. As I entered China, the Chinese government decided to close the Tibetan border and ban all foreigners from visiting, right up until two days after my Chinese visa expired. It was just not meant to be. My time will come.

Australasia

"Australia is properly speaking an island, but it is so much larger than every other island on the face of the globe, that it is classed as a continent in order to convey to the mind a just idea of its magnitude."
~ Charles Sturt (Explorer)

☑ **Learn about Māori culture in New Zealand.** *This was a great day that began with a traditional welcome of rubbing my nose against that of a Māori warrior in full traditional gear. Then, as I was chosen as the chief of the visiting tribe, I had to stand in the middle of the crowd as 'their' warriors screamed, shouted and ran at me in order to intimidate me – all in the name of tradition. Once it was determined that I was not to be intimidated, my tribe and I were then invited to sit down to an authentic hangi meal, which is cooked in the earth oven known as 'the hangi pit' with hot rocks.*

After dinner, we were treated to a cultural performance that was real, raw, emotional and full of power. Then I was invited to wander through the natural bush setting, were performers acted out and talked me through the ancient Māori customs and traditions that were part of everyday life. I learned about the carvings, music and ta moko (tattooing) and how their tattoos are used to demonstrate the strong ties that Māori people have with their cultural heritage. Then, through the medium of song and dance I learned Māori tales and legends before watching the mesmerising poi dance. Then just before I left I was given the opportunity to take part in the spine tingling haka, the Māori war dance.

☑ **Explore Franz Josef Glacier, New Zealand.** *The name 'Franz Josef' may seem quite strange for a glacier in New Zealand and it is. That is because it was given that name by a German explorer, Julius von Haast, in 1865 when he named it after Emperor Franz Joseph I of Austria. Typical boring European naming. The Māori people, on the other hand, call the glacier "Ka Roimata o Hinehukatere" which translates to "The tears of Hinehukatere". Now, that is more like it.*

For me, this was the first time I had stood at the face of a glacier and looked up as it wound down the mountain. Franz Josef Glacier has its origins high in the Southern Alps of New Zealand. Quite astonishingly, it descends deep into the lush rainforest of Westland's National Park, going from a height of 2,700 metres above sea level to only 240 metres in as little as eleven kilometres. This makes it the world's steepest and fastest flowing commercially guided glacier. It was the hike back into the local town that ended this tour perfectly as we hiked through the pristine rainforest on our way back to the hostel.

☑ **Visit the stromatolites at Hamelin Pool, Western Australia.** *There would be no point at all in me including a photograph of the stromatolites here, as they would not seem very important or interesting. However, these 3.5 billion year old rock-like structures are the earliest record of life on Earth. At first glance, these do not even seem to be alive in any way. However, each structure is actually a very slow growing microbial colony, with typical* *growth at about 0.5 millimetres per year.*

Some fossil stromatolites structures in the Shark Bay area have grown into massive pillar structures estimated to be over 3 billion years old. They now measure in at approximately 50 metres high and 30 metres in diameter, having thrived in this area for so long simply due to the water here being twice as saline as usual seawater. I know what you are thinking, where am I going with this

Uluru

and why would I want to visit what looks like large underwater rocks?

It is now scientifically accepted that around 2.4 billion years ago, the Earth's atmosphere underwent a dramatic change when oxygen levels rose sharply, in what is known as the "Great Oxidation Event." This oxygen spike marks an important milestone in the Earth's history – the transformation from an oxygen-poor atmosphere to an oxygen-rich one. This paved the way for complex

life to develop on earth and all thanks to these stromatolites.

Through the process of photosynthesis, stromatolites produce carbohydrates from carbon dioxide and water and as a by-product of the process, oxygen is released into the air. These little rock-like fossils are responsible for oxygenating this planet, thus allowing humans to survive on Earth. Therefore, the reason I trekked half way across the world to visit these stromatolites was because if it were not for them, none of us would be here. I guess that you now consider stromatolites to be a little more important and interesting? Okay, maybe not.

☑ **Search for aboriginal rock art at Kakadu National Park, Australia.** The gorges, caves and rock outliers of Kakadu are home to one of the greatest concentrations of rock art sites on the planet, with approximately 5,000 sites recorded to date. Experts estimate that this is only a fraction of what is thought to exist in the area. The paintings, dating back 20,000 years, are tantamount to one of the longest historical records of any group of people in the world.

☑ **Walk the 10.2 kilometres around Uluru, in the red centre of Australia.** A location that the Aboriginals hold dear to their hearts, Uluru is Australia's most recognisable natural icon. Also known as Ayers Rock, this world-renowned sandstone formation stands at a rather deceiving 348 metres high with a lot more than that again below the surface. The local Aboriginal Anangu tribe do not climb Uluru because of its great spiritual significance and they request that visitors to the site do not climb the rock either. This is partly due to the path crossing a sacred traditional Dreamtime track and also due to a sense of responsibility for the safety of visitors to their land.

The Anangu believe they have a spiritual connection to Uluru and feel great sadness when a person dies or is injured while climbing. Out of respect for the tribe, I had decided in advance not to climb on this sacred rock. The way I saw it was that I would not like a group of tourists climbing around on the roof of my Parish Church on a Sunday morning whilst we were saying Mass. The walk around the circumference of Uluru, however, is absolutely fascinating as it provides a close up of the twists and turns in the red rock that can never be seen from on top or from a distance.

I was quite happy with that decision when I noticed the surprisingly large number of memorial plaques placed on the rock. At the bottom of the path, many families have placed plaques in memory of loved ones that died as a result of falling whilst hiking up Uluru. Maybe the spirits that the Anangu tribe look to seriously frown upon the icon being treated as a tourist 'to-do'. After spending two nights at Uluru, I came away with the feeling that there is a spiritual mystique about this sacred rock. Something that

is hard to explain. Something that cannot be captured in a photograph.

☑ **Investigate the rugged Kimberley, Western Australia by four-wheel drive.** Covering nearly 423,000 kilometres^2, this rugged and desolate region has fewer people per kilometre^2 than most other places on Earth. Laying in the north of Western Australia the region offers everything from spectacular gorges and thundering waterfalls inland, with some of the world's most beautiful beaches and untouched coral on the coast. What I really liked best about this was the feeling of being isolated. The entire time we spent exploring the region we never met another person.

☑ **Stay on Robinson Crusoe Island, Fiji.** "This morning we witnessed a shocking spectacle. Twenty dead bodies of men, women and children were brought to Rewa as a present from Tanoa. They were distributed among the people to be cooked and eaten. They were dragged about in the water and on the beach. The children amused themselves by sporting with and mutilating the body of a little girl. A crowd of men and women maltreated the body of a grey-haired old man and that of a young women."

Breath out and relax. This is not an extract from my personal travel journal, but the writings of Rev. David Cargill, Methodist Missionary, Rewa, Fiji, 1839. Once known as the Cannibal Isles, because of its ferocious natives, Fiji had a reputation that inspired fear in sailors and explorers the world over. Thankfully, the cannibalism practiced in Fiji at that time quickly disappeared as Christian missionaries gained influence. Today Fiji could not be more different and the locals are more likely to smile and wave as they pick a low hanging fruit from the tree than, er... cook you for dinner.

During my time there I stayed mostly on Robinson Crusoe Island. This small island off the southwest coast of Fiji's main island was originally restricted as a sacred island where traditional ceremonies and important Chiefly gatherings were held. Traditionally known as "Likuri Island," it has a history dating back nearly 4,000 years, however the island was recently renamed after a yacht was wrecked on the nearby reef and the captain and his cat took refuge on the island. Well, at least that is how the story goes.

The island is surrounded by coral reefs on its seaside exposure, offering an abundance of fish and colour. On the landside exposure, the island is covered in mangrove forests, with a soft sand bar and a lagoon bearing into the Pacific Ocean, meaning that it is possible to walk around the entire island in warm water that is only knee deep. Thanks to the High Chief, the island has now opened to the world, allowing the visitation of a limited number of eco-tourists seeking to experience the Coral Coast and its

historically significant culture. As a result, we got to experience the traditional culture, customs and cuisine of the Fiji Islands as well as a spectacular local dance consisting of fire and knifes.

☐ **Explore Tasmania, Australia.** This island at the edge of the world may be Australia's smallest state, but it may also be its most beautiful. With majestic rivers, pristine deserted beaches, inspirational vantage points and even the sub Antarctic Macquarie Island, Tasmania offers something a little different from the rest of Australia. Nevertheless, beyond all of this, people tell me that it is the friendly, welcoming and relaxed pace of life that really makes Tasmania so special.

☐ **Relax on Bora Bora islands, French Polynesia.** Surrounded by a lagoon and a barrier reef with the remnants of an extinct volcano rising from the centre of the island, it is no surprise that Bora Bora has become a major international tourist destination. Just saying the name evokes thoughts of the exotic and unspoiled. Personally, I just want to stay in one of those aqua-centric luxury bungalows on stilts that sit out over the crystal clear waters so that I can wake myself up in the morning by simply rolling out of bed and falling overboard into the refreshing water.

☐ **Visit Milford Sound, New Zealand.** One day, whilst travelling through the South Island of New

Zealand, I had the chance to either visit Milford Sound or stay in bed. Sometimes a man just has to listen to his heart, I thought to myself. I stayed in bed. With its dramatic peaks and flushing waterfalls cascading down the cliffs into the dark blue waters that reach depths of nearly 300 metres, Milford Sound is the twinkle in the eye of the glacier-carved Fiordland National Park. I must have been really tired.

North America

"Guy dies and goes right to Heaven where he is given a tour. After looking around a while he turns to the Host and notes: "Yeah, it is pretty nice but it's not San Francisco!"

~ Herbert Caen (Journalist)

☑ **Watch the sun rise and set over the Grand Canyon, Arizona, USA.** *Purple. This is what comes to my mind when I think of the time I sat with my feet dangling over the edge of the Grand Canyon. I sat there observing the silence right up until sunset. As the sun sank unhurriedly in the sky, it seemed to have this implausible impact upon the stone, which stretched as far as the eye could see. It was almost as if the entire canyon had been transformed into a rainbow of purple as the dying sun breathed its last breaths for that hot June day. Despite all else that the Grand Canyon has to offer, for me it was all about the silence and the colours. Purple, to be precise.*

☑ **Explore the swamps of Louisiana, USA with the Cajun people.** *There is more to Louisiana than New Orleans. The day I spent out on the Atchafalaya Swamp with the Cajun people was a day when I was exposed to a whole new world. The people there have stuck close to their French roots, relocating to the area after leaving Nova Scotia in the 18th century. They have developed their own Cajun*

French dialect and have hung on to their vibrant culture through maintaining their recipes, music and folkways. In addition to this, they abide by laws based on the Napoleonic Code, as opposed to the English Common Law that the rest of the USA abides by.

The people there earn money on the swamp through fishing as well as harvesting crabs, crawfish, shrimp, raccoons and turtles. However, it is during alligator season in Louisiana that they earn most of their yearly income in the high-risk activity of culling alligators. Following a tradition dating back 300 years, the season begins on the first Wednesday in September and lasts 30 days. The hunters are each issued a limited number of tags that must be attached to their kills; once they run out of tags, their season is over and they may no longer kill any more alligators for the rest of the season. The swaps are a different world to anything that I have ever experienced and are certainly worth a visit if you ever find yourself in this part of the world.

☑ **Tour the Jack Daniel's Distillery, Lynchburg, Tennessee, USA.** *The tour of the Jack Daniel's Distillery was unlike any other distillery tour I have ever been on. This distillery, situated deep in the American south, takes up most of the village of Lynchburg. For such an iconic brand, it is fascinating that each bottle of 'JD' starts its life in such humble beginnings.*

We were given a good look around the village before they walked us through the barrel storage house and the areas where they create the mash and distil the whiskey. Therefore, despite the fact that I do not even like whiskey, by the end of the tour I really felt the urge to sip on a nice glass of Old No. 7. Disappointingly, it materialises that I was forbidden from sampling any of the produce. Why, you may ask? Well simply because Lynchburg is a dry county and it was a Sunday – alcohol is forbidden in Lynchburg on Sundays. We were offered a glass of orange juice instead, which is not quite the same.

☑ **"Remember the Alamo" in San Antonia, Texas, USA.** *In an old mission a small band of Texans managed to hold out the Centralist Army of General Antonio López de Santa Anna for a total of thirteen days. Following a dawn attack, the Alamo fell on the morning of 6 March 1836 and a legend was born. The death of David Crockett, James Bowie and William Barret Travis, amongst the others that have come to be known as 'The Alamo Defenders', has come to symbolise courage and sacrifice for the cause of Liberty. The cry "Remember the Alamo!" is as powerful today as when the Texan Army under Sam Houston shouted it before routing Santa Anna at the battle of San Jacinto on 21 April 1836.*

As people worldwide remember the Alamo as a heroic struggle against impossible odds, it is fondly remembered as a place where men made the ultimate sacrifice for freedom. For this reason, the Alamo remains hallowed ground for Americans and the Shrine of Texas Liberty. However, as the facts surrounding the siege of the Alamo continue to be debated, there is no doubt that the battle has come to symbolise everything dear to the American character.

☑ **Witness sunrise over Monument Valley, USA.** *As I entered Monument Valley, everything was dead black. The ground I sat on was dead black, the surrounding area was dead black and the sky was dead black, apart from the stars that gazed upon me. However, in that hour that it takes the sun to wake up and pop his head over the horizon something magical happened.*

My surroundings gradually transformed from dead black to rusty red. Initially, the sky above me turned red, starting at the horizon and climbing up the sky until it was far behind me. Next, the ground turned red, again starting at the horizon and slithering towards me, chasing away the dark. Lastly, as the sun popped its head above the horizon to say "good morning" to America, the iconic rock formations of Monument Valley, which had been boxy silhouettes against the red dirt, lit up in a bright red to complete this red world. This is one of the best sunrise experiences on the planet.

☑ **Chill out in Central Park, New York, USA.** *This is a facility that I really grew to appreciate the longer I stayed in the 'Big Apple' as I developed an instinct for the importance of the facility to the locals, now and in the past.*

Between 1821 and 1855, the population of New York City nearly quadrupled, which lead to very few open spaces being available for families to relax. As the city expanded so rapidly, New Yorkers were drawn to the graveyards as one of the few existing open spaces available, in order to escape from the noise and chaos of life in the expanding city. It was not until 1857 that the new 3.41 kilometre^2 park opened, at a cost of more than $5 million for the land alone. The result is a fantastic facility that is very much like a paradise island in the concrete jungle of NYC.

☑ **Ride a bicycle across the Golden Gate Bridge, San Francisco, USA.** *I have always believed that the best way in which to get intimate with any city is by bicycle. This is especially true of San Francisco. I had a great day completing the 13 kilometre bike ride as I set off from Fisherman's Wharf, going over the fabulous Golden Gate Bridge with a breeze in my hair and the sun on my back as I made my way to Sausalito. A great day was capped off with the return trip across San Francisco Bay to the wharf by ferry at sunset. Perfect.*

☐ **Visit Midway Geyser, Grand Prismatic at Yellowstone National Park, Wyoming, USA.** *"Hell's Half Acre" is how Rudyard Kipling, described this basin after a visit to Yellowstone in 1889. Considered to be the third largest hot spring in the world, Grand Prismatic was named as such by The Hayden Expedition to the spring in 1871 as a result of its striking colouration. Artist Thomas Moran made watercolour sketches depicting the rainbow of colours around the spring, but the sketches were dismissed as exaggerations until the geologist A.C. Peale returned in 1878 to verify the colours.*

I have a real interest in bright colours within nature, which is the main reason why I wish to visit Grand Prismatic. The colours start in the centre with a deep blue that turns into a pale blue as it gets closer to the edges, where a vivid green algae forms beyond the shallow edge. Outside the scalloped rim, there is a band of yellow that fades into a ripe orange colour, with a deep red marking the outer border. As Grand Prismatic discharges an estimated 2,200 litres of water per minute, a steam often shrouds the spring which reflects the brilliant colours in all their glory. Forget "Hell's Half Acre", this sounds more like "Heaven's Half Acre" to me.

☐ **Stand in the San Andreas Fault, California, USA.** *The San Andreas Fault is a continental transform fault that runs 1,300 kilometres through California forming the tectonic boundary between the North American and Pacific Plates. The fault extends to depths of 18 kilometres into the Earth and is recognised as a complex zone of crushed and broken rock that measures from 100 – 2,000 metres wide on the surface. It is on the broken and crushed rock that I want to stand and feel two of the planets massive plates grinding against each other.*

☐ **Visit the Bay of Fundy, Canada.** *Located between the Canadian provinces of New Brunswick and Nova Scotia on the east coast of North America, the Bay of Fundy is renowned for having the highest tides on the planet at 16.2 metres. One hundred billion tonnes of seawater is estimated to flow in and out of the Bay of Fundy twice a day. To put this in perspective, this is more water than the combined flow of all the world's fresh water rivers.*

It is as a result of Fundy's extreme tides that such a dynamic and diverse marine ecosystem exists in the area. Renowned for its coastal rock formations, extreme tidal effects (vertical, horizontal, rapids and bores) and sustainable coastal development, the Bay of Fundy is also a critical international feeding ground for migratory birds. In addition, it is a vibrant habitat for rare and endangered Right whales and is one of the world's most significant plant and animal fossil discovery regions. Sounds like a good day out, to me.

Patrick Hamilton Walsh

Latin America

"You must not judge people by their country. In South America, it is always wise to judge people by their altitude."

~ Paul Theroux (Travel writer)

☑ **Watch sunset over the lakes of San Carlos de Bariloche, Argentina.** Most of us live in a world that consists of varying shades of beige. It appears that the more affluent we are the lighter the shades of beige that surround us, while the less-well-off move around in a world of darker beige. However, as I stood in this remote corner of the world it almost seemed as if convention had been turned on its head. Let me attempt to build you a picture of this.

Imagine if we could lift New Zealand's Lake Tekapo and drop it in the middle of the Swiss Alps. Now lets bundle those two together and put them at the end of the world in the southern hemisphere. Now, if I have done my job properly, then you are starting to envisage the beauty that surrounds the town of San Carlos de Bariloche. 'Bariloche,' as it is affectionately known, sits in the Argentinean Andes, deep in the northern portion of Patagonia and there almost seems to be certain heavenliness to the area.

This small city rests on the shores of Lake Nahuel Huapi as the snowy peaks of the Andes Mountains encroach on this lake of inexpressible blue. The water was so pristine that I could lap it straight into my mouth without worry of ailment. The air was so fresh, it was part responsible for that extra spring in my step. The people were so relaxed they forced me to speculate whether the word 'stress' was ever a part of the local lexicon.

Bariloche is the ultimate outdoor enthusiast's playground. I was there during the summer months and spent all day every day exploring the cycle routes. These routes led through the truly awe-inspiring forests, valleys, mountains and fluffy white clouds and always ended up at a lake, allowing my newfound friends and I to cool off. We always finished the day on top of a hill watching as the sun dropped into the lake, causing the water to run blood red. Once we got back to town, the first stop was always the chocolatiers.

Yeah, this is home to the world famous Bariloche chocolate and it seems like every second retail store is a chocolatiers. Chocolate shops the size of grocery stores await the chocoholics of this world – I am talking to the girls here. Yes, you! From dark to white, from creamy to decadent, there is a chocolate for every taste and the price is very reasonable, due to the vast array of competition in the town.

For the five days I was there, it felt like I could stay forever. I breathed the crisp clean air of northern

Patagonia and took in the views with new friends as we hiked and cycled through the hills. Of course, we also had many chocolate breaks, ate the finest Argentinean beef and sampled the local produce from Antares microbrewery. However, no matter how nice and cosy a town seems, it is in the backpackers' mentality to keep moving. This is nice, but maybe the next town is even better?

☑ **Watch as the sea comes in and washes the streets of Paraty, Brazil.** Paraty is an old pirate town consisting of brightly coloured houses and fishing boats, which provide for a really chilled out setting. However, the best part about this town is the manner in which it was designed. Everyday at high tide the sea comes up and floods the streets in order to wash all the cobbled streets clean, as the local fishermen kick back with a cold drink after a hard days work.

☑ **Listen as the ice cracks at the Perito Moreno Glacier, Argentina.** Down in Argentine Patagonia there seems to be a whole other range of scale. Perito Moreno Glacier is a prime example of this scale. As we drove towards the park, I casually glanced out the bus window and noticed a massive iceberg floating in the river beside us. How big, I do not know, but I guess that the above-water part was bigger than a two-storey house. Based on this, I was expecting Perito Moreno Glacier to be big, but as we turned the corner and

I got my first glimpse, I was quite taken aback. I literally let out a gasp followed by a 'Wow!' Yeah, seriously, the 'gasp-wow' combo. It was that spectacular.

The terminus of the glacier is five kilometres wide, with it standing at a total depth of 170 metres and an average height of 75 metres, or roughly the size of a 15-story building, rising above the surface of Lake Argentina. As I strolled the boardwalks overlooking this natural wonder, I soon realised that the visible glacier I had got excited about as the bus pulled in was in fact only a tiny corner of the glacier. What I had not realised is that it climbs 30 kilometres up the mountain, culminating in a total ice formation measuring 250 $kilometers^2$.

What I did not know about glaciers before this day was that they are constantly moving forward from the source, like enormous, slow moving rivers of ice. They form only on land, in locations where the accumulation of snow exceeds the amount of snow that melts. Thus, over many years, often centuries, a glacier will form as compacted layers of snow turn to ice. Then in response to gravity, this river of ice will be pulled towards sea level due to its colossal weight. The result is massive chucks of ice falling off the end constantly. That is why standing in front of a growing glacier, as it very slowly crawls down the hill, is the best place to hear ice crack and break.

To avoid providing further numerical statistics to build a picture of what is surely a world wonder, I will attempt to use adjectives. So to put it another way, imagine a dust mite standing looking up at vacuum cleaner as sand falls out of the bottom and that will give you a slight insight how I felt. Even though I was having one of my happy-snapping days and captured dozens of phoneographs, I just could not get an angle that would allow me to capture how big this glacier actually was. It had that Grand Canyon feel to it, where it was hard to grasp the volume of space it takes up.

☑ **Visit Cuba before Fidel Castro dies.** *If afforded the chance to visit this defiant communist nation in the sun, then I highly recommend that you take up the opportunity as a matter of urgency. The entire country is stuck in a 1950s time warp with old cars, trucks and buses driving in front of crumbling buildings that were once the epitome of grandeur. It is somewhat reminiscent of a scene out of an old Chicago gangster movie. I fully expect that the entire country will change dramatically following the death of both Fidel and Raul Castro, thus the reason why I made sure to visit before their death.*

☑ **Survey Tierra del Fuego, Argentina.** *In the year 1520, a group of Spanish explorers led by Ferdinand Magellan approached the coast of a mysterious land for the first time. As they sailed fearfully*

through the newly discovered straits, columns of smoke from the native's scattered fires seemed to drift upon the foggy waters. It was due to this eerie backdrop that this region was cursed with its name, 'Tierra del Fuego'. 'The Land of Fire'.

Magellan and his crew did not think much of this land but from the moment I heard the name, I was horrified and fascinated in equal measure by this so-called 'Land of Fire'. I had a vision of a hell on Earth setting that one would see in an episode of "The

Perito Moreno Glacier

Simpsons". I envisioned everything would be in various shades of red, the heat radiating from burning infernos would be relentless and the smouldering bonfires with plumes of smoke would go on for as far as the eye could see.

Like many visions that I created in my vast imagination, I could not have been more wrong. In fact, Tierra del Fuego turned out to be a cold and moist archipelago situated off the southernmost tip of the South American mainland across the Strait of Magellan. It consists of a main island, ingeniously named Grande Tierra del Fuego and a group of smaller islands including Cape Horn. It is bound to the north by the imposing Martial Mountains and to the south by the unforgiving Beagle Channel.

The area is so isolated, that it was deemed the perfect location for a natural prison, where convicts guilty of serious crimes were sent to see out their life sentences, as it would be impossible to escape. Nevertheless, times have changed. This, one-time secluded and hostile region, is now a standard part of the trail for the more adventurous backpackers who meander there to witness an area of unparalleled natural wonder.

Upon arriving in Tierra del Fuego, what I found was the town of Ushuaia, the southernmost urban area in the world. The colourful wooden houses of Ushuaia, which nestle amongst the woodland, mountains and ocean combine to create a really picturesque town. So despite my imagination running wild as a child, I came away thinking that there are many worse things I could do with my holiday time than spending a few weeks exploring the wonders of Tierra del Fuego. Try it; sure, it wouldn't be the end of the world.

☑ **Climb Volcan Villarrica, Pucón, Chile.** *The snow-capped Volcan Villarrica looms majestically over Pucón at 2,840 metres above sea level. They told me that climbing to the top was non-technical and, depending on your experience, quite easy on clear days, as they handed out the essential equipment of crampons, ice axe and windproof clothing. 'Ice axe' and 'easy' are not words that I often use in the same sentence!*

The bottom half of our route up Villarrica was covered in loose volcanic ash, which is best described as large pieces of black sand. This was not quite as bad as hiking up sand, but it was the next worst thing, as the effort required was immense. After a few hours

in the black stuff, I was delighted to finally reach the ice and snow. Not only was the ground beneath us now firmer, but I also got to put on the crampons. I felt like a proper adventurer now. The 'nice' conditions lasted for all of a few minutes, as the ice disappeared below a layer of deep snow and a biting wind blew across the slope.

Battling against the cold wind, I was using the ice axe initially as a walking pole and then later as a grip to pull myself up the volcano as the incline got steeper and each knee disappeared into the deep snow. Getting to the top, it really was a sight to behold as I looked down on the small world below. Following behind were other small ant-esque teams dressed in luminous clothing, zigzagging their way up the volcano, trying to find a path offering shelter from the biting cold. It is one of the most beautiful active volcano climbs around and the climb may have been easy on the eye, but that day, I found it hard on the arms, legs and lungs.

☑ **Explore the Amazon, South America.** *I absolutely love everything about rainforest and the extraordinary flora and fauna that exist within them. I have been quite lucky that I have been able to hike through rainforest in Australia, Africa, Asia and South America. However, it may come as no surprise to anyone to learn that, the single greatest experience of all my travels was the time I spent exploring the Amazon. Words fail me. The* beauty, majesty and timelessness of Amazonia are really something to behold.

It is frustrating attempting to explain to those who have never had the experience, just how unique it is to stand in the heart of this rainforest. The best manner in which to describe the Amazonia experience is that it is as close as I have been to experiencing the at-one-ment with Mother Nature that the Na'vi people feel in the movie Avatar (directed by James Cameron). Picture any scene from Avatar and that will go some way towards describing the character and oneness of Amazonia. As depicted in the movie, you just get a feeling that everything is connected and at one. Everything is so interdependent that upsetting one part can lead to the destruction of the whole.

The great river that runs through this majestic rainforest is the other astonishing element of this part of the world. Measuring over 6,550 kilometres long, it is the equivalent to the distance between Rome and New York. This journey into the Amazon was, for me, one of my greatest feats. This is the greatest experience I have ever had. Everything else that is in this book pales in comparison to this experience.

☑ **Survive the Potosí mine, Bolivia.** I will tell you one thing that will give you an indication of how dangerous the tour of this mine is: Our guide 'forgot' that the dynamite was to be set off at noon. This is despite the fact that it is set off at the same time everyday and the resulting explosion rocks the entire town to its foundations. It suddenly dawned on him at 11:55am and he gave us the option of either running for the entrance (it had taken us over an hour to get this far) or scampering deeper into the mine where the explosion would be greatly absorbed. I went deeper. This would not be allowed to happen in Germany.

☑ **Explore Monteverde Cloud Forest Reserve, Costa Rica.** Most people come here in search of the mysterious Quetzal, a very rare and timid bird that is facing extinction. They say that the Quetzal is incredibly beautiful with its unique plumage, but as luck had it, I never got to witness the elusive Quetzal. I was not too upset about that as the main reason I visited the Reserve was so that I could stand on the continental divide, from where, on a clear day, I could see both the Atlantic and Pacific Oceans. As luck would have it, it was not a clear day and I did not get to see that either. Thankfully, the Cloud Forest is magnificent in its own right and well worth a visit, despite its more famous friends not coming out to play.

☐ **Visit The Galapagos Islands.** Made famous by Charles Darwin for the vast number of endemic species, The Galapagos Islands are an archipelago of volcanic islands straddling the equator, 965 kilometres west of continental Ecuador in the Pacific Ocean. No less engrossing now than they were a hundred years ago, much of the same flora and fauna that inspired Darwin's "The Origin of Species" still thrives on the islands today. The celebrated giant tortoises as well as the marine and land iguanas and the seal colonies of the Galapagos are among nature's most fantastic beings and are highly approachable, as their isolated evolution has not conditioned them to fear humans.

"The archipelago is a little world within itself, or rather a satellite attached to America, whence it has derived a few stray colonists, and has received the general character of its indigenous productions. Considering the small size of these islands, we feel the more astonished at the number of their aboriginal beings, and at their confined range. Seeing every height crowned with its crater, and the boundaries of most of the lava-streams still distinct, we are led to believe that within a period, geologically recent, the unbroken ocean was here spread out. Hence, in both space and time, we seem to be brought somewhat nearer to that great fact – that mystery of mysteries – the first appearance of new beings on this earth"

~ Charles Darwin, Voyage of the Beagle

General Travel Objectives

"Perhaps travel cannot prevent bigotry, but by demonstrating that all peoples cry, laugh, eat, worry, and die, it can introduce the idea that if we try and understand each other, we may even become friends."

~ Maya Angelou (Author and poet)

☑ **Visit Antarctica.** "Men wanted for hazardous journey. Small wages, bitter cold, long months of complete darkness, constant danger, safe return doubtful. Honour and recognition in case of success."

This is the advertisement that was apparently placed in a London newspaper back in 1912, by Ernest Shackleton, the Irish Antarctic explorer, while in search of a crew for his 1914 expedition to Antarctica. It was after reading this that I became encapsulated by the spirit of the great white continent and the challenges that lay there. It was a challenge that held great appeal for many others too, as nearly 5,000 applicants, including three women, signed up for Shackletons expedition at a frantic rate. Ultimately, a grand total of 56 men were selected for the expedition.

Antarctica

In the early stages, the expedition was confronted by unforeseen circumstances, as the ship, Endurance, became wedged in the ice pack. This left Shackleton with no choice but to sit tight with the ship throughout the winter, with the hope that the spring thaw would allow the cross-continental trek to continue. Unfortunately, the thawing and moving ice floe began to crush Endurance, until the ship sank below the sea, leaving the men stranded on the ice.

With the ice floe thawing under their feet and it seeming like all hope had gone, in an act of magnificent leadership, Shackleton went on to complete an extraordinary survival story that is without parallel. In an epic struggle between man and nature, Shackleton managed to protect all his men from certain death in the face of intolerable conditions and hardships that defy belief.

Shackletons desire to maintain his men's morale while stranded on ice without hope of rescue is a unique achievement in the annals of exploration. Ultimately this fight for survival came down to the relentless battle of unwavering optimism overcoming the onslaught of crushing defeats. He will forever be remembered as a man of supreme resilience who protected his men to the point of risking his own life to ensure he eventually brought every single man home safe and sound.

It was only when I was personally exposed to the elements in Antarctica that I truly appreciated the gravitas of their mission. It is the most inspiring place on this planet and unique in so many ways. All at the same time it is the coldest, driest, steepest, highest, darkest, windiest, least accessible, most elevated, least known, most compressed, most reflective, most changeable, least humid part of our world. The only word that does Antarctica justice has become an overused cliché, stale from hyperbolic excess. That word is 'awesome.'

☑ **Travel extensively around each of the world's seven continents.** *Yes, I did it! As I set foot on Antarctica in March 2009, I had achieved my childhood dream of travelling to each of the world's seven continents. For many of my travel companions, setting foot on the continent of Antarctica was the culmination of a life long dream of travelling to the seven continents. To celebrate, an older German man, who had been to more than 200 countries around the world, had brought an old bottle of fine whiskey.*

When I told him that he should hold back on the celebrations until I had sourced for him, from the continent, a chunk of ice so pure that it is nearly alien to this modern world, his face lit up like a child on Christmas morning. In Antarctica, you can find ice that is hundreds of thousands of years old. It has been compressed so tightly for so long that it is now completely transparent. On the continent itself, this ice is buried beneath hundreds of metres of snow. However, whilst in the zodiac going to and from the Antarctic continent I would occasionally find some really clear and compacted ice, the remnants of an iceberg that had broken away from the continent many years prior.

After scooping one chunk of ice out of the sea and looking right through it, I knew that this was the perfect ice for the refreshing glass of whiskey my German friend had desired after a hard day exploring and a lifetime

of desire. Our guide estimated that the ice we had crudely broken up and plopped into our plastic cups of whiskey was around 200,000 years old. It is not every day that you get the chance to sip on a whiskey with ice made from the purest of water. "Prost", to you, my German friend.

☑ **Witness the Milky Way as clear in the sky as it can possibly be.** *A perfectly clear night-sky deep in the Amazon, with no streetlights for thousands of kilometres, is the perfect way to experience the Milky Way. The Milky Way snaked across the sky from one horizon to the other with more stars than I ever could have imagined I would see on a single night. Without speaking a word, we lay there on a hammock looking towards the heavens until sunrise, just staring in awe at the sky and wishing on the many shooting stars.*

☑ **Cross the equator by land.** *I first crossed the equator by land on the Island of Sumatra, Indonesia, which meant one thing: I had to shave my hair off!*

Let me explain. One night, I was out in Cusco, Peru when I noticed that a large group of friends all had skinheads. Not only the boys, but the girls also. I had to enquire. They told me about them sailing across the equator for the first time and the tradition of all first timers across the equator shaving their heads. I pledged there and then to the group that I would carry on this tradition whenever I first crossed the equator by land or sea. It was the least I could do, considering all these beautiful girls had shaved their lovely long hair completely off in the name of tradition.

Upon arriving at our guesthouse on the Island of Sumatra, having just crossed the equator, I dumped my bags and went straight to the local barber and had her shave my hair totally off. As it was November of that year, I was already partaking in the 'Movember' festivities. So, to the locals of this isolated island who had never seen a white person before I did look quite strange: I had a skinhead combined with a huge handlebar moustache that ran all the way to my Adam's apple. I received some very strange looks indeed. I hope they did not think that it was a popular trend in Europe and feel the need to be part of it.

The last time I got to drive across the equator was in Kenya and as I had been in Antarctica only a few months before crossing the equator, I decided to act the fool. I pulled out all of the warm clothing I had used in Antarctica: Jacket, gloves, hat and scarf. Then, much to the amusement of the locals, I put them on and had my photo taken with one foot on either side of the equator. I think that it may be safe to say that it was the first time that the locals had ever seen such a jacket.

☑ **Visit the Mausoleums of the Communist leaders: Lenin (Moscow), Moa (Beijing) and Ho Chi Minh (Ho Chi Minh City).** *From what I learned as I visited each of the Mausoleums, each of these*

Communist leaders had requested to be buried with their respective families. However, the members of the Communist party they left behind had other ideas and chose to go against their wishes, something they would have been reluctant to do when these men were alive.

☑ **Circumnavigate the globe in less than 80 days.** *Very few people ever truly traverse the entire globe due to time and/or money restrictions. However, whilst living in Sydney, I wanted to go home for Christmas so I then got the opportunity to complete a full circle of the globe, when it materialised that an 'Around The World' ticket would be cheaper than a return flight to Ireland. So in the space of 56 days, taking some time to explore each location, I completed the following trip: Sydney – Christchurch – Los Angeles – London – Dublin – Stockholm – Hong Kong – Sydney. Take that Phileas Fogg!*

☐ **Explore Easter Island.** *Despite being a 'special territory' of Chile, this triangle of volcanic rock in the South Pacific Ocean is one of the most isolated locations on Earth, with its closest inhabited neighbour being over 2,000 kilometres away. Romantically know as "Te Pito O Te Henua" (The Navel of The World), it was Admiral Roggeveen, who came across the island on Easter Day in 1722 that renamed it Easter Island. My desire to travel to such a remote location is based on the 887 enormous statues, known as Moai, which made the island world famous.*

☐ **Witness the Aurora Borealis and the Aurora Australis.** The Aurora Borealis are more commonly known as the "Northern Lights" and despite spending a reasonable amount of time high in the northern hemisphere, they have never appeared for me. I once visited Iceland at the peak of winter during a time of enhanced solar activity to see this phenomenon and despite the Northern Lights lighting up the sky I never got to see them due to thick cloud cover. Even when they appeared in my home country of Northern Ireland in March 2011, I was not around to witness them.

The Aurora Australis are better known as the "Southern Lights" and these have also eluded me. When I was in Antarctica, it was during Southern Hemisphere summer time, thus the wrong time of the year to see the Aurora Australis. However, I was still hoping that they might appear during an Antarctic summer for the first time ever. They didn't! As it stands I have never bore witness to the great natural wonders that are the Aurora Borealis and Aurora Australis. My time will come.

☐ **Stand at the North and South Poles.** No, not at the same time... that would be quite a feat. Actually, it would be quite a feat to stand on any of the North or South Poles at the same time. Let me explain using the South Pole as an example. (If you are a knowledge geek, as I am, then continue reading. Everyone else, I advise you to skip the next few paragraphs and continue reading again were it says 'CouchSurf').

Everyone that watched cartoons as a kid knows that The South Pole is just a red and white Barbershop pole sticking out of the snow at the southernmost point on the Earth with a lazy penguin sleeping up against it. Well, we also know that adults like to make things more complicated than they should be and the subject of The South Pole is no different, as there are in fact four South Poles as defined in one of several ways.

The point that is usually assumed when an unspecified "South Pole" is mentioned is what is known as The South Geographic Pole. This is the southern end of the Earth's axis of rotation situated at 90° South. At present, Antarctica is located over The South Geographic Pole, although due to continental drift this has not always been the case.

In 1909, an expedition led by Ernest Shackleton found what became known as The Magnetic South Pole. The Magnetic South Pole does not coincide with The South Geomagnetic Pole, as it is the point nearest The South Geographic Pole where the field lines of the Earth's magnetic field point directly into the ground. In short, it is the "South Pole" that compasses point to. The Magnetic South Pole is not fixed and its position moves about 10 to 15 kilometres per year, presently in a north to north-westerly direction. However, you will know when you are on it, as the needle on the compass will spin in circles.

To further confuse you, we then have The South Geomagnetic Pole. This is one of the two magnetic poles of the Earth's magnetic field and it is approximately 2,900 kilometres away from The South Geographic Pole. Its exact location is gradually shifting and in 2012 the location of The South Geomagnetic Pole was 64.43° S and 137.14° E. The Earth's geomagnetic field can be determined by using a tilted dipole (a bar magnet). The location of The South Geomagnetic Pole is measured as the point on the Earth's surface where the axis of this best-fitting tilted dipole intersects the southern hemisphere.

Finally, we have what is known as The Southern Pole of Inaccessibility as defined by the point that is the farthest distant from the Southern Ocean and the most challenging to reach owing to its remoteness. It is currently located at 82°06' S and 54°58' E on the surface of the Antarctic continent. It was not reached until 1958, at which time a Soviet Antarctic Expedition marked the spot with a golden guestbook for visitors to sign and a bust of Vladimir Lenin, facing towards Moscow.

Did I say four? Silly me, there are actually five if we count what is known as The Ceremonial South Pole. This "South Pole" is not too far from The South Geographic Pole and, as you can probably tell by the name, it is an area set aside for photo opportunities. It consists of a red and white Barbershop pole sticking out of the snow with the flags of the countries that signed the Antarctic Treaty placed around it in a circle. There may or may not be a lazy penguin sleeping up against it when you visit.

☐ **CouchSurf.** CouchSurfing is a service that offers people the opportunity to sleep in the home of another for free. People usually offer up whatever spare space they have available, which can range from their floor or couch to an en suite bedroom or even a full apartment. Guests generally stay for a few days in a location before moving on to the next house in another location. The agreement is consensual between the host and guest, with the duration, nature and terms of the guest's stay generally agreed in advance. The guest benefits from the low cost (usually free) place to stay for a few nights, whereas the host gains a new friend.

I have attempted to 'CouchSurf' on a few occasions, but because I have no personal references from people that have previously hosted me, I have been rejected on each occasion. Fair enough, I suppose, but how am I supposed to get a reference if I cannot get a host because I have no references? However, leaving that aside, I really need to get out and do some CouchSurfing. There is no excuse for this, considering the amount of travel I have completed to date. Therefore, if you are a Couchsurfer then do me a favour and get in contact at 'Patrick Hamilton Walsh', as I may be passing through your way soon... or vice versa.

The Giants Causeway

Seven Wonders

"The hand is the cutting edge of the mind. Civilization is not a collection of finished artefacts, it is the elaboration of processes. In the end, the march of man is the refinement of the hand in action. The most powerful drive in the ascent of man is his pleasure in his own skill. He loves to do what he does well and, having done it well, he loves to do it better. You see it in his science. You see it in the magnificence with which he carves and builds, the loving care, the gaiety, the effrontery. The monuments are supposed to commemorate kings and religions, heroes, dogmas, but in the end the man they commemorate is the builder."

~ Jacob Bronowski (Author)

When I was growing up, I had heard a lot about the Seven Wonders of the World and even though I had never known what they actually consisted of, I always had a great desire to visit them. It was the great mystique of the name that led me to researching the "Seven Wonders" to determine where they were located. I was quite surprised to find that there were over fifty locations that were deemed "Wonders of the World". Let me explain:

Seven Wonders of the Ancient World

At the Museum of Alexandria in Egypt, the scholar Callimachus of Cyrene and the historian Herodotus, made early lists of what they considered to be the Seven Wonders of the World. The list was based on locations popular among ancient Greek sightseers and as a result, the list only includes works located around the Mediterranean rim. The list was limited to seven because the Greeks believed seven to be the representation of perfection.

Unfortunately, the Great Pyramid of Giza is the only wonder of the ancient world that is still in existence today. Despite this, I still wish to visit the sites of all Seven Wonders to get a sense of what the great architects of that time had in mind when designing and building these wonders. The list that Callimachus and Herodotus drafted consisted of the following:

☑ **Great Pyramid of Giza, Egypt.**

☑ **Temple of Artemis at Ephesus, Turkey.**

☑ **Lighthouse of Alexandria, Egypt.**

☐ **Colossus of Rhodes, Greece.**

☐ **The Hanging Gardens of Babylon, Iraq.**

☐ **Mausoleum of Maussollos at Halicarnassus, Turkey.**

☐ **Statue of Zeus at Olympia, Greece.**

Seven Wonders of the Medieval World

During the 19th century many lists were created based on structures that were built during the Medieval Ages. From what I can see, these are the constructions that seem to be included in lists of the Seven Wonders of the Medieval World most consistently:

☑ **The Colosseum of Rome, Italy.**

☑ **The Great Wall of China.**

☑ **Stonehenge, England.**

☐ **The Catacombs of Kom el Shoqafa, Alexandria, Egypt.**

☐ **The Leaning Tower of Pisa, Italy.**

☐ **Hagia Sophia, Turkey.**

☐ **The Porcelain Tower of Nanjing, China.**

Seven Wonders of the Underwater World

CEDAM International, a non-profit group for divers dedicated to ocean preservation and research compiled a list of 'Underwater Wonders' in 1989. A panel of marine scientists chose seven underwater areas that they considered to be most worthy of protection:

The Backpacker who sold his Supercar

In 1995 The American Society of Civil Engineers decided that it was time to compile yet another list of Wonders of the World. They listed the Seven Wonders of the Modern World as follows:

☑ CN Tower, Canada.

☑ The Empire State Building, USA.

☑ Golden Gate Bridge, USA.

☑ Itaipu Dam, Paraná River, Brazil and Paraguay.

☑ The Panama Canal, Panama.

☐ The Zuiderzee Sea Protection Works, The Netherlands.

☐ Channel Tunnel, English Channel.

Seven Natural Wonders of the World

Similar to the other lists of wonders, there is no consensus on a list of the Seven Natural Wonders of the World. One of the many lists compiled is as follows:

☑ Grand Canyon, USA.

☑ Great Barrier Reef, Australia.

☑ The Giants Causeway, Northern Ireland.

☑ Mount Everest, Nepal.

Petra, Jordan

☑ The Belize Barrier Reef, Belize.

☑ The Great Barrier Reef, Australia.

☑ Lake Baikal, Siberia, Russia.

☑ The Northern Red Sea, Sinai Peninsula, Egypt.

☐ Deep-sea hydrothermal vents, Ecuador.

☐ Palau.

☐ The Galápagos Islands.

Seven Wonders of the Modern World

☑ **Victoria Falls, Zambia and Zimbabwe.**

☐ **Aurora Borealis and Australis (Northern and Southern Lights).**

☐ **Volcán de Parícutin, Mexico.**

Seven Wonders of the Industrial World

Then the 'Wonders of the World' lists expanded yet further. British author, Deborah Cadbury, wrote a book on the great feats of engineering that went into producing the wonderful structures of the 19th and early 20th centuries. This is her interpretation:

☑ **The Brooklyn Bridge, USA.**

☑ **The Panama Canal, Panama.**

☑ Hoover Dam, USA.

☐ The London sewerage system, England.

☐ **The First Transcontinental Railroad, USA.**

☐ **SS Great Eastern, London, England.**

☐ **Bell Rock Lighthouse, Scotland.**

New Seven Wonders of the World

The New7Wonders Foundation, based in Switzerland, decided in 2001 that it was time to update the concept of the Seven Wonders of the World. They wanted a list of man-made wonders according to the modern mind. Therefore, they ran a worldwide poll to determine what the winners should be and after 100 million votes were cast this is what they came up with:

☑ **Chichen Itza, Mayan City, Mexico.**

☑ **Christ the Redeemer, Brazil.**

☑ **The Great Wall of China.**

☑ **Machu Picchu, Peru.**

☑ **Petra, Jordan.**

☑ **The Colosseum of Rome, Italy.**

☑ **The Taj Mahal, India.**

New Seven Wonders of Nature

'The New7Wonders of Nature' campaign began in 2007, immediately after the campaign to elect the man-made 'New7Wonders of the World' had been finalised. It looks as if this 'New7Wonders' thing is going to keep running too, as it seems like this organisation has came up with an ingenious way to visit all the worlds great locations. Whatever is said about their process, it seems to have captured the public's imagination. Despite some controversy, here is what was elected as the official winners of the New7Wonders of Nature:

☑ **The Amazon, South America.**

☑ **Ha Long Bay, Vietnam.**

☑ **Iguaçu Falls, Argentina and Brazil.**

☑ **Table Mountain, South Africa.**

☐ **Komodo National Park, Indonesia.**

☐ **Puerto Princesa Underground River, the Philippines.**

☐ **Jeju Island, South Korea.**

The Seven Blunders of the World

Although not directly related to the locations of the Wonders of the World, this may be the most important list of them all for human kind. It was published by Mohandas Gandhi in 1925 and given to his grandson, Arun Gandhi, shortly before he was assassinated. 'Gandhi's Seven Blunders', that I do not ever wish to tick off, are:

☐ **Wealth without work.**

☐ **Pleasure without conscience.**

☐ **Knowledge without character.**

☐ **Commerce without morality.**

☐ **Science without humanity.**

☐ **Worship without sacrifice.**

☐ **Politics without principle.**

Patrick Hamilton Walsh

Urban Wonders

I enjoy being around people, hence I love being in cities. I love the buzz of the urban landscape and the energy it generates in its relentless chase of tomorrow and the 'next big thing.' I love the chaos and the confusion. I am fascinated by the fact that, despite being surrounded by millions of people, cities can be the loneliest place to live. Cities are our urban jungles, where the inhabitants are involved in the constant urban warfare with their friends, their foes and, of course, themselves. I love when cities get it right and I love when cities get it wrong. Cities are urban wonders. I love cities, thus my contribution to the lists of Wonders is, *'The Seven Urban Wonders of the World'.*

"Living in cities is an art, and we need the vocabulary of art, of style, to describe the peculiar relationship between man and material that exists in the continual creative play of urban living. The city as we imagine it, then, soft city of illusion, myth, aspiration, and nightmare, is as real, maybe more real, than the hard city one can locate on maps in statistics, in monographs on urban sociology and demography and architecture."

~ Jonathan Raban (Writer and novelist)

☑ **The Magic Roundabout, Swindon, England:** *The world's* most confusing intersection. To be honest, despite its unique layout, this roundabout has been so well designed to reduce overall congestion that it is marvellously functional. It looks like a nightmare in pictures, but as I drove it, I just seemed to cruise through so easily. However, as it is certainly an urban wonder it may be highly perplexing to those unfamiliar with roundabouts. Check it out on Google Earth to see what all the fuss is about.

☑ **Baldwin Street, Dunedin, New Zealand:** *The world's steepest residential street. As with*

The world's steepest residential street

many other parts of New Zealand, the streets were laid out in a grid pattern by planners in London with no consideration for the terrain. The result is roads, like this, that lead up a mountainside.

☑ **Lombard Street, San Francisco, USA:** *The world's most crooked road. Lombard Street is famous for the eight sharp turns on Russian Hill between Hyde Street and Leavenworth Street. This part of the street has been highlighted in many movies, usually featuring fleeing villains in car chases. So, there you go, the most crooked* road in the world is not Wall Street after all!

☑ **9 de Julio Avenue, Buenos Aires, Argentina:** *The widest avenue in the world. At just under 100 metres wide, 9 de Julio Avenue occupies what could be an entire block in the city grid. Crossing the avenue can often take up to five minutes by foot, as there are up to three sets of traffic lights that must be passed through to cross its twelve lanes of traffic.*

☑ **Yonge Street, Toronto, Canada:** *The longest street in the world. Yonge Street was built for military purposes in case of conflict with the United States. Construction, performed by local farmers and convicts, begun in the late 1700s and today the street is a hub of activity in central Toronto.*

☑ **O'Connell Bridge, Dublin, Ireland:** *The only traffic bridge that is as wide as it is long. The bridge spans 45 metres across the River Liffey, yet it is 50 metres wide. How Irish is that?*

☐ **Parliament Street, Exeter, England:** *The narrowest street in the world. The street, dating back to the 14th century, is 50 metres long and links the High Street to Waterbeer Lane. The street is approximately 115 centimetres at its widest and less than 63 centimetres at its narrowest.*

Buildings and Monuments

Europe

Many times over the years, in towns and cities all over the world, I have found myself saying goodbye to the people that I have been travelling with as I set out through the streets and alleyways in search of a particular building or monument. The writer Carson McCullers summed it up perfectly when he stated: *"We are torn between a nostalgia for the familiar and an urge for the foreign and strange. As often as not, we are homesick most for the places we have never known."*

I know exactly how this feels. In fact, I would detour hundreds of kilometres simply to go and admire a piece of architecture or a statue that sparked my interest. Despite this, I am usually forced to go alone, as my temporary travel companion at the time shows no interest in the slightest. Undeterred, I will enthusiastically set out to visit these buildings and monuments as if they were a long lost friend. When I get to the structure I simply stand and admire. After all, architecture is the mother art.

"After about the first Millennium, Italy was the cradle of Romanesque architecture, which spread throughout Europe, much of it extending the structural daring with minimal visual elaboration."
~ Harry Seidler (Architect)

☑ **The Kremlin, Moscow, Russia.** *Russia's symbol of the 20th century, The Kremlin, returned to pre-eminence in March 1918 when the Bolsheviks' choose Moscow over St. Petersburg as their capital. It was during Soviet rule that The Kremlin returned as the centre of power as a city within a city, containing a multitude of palaces, churches, armouries and a medieval fortress. Walking around inside is quite surreal as it always seemed to be so closed off to 'outsiders' like me and yet there I was strolling around as if I owned the place (well in my own head at least).*

☑ **Duomo di Milano, Italy.** *In Milan during 1386, Archbishop Antonio da Saluzzo began construction of Duomo di Milano after the previous buildings on the site were destroyed in a fire in 1075. On 20 May 1805, over four centuries after work had begun, Napoleon Bonaparte, in his great enthusiasm, about to be crowned King of Italy, ordered the façade of this great building to be finished. He assured that all expenses would fall to the French treasurer, who would* *reimburse the Fabric for the real estate it had to sell. Despite the fact that this reimbursement is still to be paid, it meant that the Cathedral had its façade finally completed.*

Work on the Gothic cathedral proceeded for generations, taking nearly six centuries to complete with the result being the fourth-largest church in the world, designed to host up to 40,000 worshippers. The last details of the cathedral were finished late in the 20th century with the last gate inaugurated on 6 January 1965. This date is considered the very end of a process, which had proceeded for generations, although even now, some uncared blocks remain to be turned into sculpture and completed as statues.

This great building is known for its remarkable façade and the thousands of pinnacles and statues that are placed at the sides of the roof. However, there are many astonishing places of worship throughout the world, with fantastic interiors and majestic exteriors. Nevertheless, the Duomo di Milano has one feature that makes it unique from all other cathedrals in the world. For here in Milan, tourists are actually encouraged to go up and walk about on the roof of the cathedral.

The street plan of Milan, with streets either radiating from the Duomo or circling around it, indicates that the Duomo occupied the most important site in the

ancient Roman city of what was then called, Mediolanum. Moreover, the views from the roof certainly prove it. Walking on the roof of such a prestigious historical monument is such a special experience that I would recommend you make the most of it quite soon, as I expect the 'Fun Police' to eventually step in and forbid this unique spectacle. After all, it is not everyday that you are invited to walk on the roof of a cathedral.

☑ The Acropolis, Athens, Greece. *Sitting on the edge of a cliff overlooking Athens, with my back against the Acropolis was a special moment for me as I maintain a profound appreciation for Ancient Greece. A lot of what is good about the world in which we live today is due to the contributions of the men and women that walked the corridors of buildings like The Acropolis. Democracy, biology, mathematics, physics, philosophy, astrology and theatre are only a few of the contributions that they passed through the ages.*

The words and thoughts of great Greek men such as Socrates, Pythagoras, Plato and Aristotle are still relevant and taught in universities throughout the world to this day. The fantastic buildings and monuments in their great cities have withstood the powers of nature for thousands of years. As a testimony to the great minds of Ancient Greece, these buildings still stand for us to explore in wonderment. This was a great civilisation, far ahead of its time, whose beauty and knowledge will live on for many generations to come. For me to go to mainland Greece and not visit The Acropolis would be unthinkable.

☑ **Gaudi's La Sagrada Familia, Barcelona, Catalonia.** Although construction of this great building commenced in 1882, with Gaudí getting involved a year later, it still is not finished. In fact, it is estimated that construction only passed the mid-point in 2010 with some of the project's greatest challenges remaining. It is anticipated that construction of this unique church, combining Art NouveauGothic and curvilinear forms, can be completed by 2026 to coincide the centennial of Gaudi's death.

I spent a long time sitting on the pavement outside it, just looking up and admiring the complexity of the task in hand and searching for evidence were the newly constructed sections of stonework are clearly visible against the stained and weathered older sections. As I sat there, the words of Friedrich Wilhelm Joseph Von Schelling never seemed more appropriate; "Architecture is music in space, as it were a frozen music."

☑ **Kylemore Abbey, Connemara, Ireland.** What was once 'Kylemore Castle' is situated far off the beaten track in the rural west of Ireland, in a place of peace and tranquillity. The 1,000 acre estate was originally built in 1867 by Mitchell Henry as a romantic gift for his beloved wife and encompasses a mountain, a lake teeming with salmon and a Gothic church. It is now home to the Benedictine order of nuns, who have resided here since 1920, when they were forced to flee here from the Abbey at Ypres, Belgium as the first bombs were dropped in the area during World War I.

Thus, the Castle became an Abbey and the nuns opened an international boarding school and established a day school for local girls, just as they had at Ypres. The daughters of diplomats and dignitaries were always well represented at Kylemore over the years. It was rumoured that Madonna had listed her daughter, Lourdes, to attend the Abbey for her secondary education, but unfortunately, the school was forced to close in June 2010. The diminishing number of women taking the vocation to become a nun was held as the reason for the school's closure.

Today, there are just twelve Benedictine nuns left at Kylemore and thankfully, they have opened the Abbey and Estate to give visitors the chance to explore the grounds and buildings. The Abbey must suffer now with the absence of energy and enthusiasm that the schoolgirls running around in their blue uniforms would have brought to the estate. Nonetheless, the iconic image of the castle reflected in the lake, the award winning gardens and the world-class fishing on *offer within the estate ensure that Kylemore will be enjoyed for a long time to come.*

☑ **The Sibelius Monument, Helsinki, Finland.** *Dedicated to the Finnish composer Jean Sibelius (1865–1957) and designed by Eila Hiltunen, it consists of a series of 600 hollow steel pipes welded together in a wave-like pattern. The essence of the piece was to capture the spirit of the music of Sibelius, but for me I just treasured the design and setting.*

☑ **'The House of Ceaușescu', Bucharest, Romania.** *Every so often, an individual with just the right personality comes along and proves how absolute power can corrupt absolutely. Step forward Mr.*

Nicolae Ceaușescu, the Romanian dictator who built the world's largest house. Ceaușescu wanted his new residence to be right in the city centre of Bucharest so the building of "Ceaușescu's Palace" commenced in 1983 when the starving people of Bucharest were forced from their homes so that Ceaușescu could build his. The fact that much of the city's historic district had to be demolishing for his new home to be built was of no concern to him.

The demolition went ahead, destroying 30,000 residences, 19 Orthodox Christian churches, six Jewish synagogues and three Protestant churches, with a further eight churches relocated. When the House of Ceaușescu was eventually

completed, it consisted of 1,100 rooms covering twelve floors and measured 270 metres by 240 metres, with 86 metres above the ground and a massive 92 metres underground. The total spend in the construction of the house came in at over $10 billion. As well as being the largest house ever built, it is listed in the Guinness Book of World Records as the world's heaviest building, the most expensive administrative building and the largest civilian administrative building.

To think that a man used the money of the people to build a house of this size, as they starved outside is upsetting. The only surprise is that the people starving on the streets waited until the winter of 1989

to overthrow Ceauşescu. On 25 December 1989, Ceauşescu and his wife were sentenced to death by a military court on numerous charges that ranged from genocide to the illegal gathering of wealth. The pair was executed by a firing squad that began shooting as soon as they were in position against the wall. It is said that hundreds of people volunteered to be executioners. Let us hope that a long time passes before the next Ceauşescu comes along.

☑ **The Mother Motherland monument, Kiev, Ukraine.** This cold grey titanium statue stands at 108 metres high, on top of the Museum of the Great Patriotic War, as she looks over the Kiev skyline towards Moscow. With her right arm extended above her head, she holds a sword, 16 metres long, weighing nine tons. In her left hand, she holds a shield, 13 metres by eight metres, emblazoned with the Soviet Union coat of arms. She weighs a total of 560 tons and is quite an imposing lady.

During the period of Soviet rule, the leaders in Moscow built large, unwelcoming, cold monuments all over the former USSR. It was said that they did this to encourage a notion of solidarity in the countries under communist rule. Maybe they also did it to remind the citizens below that Big Brother was watching. Mother Motherland was the name given to several monuments in cities throughout the former USSR. My local friend referred to the statue as "Baba Moskva," as he flicked his hand at

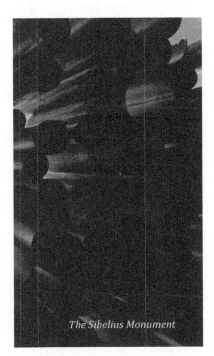

The Sibelius Monument

it in disgust. Translated it means "Old Granny Moscow," an impolite phrase, showing a slight glimpse of the disdain the people of Kiev have for their former rulers.

☐ **The Alhambra, Granada, Spain.** In the late middle ages, the Moors sought to create their own version of paradise on Earth. They built these wonderful palaces inside a fort for the last Muslim Emirs in Spain and the court of the Nasrid dynasty. Just recently, the strange writings on the walls of The Alhambra were deciphered, which will make for an even more interesting visit when I eventually get the chance to travel there.

☐ **The Bosnian Pyramids, Visoko, Bosnia.** At Visočica hill stands the first known European pyramid to be discovered. Standing at 213 metres, it is said to be the largest ancient pyramid on Earth. What is nothing more than a mound of clay at the moment has all the elements of a pyramid with four perfectly shaped slopes pointing toward the cardinal points, a flat top and an entrance complex. Despite some arguing that it is a natural mound, experts have nicknamed it "the Bosnian Pyramid of the Sun" because of its similarities to the Pyramid of the Sun in Teotihuacan, Mexico. On the same site, there are four other ancient structures, which have been named "the Bosnian Pyramid of the Moon", "Temple of the Earth", "the Bosnian Pyramid of the Dragon" and "the Bosnian Pyramid of Love".

The Middle East

"Most of people talk, we do things. They plan, we achieve. They hesitate, we move ahead. We are living proof that when human beings have the courage and commitment to transform a dream into reality, there is nothing that can stop them. Dubai is a living example of that."
~ HH Sheikh Mohammed Bin Rashid Al Maktoum, (Ruler of Dubai)

☑ **The Dome of the Rock, Jerusalem.** Seen from all over the city, the Dome of the Rock is the most famous Islamic site in Jerusalem. I was surprised to learn that this impressive edifice is not a mosque but a Muslim shrine. It is revered in the same way as the Kaaba in Mecca is, due to it being built over a sacred stone believed to be the place from which the Prophet Muhammad ascended into heaven during his Night Journey. The sacred rock over which the Dome of the Rock is built was considered holy before the arrival of Islam. Jews believe that the rock is the spot where Abraham prepared to sacrifice Isaac and to be the site of both Herod's and Solomon's Temples.

☑ **The Wailing Wall, Jerusalem.** Constructed by Herod the Great, this is the most famous wall in the world and is arguably the most sacred site to those of the Jewish faith. Jews believe the wall to be part of the 'Second Temple'. However, like most things in this region, it is a source of much dispute, as Muslims consider it to be the wall to which the Prophet Muhammad tied his winged steed during his Night Journey. The Photographer, Ken Duncan perfectly summed up the feeling that exists around this wall when he stated, "Spiritually, the Holy Land really stirs you up and starts awakening many things in your life." *I have to agree. There is a really nice vibe around the wall, despite the abundance of security personnel.*

☑ **The Basilica of the Annunciation, Nazareth.** *This is the site where Roman Catholics believe the Annunciation took place while Mary was drawing water from a local spring. The Greek Orthodox tradition has erected a church at an alternate site, just up the road, where they believe the Annunciation took place. In Catholicism, the Annunciation was when the angel Gabriel visited the Blessed Virgin Mary to inform her that she would conceive and become the mother of the Son of God, whom she was to name Jesus. There is a massive event held here on 25 March each year, being nine months before Christmas day.*

☑ **The Church of the Nativity, Bethlehem.** *The church is build over the holy site, known as the Grotto, which is believed to be the birthplace of Jesus. It is one of the longest continuously operating churches in the world. Following numerous additions* over the centuries, it truly is now a remarkable basilica that provided a feeling of peace and calm, after a day spent exploring the West Bank.

☑ **The Church of the Holy Sepulchre, Jerusalem.** *The site is respected as the location where Jesus was crucified and is said to contain the place where he was buried (the Sepulchre). In addition to that, it is also the purported site of the resurrection of Jesus. Despite the heaving masses of people in the church, there is a very positive energy within the building.*

☑ **Burj Khalifa, Dubai, UAE.** *Standing at 830 metres, this is currently the tallest structure in the world. It is so tall that it measures more than the height of the, once standing, World Trade Centre towers stacked on top of each other. I was there just before it opened, so I never actually got inside it. However, to stand at the bottom and look up was good enough for me, as it is not like the Empire State Building, where you look over one of the world's great cities. At the top of this, I can imagine that it will be mostly ocean or desert on view, which is not as exciting.*

The building officially opened as the tallest man-made structure ever built on 4 January 2010, but its grand title will be short lived. The Chinese have drawn up plans for a building that will measure close to 1,000 metres in height.

☑ **King Abdullah Mosque, Amman, Jordan.** *The roof inside this mosque is spectacular. After a hard day spent exploring the city of Amman, I just lay on the floor staring up at it. I find the inside of Mosques to be very relaxing when they are empty. However, they can also be quite a nice place to visit at prayer time on a Friday, as away from the worship of the "God of Shopping" that now dominates in the Christian world, you find people that take the time pray to a God that dominates every facet of their lives. The level of faith that Muslims have always astonishes me.*

☐ **The Great Mosque of Damascus, Syria.** *Officially known as Umayyad Mosque, it is one of the largest and oldest mosques in the world and holds the distinction of being considered the fourth-holiest place in Islam. To this day, the Great Mosque holds a shrine that is said to contain the head of John the Baptist, a man that is honoured as a prophet by Muslims as well as Christians. In addition, this is believed to be the site where Jesus (Isa), who is also considered a prophet by Muslims, will return to at the End of Days.*

☐ **Al-Masjid al-Harām, Mecca, Saudi Arabia.** *This "Sacred Mosque" is what surrounds Islam's holiest place, the Kaaba, in the city of Mecca. It is the largest mosque in the world and, as one of the Five Pillars of Islam, every able bodied Muslim must perform the Hajj pilgrimage at least once in their lifetime if possible and circumambulate the Kaaba. The*

current structure, covering 356,800 metres^2, can accommodate up to four million worshipers during the Hajj period, making it one of the largest annual gatherings of people on the planet. Muslims pray five times a day and when they pray every single one of them will turn and face the Kaaba during their prayers. That is how sacred this location is.

Africa

"When the missionaries came to Africa they had the Bible and we had the land. They said, 'Let us pray.' We closed our eyes. When we opened them we had the Bible and they had the land."

~ Bishop Desmond Tutu

☑ **El Djem, Tunisia.** *This little town is home to the most impressive Roman remains in Africa, including its very own Colosseum. Actually, despite the fact that it looks very similar to the Colosseum in Rome the locals take great care to ensure that it is called an amphitheatre and not a Colosseum. The reason for this is that Colosseum is the Latin word for 'that thing by the Colossus'. Therefore, technically as there is no Colossus in El Djem, it is an amphitheatre with a seating capacity for 35,000 spectators.*

☑ **The Red Pyramid of Dahshur, Egypt.** *This is arguably the most impressive of all the pyramids in Egypt. It was totally inaccessible up until 1996 due to its location being within a military base and it still appears to be relatively unknown outside archaeological circles to this day. I jumped in a taxi and paid a small sum to the driver to take me out to the region for the day. What I saw amazed me.*

Here was this massive, yet beautiful, pyramid in the middle of the desert

The Red Pyramid of Dahshur

with not a single person around. I was free to climb all over it, go inside and explore and ultimately just stand at the base of it and look up. I never met another person. There is no cover charge, no hawkers selling postcards and no tourists concerned only with getting that perfect Facebook profile picture. This is a total pyramid experience. It is how I imagine the Great Pyramids of Giza would have been 100 years ago, with the sand blowing up around it, covering its base.

I recommend this as a must do and I would nearly go as far as to say, skip the Great Pyramids of Giza as the only thing that they have to offer over this pyramid is that they are bigger. The structure of the Red Pyramid of Dahshur is the third largest pyramid in Egypt and, to be honest, they are all so vast in size that it is hard to tell what is bigger when standing at the base. Put this on your Carrot list now.

☑ **Karnak Temple, Luxor, Egypt.** Luxor, under its previous guise, Thebes, once held the grand title as the "Capital of the Known World". Therefore, to go with this grand title they needed great temples, so they built six. The four on the left bank of the Nile are known as Goornah, Dayr-eh-Baharee, Medinet Haboo and the Ramesseum; with the two temples on the right bank known as Karnak and Luxor. It is a fascinating area and because it is so far south from Cairo, most visitors to Egypt make do with the Great Pyramids at Giza and leave this area relatively tourist free by comparison.

☑ **The Pyramid of Djoser, Egypt.** This stepped pyramid was the first of the 118 Egyptian pyramids to be built. This is a fascinating location to visit despite the fact that it is currently covered in scaffolding, as the authorities have finally seen the value in repairing the site.

☑ **The Bent Pyramid of Snofru, Egypt.** This is believed to be the first Egyptian pyramid that was intended to be smooth-sided and non-stepped. Yet, ultimately it all went wrong so they changed the design to a stepped pyramid and had the steps filled in before concealing the 'mistake' with an outer casing. The result is comical.

Asia

"The superior man is modest in his speech, but exceeds in his actions."
~ Confucius (Teacher and philosopher)

☑ **Swayambhunath, Stupa Kathmandu, Nepal.** *Sitting high on the hill, the soaring white dome and glittering golden spire of the stupa are visible from all over Kathmandu. The stupa has been an important Buddhist pilgrimage destination since before the fifth century, however the origins of the stupa date to a time long before the arrival of Buddhism in the region.*

Although the site is considered Buddhist, the temple is sacred to both Hindus and Buddhists, which I found fascinating in a world where religious intolerance is on the increase. Having adopted the temple along side the Buddhists, the Hindus have constructed their own shrines in harmony with the Buddhist Temple, which merge beautifully. In what is a healthy example to mankind, the two religions of Kathmandu peacefully share this spiritual site, with their shrines and statues amalgamating amicably.

Before first light each morning, countless Hindu and (Vajrayana) Buddhist pilgrims climb the 365 steps that lead up the steep hillside, passing the two lions guarding the entry way. At the top colourful prayer flags flutter overhead as the devotees shuffle around the stupa in a clockwise fashion (Newari Buddhists circle in a counter-clockwise direction).

The weather-beaten faces of the pilgrims provided an insight into the daily struggles of life in Nepal. Their sparkling eyes and honest smiles show that the dedication that they have to their God fills them with a deep contentment. As a part of their daily ritual, whilst circumambulating the stupa, their leathery hands spin the decorated cold metal prayer wheels as the mantras they mutter float heavenward towards their God.

The dawn visit to Swayambhunath stupa was certainly a priceless experience and I was glad that I made that climb up the historic staircase and safely navigated past the 'holy monkeys'. It was only through reaching the top that the entirety of this most enigmatic and ancient of holy shrines was revealed in all its splendour and I got to enjoy the astounding vistas over the vast city below. Right then I made a pledge to someday return to this most holy of temples.

☑ **Patouxai, Vientiane, Laos.** *Strategically built in the heart of Vientiane city, the Patouxai, which has a strange resemblance to the Arc de Triomphe is situated in the middle of a roundabout. It lays at the end of the grand Lang Xang Avenue, a long straight road that has a strange resemblance to the*

Champs Elysees. It is a fabulous monument in a very nice part of town, yet it remains unfinished. The locals do not seem to see the beauty in the structure as they use the monument as a great location to shade their mopeds and bicycles from the sun. Therefore, just in case you were wondering, Laos was a French Colony at the time Patouxai was built.

☑ **The Terracotta Warriors, China.** *Irish funerals can be quite grand occasions as we celebrate the life of the recently deceased. However, nothing can compare to the send off that Qin Shi Huang, the first Emperor of China, had. When he died, in the third century BC, he had an entire army sculpted in clay and buried with him in his mausoleum in order to protect him in the afterlife. In addition to warriors, he also had full-scale horses with accompanying chariots buried with them. In total, it is estimated that there were more than 8,000 soldiers, 150 cavalry horses and 130 chariots with 520 horses individually sculpted and carefully placed underground to protect the Emperor.*

However, he did not stop there as there were also other non-military figures found including officials, musicians, acrobats and even strongmen. I was really looking forward to seeing the magnificent Terracotta Warriors up close since the day I learned about them. Unfortunately, I came away feeling short-changed. I think that I had just built them up so much in my

mind and they did not quite live up to my, obviously unrealistic, expectations.

☑ **The Shanghai World Financial Centre, China.** *"SWFC", as the locals know it, is one of the new style of mixed-use skyscraper, consisting of shopping centres, offices, hotels, and, the now obligatory, observation deck. It officially opened just after the Olympic games on 28 August 2008, as the tallest building in mainland China. However, as it was 'only' measured at 492 metres it was 'only' the second-tallest building on the planet at that time.*

Of course, boys being boys, they had already begun building the Shanghai Tower right next to it when I visited the city, which is set to dwarf SWFC upon completion. I was really impressed by the building and the design despite it looking to me like the world's largest bottle opener. I am not sure if that was the look they were going for.

☑ **The Forbidden City, Beijing, China.** *For nearly 500 years "The Purple Forbidden City," to give it its full translation, served as the palace of emperors and the power base of the Chinese government. Built in 1406 and covering 720,000 metres^2, this imperial palace housed all Emperors from the Ming Dynasty right up until the Qing Dynasty. This walled city within a city derived its name from the fact that no one could enter or leave the palace without the Emperor's permission.*

However, it certainly is not forbidden these days. This is the one destination that had the most tourists in any single place that I have ever been. Even Disneyland was not as crowded with tourists as this, so called, Forbidden City. However, what was great about this was that 99 percent of the tourists within the city were local Chinese people, which was great to see and really refreshing.

☑ **Sahib Golden Temple, Amritsar, India.** *Sri Harmandir Sahib, known as the Golden Temple due to its scenic beauty and golden coating, is a place of worship for Sikhs. Construction of the Temple began in 1574 with the building project overseen by the fourth and fifth Sikh Gurus until its completion in 1601. Restoration and embellishment continued over the years culminating with 100 kilograms of gold being applied to the inverted lotus-shaped dome in the early 19th century, at a time when decorative marble was added.*

All this work took place under the patronage of the legendary warrior king, Maharaja Ranjit Singh. The Sikh community and the Punjabi people remember him with much affection as he was the major donor of the money and materials that helped the shrine become such a fantastic building. After I arrived in Amritsar and booked into a hotel close to the temple, I learned that travellers are allowed to stay the night and eat for free in the temple.

This appealed to me as one of the great travel experiences.

After enquiring at the Temple I was handed a mat and directed to a large hallway were many pilgrims lay on the floor. I found myself a space on the floor, were I laid my mat out before going off in search of the free food. In a large dorm filled with tables, I was handed a wooden bowl and joined the queue to collect the rice on offer. Finding a space among some of the poorest people imaginable I ate the rice with my hand whilst trying to absorb this experience before going back to lay my head down on the hard marble for the night.

☑ **Two International Finance Centre (2IFC), Hong Kong.** *2IFC officially has 88 floors but the reality is quite different. In Chinese culture, certain numbers are believed by some to be lucky based on the Chinese word that the name of the number sounds similar to. Lucky numbers are based on Chinese words that sound similar to other Chinese words. The numbers "six," "eight" and "nine" are believed to be lucky because their names sound similar to words that have positive meanings.*

If we carried on this tradition then the best example I can think of is that the number "six" would be lucky due to it sounding similar to the word "rich". It is based on this logic that the word for "eight" is deemed lucky due to it sounding similar to "fortune". As a result, the

Chinese people attempt to include the number eight when possible. An example would be the opening ceremony for the 2008 Olympic games held in Beijing. The official starting time for the games was 8:08pm on 08/08/2008.

Another example where the number eight has been utilised to great effect is in the 88 floors of 2IFC building. The building actually has 110 floors in total, but to reach the magic number of 88, some floors have been numbered as 13A, 13B, et cetera to attain the lucky number of 88. However, there are also a few numbers omitted due to the fact they sound unlucky. The aptly named "taboo floors" such as 14 and 24 have been excluded. In Cantonese, the word for "fourteen" sounds like "definitely fatal" whilst "twenty-four" sounds like "easily fatal."

☑ **The Genghis Khan Statue, Mongolia.** *Nearly 800 years after Genghis Khan conquered all that lay before him, the people of Mongolia erected the world's largest equestrian statue in his likeness as a mark of honour. Standing 40 metres tall atop a ten metres high visitor centre and symbolically pointing south toward China, the statue commemorates the site where legend says Chingis (as he is fondly known) found a golden whip. Personally, I cannot quite decide if it is a beautiful or terrible statue, but it was certainly well worth the detour through the steepes.*

☑ **National Stadium, Beijing, China.** *You may know it as the "Bird's Nest" and we all know how fantastic this stadium was as the venue of the 2008 Olympic games. In my opinion, it is the greatest multipurpose stadium ever built. It has certainly caught the public's imagination with some 25,000 people per day joining the stadium tours. At a price of around €6 per person the tours certainly cover the estimated €6.5 million per annum running costs. Unfortunately, I was too late to join the final tour of the day and with little sympathy from the guards, I only got to walk around the exterior of the National Stadium and the nearby National Aquatics Centre, which still impressed me no end.*

☐ **The Pyramids of Shǎnxī Province, China.** *These pyramids are ancient mausoleums built to house the remains of several Emperors of China and their relatives. There are 38 of them northeast of Xi'an, close to site where the Terracotta Army was found. The pyramids have flat tops, similar in shape to the Teotihuacan pyramids in Mexico as apposed to the pyramids in Egypt.*

The Genghis Khan Statue

The Americas

"If you seek Hamilton's monument, look around. You are living in it. We honour Jefferson, but live in Hamilton's country, a mighty industrial nation with a strong central government."

~ George F. Will (Author and journalist)

☑ **The White House, Washington, D.C., USA.** *In December 1790, President George Washington signed an Act of Congress declaring that the federal government would reside in a district "not exceeding ten miles square...on the river Potomac" and together with the city planner chose the site, on 1600 Pennsylvania Avenue, for the new Presidential residence. Nine proposals were submitted regarding the building of the "President's House", but it was Irish-born architect James Hoban's design that won the gold medal due to its practical and handsome design.*

As a result, there are 132 rooms and 35 bathrooms spread over six levels in the residence, with 412 doors, 147 windows, 28 fireplaces, eight staircases and three elevators. 570 gallons of paint is required to cover the outside surface of this famous white house. For recreational purposes, the White House has a wide selection of facilities available to keep its residents entertained, including a tennis court, jogging track, personal cinema, swimming pool and bowling alley. Now, for

more than 220 years the White House has stood as a symbol of the President, the United States government and the American people, and I for one, quite like it.

☑ **Capitol Hill, Washington, D.C., USA.** *After being built, burnt, rebuilt, extended and then restored, the Capitol building is now one of the most symbolically significant in the world. Not to mention that it is one of the grandest architectural achievements of the past few centuries. Capitol Hill is home to the United States Senate, House of Representatives, Supreme Court, Capitol, Library of Congress and Botanical Garden. Therefore, things get done around here.*

☑ **Alcatraz Island, San Francisco, USA.** *I was fortunate in that I managed to get booked on the night tour to Alcatraz Island. Setting off from San Francisco at sunset allowed us to enjoy the beauty of the Golden Gate Bridge silhouetted by the departing evening sun as we chugged towards "The Rock". I have only ever visited this most famous of Islands at night, so I cannot really compare it to the normal day tours, but we seemed to experience the many moods of the island that winter evening. As it was the final tour of the day and we were the only people on the island, it just seemed a little bit more eerie.*

☑ **Copán, Honduras.** *All the Maya sites are so different and offer such unique insights into the ancient Maya mindset. This site provides a* close up of the intrinsically carved stelaes, which depict the 16 rulers of this once magnificent and influential city. In addition, the spectacularly carved staircase, ball courts and stelaes are situated around an enormous main plaza.

☑ **Tikal, the Petén Basin, Guatemala.** *The breathtaking Maya site of Tikal was once the capital of a conquest state that became the most powerful kingdom of the ancient Mayan's. This complex is one of the biggest Maya sites discovered, with its 3,000 structures covering an area greater than 16 kilometres^2, during its heyday. When creating these imposing structures an emphasis was placed on height, due to the Maya belief that the higher the building the closer they were to the Gods. In my opinion, this is the greatest Mayan site of them all.*

☑ **The Cathedral of Rio de Janeiro.** *Built in 1979 and located in the centre of the city it looks like an* upside down concrete bucket from the outside. It is not very appealing to the eye, but despite this, I just had to look inside. It was here that the magnificence of the building showed itself. The cathedral has standing-room capacity for 20,000 people who are greeted with four rectilinear stained glass windows standing at 96 metres, soaring from floor to ceiling. This creates a magnificent light filled cross that allows the sun to shine in, no mater the time of day and fills the Cathedral with an array of colour. It is a wonderful spectacle, indeed.

☑ **F&F Tower, Panama City, Panama.** *This controversial "corkscrew" tower complex of modern offices is the latest addition to Panama's high-rise buildings, which are transforming the city into a modern metropolis. Consisting of 52 floors of tinted glass and reinforced concrete, this was the first thing that I went in search of upon arriving in Panama City. I see it as a magnificent*

F&F Tower

example of contemporary urban architecture, despite it raising a few eyebrows with critics.

☑ **The Basilica of Our Lady of Guadalupe, Mexico City.** *This was built in 1976, right next to the Old Basilica, which is sinking into the city's marshy ground and dangerously falling apart. The new Basilica is the 'football stadium' of churches. It has sitting space for 10,000 people inside, however temporary seats are often brought in to allow as many as 40,000 people to attend Mass. Based upon the large number of pilgrims that visit every year the Basilica is considered second only to the Vatican City as the most important sanctuary of Catholicism.*

☐ **Statue of Liberty, New York, USA.** *Despite always wanting to climb inside this great status symbol, when I visited the city of New York, going over to have a look at the Statue of Liberty just did not appeal to me. There just seemed to be too many other things to do in this city. In addition, I did not go in search of the Statue of Liberty in Paris or Tokyo either. I do not know why. The Statue of Liberty in Las Vegas is pretty hard to miss, though.*

☐ **Mount Rushmore, South Dakota, USA.** *Local historian Doane Robinson is the person credited with conceiving the idea of carving the faces of famous people into the Black Hills of South Dakota in order to promote the region as a tourist destination. Robinson's*

initial idea for the sculpture was to feature the faces of Western heroes like Buffalo Bill and Red Cloud. However, it was eventually settled that they would carve 18 metre high sculptures of the heads of former US presidents Abraham Lincoln, George Washington, Theodore Roosevelt and Thomas Jefferson. Robinsons plan was successful, as now the site attracts approximately three million people annually.

As you can see from the buildings that I have visited, I feel equally comfortable in the mosques, synagogues, churches and temples of all the world religions. Some people find this strange. However, I have noticed a familiar pattern whilst visiting these places of worship and talking to people of all beliefs from all over the world. It is that all religions are basically the same. When we strip them back to their basics, focus on the similarities as opposed to the differences, then they all preach a similar message. From what I have learned that message is: *have respect for yourself and show respect to others.*

V

Adventure is
what helps us to overcome
our fears

Bronnie Ware, an Australian palliative care nurse has spent many years working in retirement homes comforting people during their final moments. When these people entered their final days and looked back over their lives Mrs. Ware noticed a pattern emerging. In her book, *"The Top Five Regrets of the Dying"*, she revealed the most common regrets we have at the end of our lives. She found that the number one regret that people declared on their deathbed was; *"I wish I had the courage to live a life true to myself, not the life others expected of me."*

In short, they were afraid. It was only as they approached death's door that they could openly admit that they were more afraid of the thoughts of others than stepping outside of the group and doing what would make them feel truly happy and complete. I believe that we can all relate to this, as we all live with this fear to a certain extent.

I know that during the early years of training to be an accountant I wanted to fit in and sometimes I would hold back from stating an opinion that would go against the group. I acted in certain ways that I normally would not act. Other people in the group went even further and somehow managed to change their personality and even their accent just so that they could sound like the others.

Then I came to the realisation that none of us were actually being ourselves. The group had become the sum of all of us. I felt that this was a ridiculous way to live. I pondered on the situation for a while and came to understand that every one of us was individually greater than the group, but we had all chosen to shrink to fit the confines of the group structure.

I came to understand that, throughout our lives, we will be constantly presented with our fears so that we can overcome them and grow bigger and shine brighter as individuals. With this awareness, I began to actively look for the circumstances in life where I was afraid to be myself. I would then set out to confront and overcome that fear. Once I overcame a fear that had been creating a block in my life, I then felt freer, bigger and more expansive.

This realisation has transformed my life. Now I live a life that is true to who I am as a person. I am perfectly healthy and filled with energy and I intend to use these gifts to ensure that none of my dreams go unfulfilled. Now, instead of wanting to be a part of a group, I love to stand-alone, proud of the person I am. Adventures that seemed so far out of my comfort zone only a few years ago are now easily conquered. I still have what I would consider a comfort zone, but the reach of this zone is ever expanding to encapsulate and enjoy more of what the world has to offer.

The first step in achieving this was for me to confront my fears. To do this I wrote down a list of challenges that I would like to experience and overcome. What follows are some of the adventures that I have taken on and others that I look forward to facing in the coming years. These adventures have provided me with a fun way in which to confront and ultimately overcome my fears and develop into a better and more balanced person.

Adrenaline

The one thing that defeats more people than any other is fear – we sometimes forget that we are always in control of our emotions and fear is only as strong as we allow it to be. The one quote that best sums up how we should all approach fear was spoken by Will Smith's character, Cypher Raige, in the movie 'After Earth':

"Fear is not real. The only place that fear can exist is in our thoughts of the future. It is a product of our imagination, causing us to fear things that do not at present, and may not ever, exist. That is near insanity. Do not misunderstand me, danger is very real but fear is a choice."

Too many people now live in fear of fear itself. Too many people believe that the worst thing that can happen is that we die. Personally, I think that death is overrated. It gets way too much publicity for my liking and the fear of death stops too many people from taking on so many great challenges. Life is where it is at for me. That is what I focus on.

Ultimately we are spiritual beings here to experience human life on this planet, so whilst we are here we may as well experience everything possible – including the stuff that gets the heart pumping – because the chance of dying in most extreme sports is incredibly

small. Thus, I do not focus on what could go wrong; I focus on how great I am going to feel during and after the event.

"If you think you are beaten, you are. If you think you dare not, you don't. If you would like to win but think you can't, it's almost certain that you won't. Life's battles don't always go to the stronger woman or man, but sooner or later, those who win are those who think they can."

~ Anonymous

☑ **Black Water Raft through the Ruakuri Caves, Waitomo, New Zealand.** *A day spent falling down underground waterfalls whilst navigating pitch black caves, lit up with nothing but glow-worms in freezing water is my idea of a day well spent. This is the type of fun that you can only experience in New Zealand, because everywhere else in the world the 'Fun Police' would have introduced 'regulations' to save us from ourselves.*

☑ **Skydive over the Great Barrier Reef, Australia.** *I have never heard of anyone coming down from their first skydive saying, "that was a waste of time!" Everyone always gushes about how great it was. Therefore, I booked my first Skydive to be over the Great Barrier Reef and the rainforests of Queensland, providing me with the view to beat all views. In the hostel, people kept asking me if I was nervous.*

My answer was "What is the point of being overly nervous? I need some nerves because they provide the buzz. If the parachute does not open, after me jumping out of an airplane at 4,500 metres, then I might as well enjoy the ride, as I will not feel a thing when I hit the dirt. It's game over... nothing to worry about." This may sound like male bravado, but I am not being macho – simply put, that is the reality of skydiving.

Going up in a flimsy airplane that had the door wide open was actually the scariest part. Dangling my feet out the side of the plane as I prepared to jump was when the buzz kicked in, leaving me with a smile on my face as wide as the horizon in front of me. Sitting there looking down, I was just happy. I felt blessed to be in a position where I was able to choose these types of experiences. Therefore, with my goggles over my eyes, a parachute strapped tightly to my back and a big smile on my face, I dived out and said goodbye to that flimsy airplane.

☑ **Bungee jump off the Victoria Falls Bridge, Zimbabwe.** *From what I learnt about bungee jumping in New Zealand, the company there purchases cord that can be used for a maximum of 5,000 jumps. In New Zealand, to be extra safe, they will change each cord after 500 jumps. With that in my mind, I find myself sitting on a stool on a platform high above the middle of the Zambezi*

Bungee jump off Victoria Falls Bridge

River, as two locals tie the bungee cord to my ankles. As I look at the cord, I am thinking to myself; "That cord has seen more than 10,000 jumps."

The once white cord was now a filthy grey and there was not one centimetre of it that was not frazzled and had broken ends sticking out of it. I was attached to the cord by a towel tied around my ankles with the cord in a choke knot, with the plan being that the cord would grip my legs tighter as I fell and I would eventually bungee back up again. Great plan, and everything went accordingly that day. The dodgy cord combined with an untrained team and me jumping

off a relatively safe platform culminated in a great buzz.

However, a few months after I did the bungee jump there, the dodgy cord finally broke as an Australian girl plummeted 111 metres into the raging Zambezi below. Despite hitting the water hard, she was able to swim downriver and to the shore, with the cord still tied to her ankles. She was lucky to survive; yet, after the event the Zambian tourism minister was quoted as saying that despite the incident, Zambezi River bungee jumping remains a "viable operation."

☑ **Learn to Surf.** *Despite being over six foot tall, it turns out that I am quite a good surfer, which surprised many people, including myself. However, I still have a lot to learn on the larger waves as where I learned, in Australia, would be considered small to medium sized waves. I really want to get more surfing experience because my ultimate surf dream is to surf the famous Pororoca, the longest wave in the world.*

Pororoca is caused by the tides of the mighty Atlantic Ocean meeting the mouth of the Amazon River in Brazil. This tidal bore only breaks twice a year, in February and March, yet it generates waves up to four metres high which can last for over half an hour. The name "Pororoca" comes from the indigenous Tupi language. It translates to mean "great destructive noise" due to the wave being heard up to 30 minutes before it arrives. *Pororoca is so powerful that it destroys everything in its path. Better to be on it than under it I suppose.*

☑ **Complete the Flying Fox jump from Zimbabwe to Zambia.** *One glance across the river told me that I was in for the ride of a lifetime. I was standing in Zimbabwe, my destination was Zambia and the obstacle was the raging Zambezi River more than 100 metres below. I had a harness around my chest and it was attached to a zip line that ran between the two countries. All I had to do to get the adrenaline pumping was run as fast as I could until there was no more ground below me. With a deep breath, I set off sprinting.*

Within a few metres, the ground dropped out from beneath me and I was sent plunging towards the mighty Zambezi River, until my harness extended fully and I changed direction from falling vertically to zipping along horizontally. As I flew through the air with the swollen river roaring below me, I attempted to let out a good scream, but was prevented from doing so due to the air rushing past my face and into my mouth. As I passed the three quarter mark of the ride, I started to slow down as the zip line rose up to meet the land. As I touched down, ungracefully, in Zambia I had tears running down my face from the wind blasting in my eyes. I was not crying, I promise.

☑ **Paraglide over Rio de Janeiro harbour.** *After running off a*

mountaintop overlooking the famous Rio de Janeiro harbour, I can now tell you what it is like to fly like a bird and smell the clouds: it is majestic.

☑ **Bungee swing over Victoria Falls, Zimbabwe.** *The scale here is massive. Right in front of me, the falls hissed and roared like a possessed cat, whilst simultaneously rumbling like thunder and crashing like lightening. As the locals tied a cord around my waist our African guide, Moses, who brought us to the falls, was behind me and he was not impressed. He scowled, "That waterfall has been there for thousands of years and Africans have never even considered to jump off it. Then the Mzungu (Literally translated as "aimless wanderer" of European descent) come and start swinging and jumping off it like it is some sort of fun. White people are crazy."*

I knew he was right. Why do we feel the need to get a buzz from such extremities? What is missing in our lives? At that moment, I did not have the answer for him, as it was not really the time to be analysing the workings of my inner mind, with the weight of the massive cord pulling me closer to the edge of the platform. Even the spectacular reputation of Victoria Falls seems unbefitting of the sight that confronted me at that moment, as the shear force of 546 million cubic metres of water per minute plummeted over the edge of the widest curtain of falling water in the world.

With my eyes looking down so that I could get the full impact of what I was about to do, I stepped off the edge. Then I was gone, free falling, feet down, head up as vast clouds of steam spewed and billowed out from the seething cauldron in front of me. This is the scariest thing I have ever had the pleasure of doing. Yet, I thoroughly enjoyed every split second of it. It just seems to be a much 'cleaner' buzz than any bungee or skydive I had experienced prior or since. I could never really explain why to Moses, but I highly recommend this.

☑ **Fly over the Grand Canyon in a Helicopter.** *I did not like this at all. The Grand Canyon and the unique vistas on offer were fantastic. It was the helicopter that freaked me out. It was a big sturdy helicopter, piloted by a man with countless flying hours earned since his time flying in the Vietnam War, but I just did not feel safe.*

☑ **Mountain bike 'Death Road' in Bolivia.** *Officially known as the North Yungas Road, it connects the Amazon rainforest in northern Bolivia, to the capital city of La Paz. As I had agreed to mountain bike down this road, I found myself high in the Andes as the sun began to rise for the day. As light broke through, the extent of what lay ahead became real. In front of me lay a 3,400 metre descent over a spectacular 64 kilometre trail from the snow-covered plains of the Bolivian Andes to the sub-tropical Yungas and the one-street town of Coroico.*

Not only is the road extremely steep, but it also has extreme drop-offs of up to 450 metres and a distinct shortage of crash barriers. In addition, most of the road would average no more than three metres wide. An abundance of loose rocks litter the road and depending on the weather the entire road surface can be mucky with mudslides from above a real threat. In addition to this, fog, low cloud and dust make for precarious visibility. This road is a recipe for disaster.

Indeed, disasters do happen, with a fatal accident being reported with concerning regularity. It is estimated that more than 100 people lose their lives on the road each year – thus I concluded that the road has been accurately named – Death Road. With this information running through my mind, I looked to my left and noticed that the eight people sitting silently on their bikes with their eyes focused on nothing in particular were having the exact same thoughts.

As the Andes soared majestically all around and turkey vultures circled high overhead, our guide let out a scream: "LETS DO THIS!" and off he went, cycling frantically down this road of death. With that, the remaining eight of us raced after him, heads down, bums up, building up as much speed as possible before reaching the first blind corner...

☑ **Climb the Sydney Harbour Bridge.** *As I had spent a long time travelling overland from London to Sydney, reaching Sydney and* witnessing the Opera House and Harbour Bridge was the proverbial cherry on top after such a great journey. However, it was not until I arrived in Sydney that I realised that I could become the cherry and climb on top of this 'giant coat hanger' bridge.

I was adamant that I would experience this before leaving Sydney and I was quite lucky when, one night in a club, I got talking to a girl that worked as a guide on the climbs. It got better when she agreed to get me on the tour at a 'friends and family' rate. She was true to her word and I was delighted when she managed to obtain for me, a ticket on the popular sunset tour. This tour is the one I would recommend as it involves climbing up in day light, being at the top for sunset over Sydney Harbour and coming down in the dark, providing three unique experiences.

Sydney is one of the worlds most exciting and vibrant cities, with a constant flow of tourists passing through, providing a great buzz. However, the climb on the Sydney Harbour Bridge provided me with a completely different perspective of the city. The chatter of the tourists, the click of the cameras, the didgeridoos, the busy streets, the traffic and the constant noise that this great city generates had disappeared. What remained was the sea, the buildings and the lights, merging to create a beautiful cityscape and providing me with a brand new insight into the city. Silence always tells the best stories.

☑ **Go snowboarding in Australia.** *I bet you never thought that you could snowboard in Australia? Well you can, in the rather aptly named Snowy Mountains in New South Wales. This is where Australians go for their yearly bout of snow fun. When I visited, the 'snow' was described as the best that they had experienced for quite a long time, but to me it felt very icy and hard and not powdery at all. In fact, it was so hard, that on my last run down the slope I fell and completely snapped my left humerus, half way between my shoulder and my elbow. I was screaming like a pig as I lay on the slope wriggling in pain, unable to get up. It was a great day up to that point. The Après ski never happened.*

☐ **Live the Gibbon Experience canopy tour in Northern Laos.** *There is a place deep in the jungle of northern Laos where people live in treetop houses and fly from tree to tree. It is the ultimate zip lining experience. The only problem is that it is booked solid months in advance, which unfortunately I found out the hard way.*

☐ **Run with the bulls in Pamplona, Spain.** *Pamplona's famous "Running of the Bulls" and the follow up party, the Fiesta San Fermin festival, has all the ingredients for the perfect celebration – history, drama, action, dancing and sangria. This event has its origins in the basic requirement of transporting the bulls to the bullring. It was during* *this relocating that the youngsters of the village would jump among the bulls, as they made their way through the streets, to show off their bravado. This has now transformed into a massive street party that is attended by people from all corners of the world. I had better get into training as I have no intention of watching from the sidelines during the relocation.*

☐ **Mountain bike the Himalayas of Bhutan.** *This tiny, unspoilt Himalayan country, known as the "Land of the Thunder Dragon", is one of the most mystifying on the planet. It completely shut itself off from the outside world to the point that the ban on both television and Internet access was only lifted in 1999. It is this isolation that now makes Bhutan so attractive to visitors. The country is totally underdeveloped and that combined with its hilly landscape makes it the greatest location on the planet for mountain biking.*

☐ **Do a base jump.** *This is as extreme as I am willing to go. The objective of the people that base-jump is to have as much fun as possible before their short lives come to an end. They say that the buzz from this is so great that after the first jump is completed the next objective is to complete a jump from each of the four objects in the acronym 'base'. Thus, it is from buildings, antenna, spans [i.e., bridges and dams] and earth that they must overcome all their natural instincts, whilst standing on top of one of these and jump outwards. The only safety net built into this is the parachute on their backs and their ability to calculate the right time to pull the cord. Too early or too late and death is a real possibility.*

However, like all other things, this gets to the point when the buzz wears away and it is no longer extreme enough to provide the rush it once did. To help them maintain the buzz and take it to the next level there is 'proximity flying'. This involves jumping off a mountain in much the same way as base-jumping, but the difference is that they wear a wingsuit. This wingsuit allows them to 'fly' along the side of the mountain at a ratio of two-and-a-half metres forward for every one metre down until they get to an area where it is safe to pull the cord on their parachute.

Travelling at speeds of 200 kilometres per hour, the closer they fly to the mountain the more intense the buzz. There has been 197 people killed doing this in the last three decades, but in a worrying trend, 59 of those have died in the last three years, as they attempt to enhance the buzz by 'skinning' the mountain. People may criticise these boys and girls, but at least they are living their lives to the maximum and when they do hit that mountain at 200 kilometres per hour they are hitting it with a smile on their face and a life filled with experiences that most of us could never imagine.

Machines and Rafts

If it keeps up, man will atrophy all his limbs but the push-button finger.
~ Frank Lloyd Wright (Architect and writer)

Men and machines go together like a hand and a glove. Therefore, it should not be a surprise that I have included a section on the great experiences involving mechanical inventions and rafts that have sparked my interest.

☑ **Jet Boat through the canyons of Queenstown, New Zealand.** *Those Kiwis' really are extreme. They designed and built a jet boat that can travel at speeds of up to 85 kilometres per hour through narrow and dramatic canyons. The jet boat I was in could speed through less*

Cappadocia, Turkey

that 10 centimetres of water and was often even closer that than to the walls of the canyons. That is not to mention the full 360° spins that the boat was required to do quite often. If only more nations had the same 'can do' approach to life as the Kiwi's, this would be a much better world to live in.

☑ **Fly in a hot air balloon over Cappadocia, Turkey.** *Setting off at sunrise with a sustained blast of fire filling the balloon with hot air, we were sent soaring high into the sky. We were afforded excellent flying conditions that allowed us to drift gently above and between the rock formations and fairy chimneys, past vineyards, valleys and rippled ravines providing unequalled vistas. Cappadocia has a landscape that is unparalleled anywhere on the planet. I cannot remember anyone uttering a word the entire time that we were in the balloon, but once the champagne bottle popped back on the ground, the chatter was deafening.*

☑ **Raft the Source of the Nile at Jinja, Uganda.** *This was quite an eventful day. The source of the Nile in Uganda is anything but humble. It is full of force and power as it rages thousands of kilometres from its starting point in the centre of Africa towards the Mediterranean Sea. In my arrogance, I believed that I could 'tame' this great river as I rafted over her rapids and down her waterfalls. However, the day that I rafted the powerful River Nile at its source was the day I came closest to death.*

The rapids on this river border on the ridiculous, as the water is unbelievably powerful. After being flung far from the raft and forced to 'hang out in the green room' (trapped under a rapid) for a little too long, I soon realised who did the taming around here. When the Nile eventually spat me back out and I climbed back into the raft, I just lay there speechless, the arrogance had been washed out of me, replaced with respect. I have not been involved in any rafting since that day, however, what does not kill me makes me stronger... and more careful.

Some days are just very eventful – this day certainly was. It began with me being dragged out of our bus, on the way to the river, by a teenage Ugandan soldier, forced to my knees and told to put my hands behind my head. Whilst in the surrender position this nervous young soldier repeatedly screamed, "What tribe are you from?" at me as held his machine-gun to my head. It was one of those days. I went to bed early that night.

☑ **Raft the Tully River, Australia.** Thanks to the heavy rainfalls that this region receives, the Tully River boasts great volumes of water, which creates the best rafting experience in northern Queensland. When I rafted this river, I made the mistake of not booking on the 'extreme' run which left me chugging along behind a queue of other rafts instead of hammering down the river at full speed.

I was a bit disappointed with that, but then again it gave me more of a chance to have a laugh with my fellow rafters as we cruised through pristine tropical rainforests and past remarkable basalt formations and waterfalls. However, if you want to make the most of the fast flowing torrents and the thundering Class III and IV rapids I highly recommend booking on the 'extreme' package.

It will be the difference between having a good day and a brilliant day.

☑ **Ride a dune buggy through the desert.** I have explored the desert whilst sat on the back of a camel and from the back of a horse and I even got to walk through a desert. However, the most fun way to experience the desert is from behind the wheel of an adrenaline-charged dune buggy. I experienced this in the Namib Desert, Namibia, were the infamous Skeleton Coast meets the desert. The buggy came equipped with roll cages, seatbelts, goggles and helmets, but once I got behind the wheel and went burning through the desert in this wild-looking vehicle, it was every man for himself. A wild experience indeed and because it was Africa, health and safety was no big deal, allowing us to put the foot down, without the worry of speed restrictions.

☑ **Raft the Ocoee River, Tennessee, USA.** Having been chosen as the river to host the 1996 Olympic Canoe and Kayak slalom events, this is without doubt the premier white-water river in the south-eastern United States. What makes it even more impressive is that the perfect water level is always guaranteed on this 16 kilometre run. I was there during the peak of summer and dam-controlled releases ensured that the Ocoee's flow was perfect throughout as we hit the Class IV rapids as hard as we could.

Rafting is so much fun because, not only is it one of the great adrenaline sports, but it is relatively fast, the power comes from the river and there is no need to worry about the weight of food and supplies. This was a great experience throughout as white-water rafting with some crazy Americans is about as good as it gets. Good people, good river, great times.

☑ **Raft Sun Kosi River, Nepal.** Flowing eastwards between the Mahabharat Lekh Mountains and the great Himalayas, the Sun Kosi is deemed to be one of the ten best rafting experiences to be had anywhere. The ever-changing scenery combined with warm water, Class IV rapids and joyous locals waving from their waterside villages create some great memories.

The river gathers strength as it flows east as the tributaries from the world's highest mountains flow into the Sun Kosi until it crosses onto the northern plains of India and joins the mighty Ganges. The rapids on this river are great when they arrive, but there can be long stretches of slow flowing water in-between. There is more to Nepal than just hiking, as I found out the hard way after this river gave me a really good work out.

☑ **Dive in a submarine.** We know more about outer space than we do about our oceans, with just over two percent of the world's deep waters explored to date. I had always wanted to explore the deep seas, but when I dreamed of one day diving in a submarine, I had this vision of being on board one of

those big black nuclear-powered war machines. A homemade yellow submarine was not in my thoughts if I am honest. However, the great thing about this life is that we never know when a great opportunity may appear.

Therefore, as I lazed around on the island of Roatan, off the coast of Honduras, I learned that Karl Stanley, a 35-year-old self-taught engineer, had built a homemade submarine and had safely logged over 1,300 dives. The words 'homemade' and 'submarine' in the one sentence would be enough to scare most people away, but for me this was a great opportunity to finally make a dream come true. The fact that the submarine was homemade made it even more exciting for me. The following morning, after convincing Karl to take me deep under water, I found myself squeezing into the yellow submarine 'Idabel'.

Looking out through the 10 centimetre thick domed viewing window, Karl and I were lowered into the ocean before setting off to illuminate places that have never known any light – places human eyes have never seen. It was incredible to experience as the blue ocean at the surface faded to black as we descended. We sank 350 metres beneath the ocean surface, to where most of the life forms have evolved to develop the ability to generate their own light, many through chemical pathways. The life I witnessed down there *demonstrated 230 million years of evolutionary triumph – accounting for almost half the time that there has been life on earth.*

Karl's comprehensive knowledge of everything that unfolded made this experience even better. Not only did he know all the extraordinary life forms we came across, but as the depth gauge read 150 metres, on our return to the surface, he turned on the lights to reveal the decomposing body of a scuba diver that committed suicide by cutting his lines. Karl informed me that he was a New Yorker called Bugsy. He cut his lines and sank below the surface never to be seen again. The nylon straps of his gear rose and fell in the current, like a dead man's wave, as we ascended past him towards the surface.

Thanks to Karl, I was able to enter another world, one that only the very luckiest people will ever get to witness. It was astounding. If it were not for people like Karl and their desire to go further and push boundaries, we humans would still be living in caves. Thus, upon returning to the surface, unlike poor Bugsy, I had never felt more full of life.

☐ Glide through the skies in an unpowered aircraft.

☐ Land beside the beach in a seaplane.

☐ Ride in a Formula One race car.

☐ Hovercraft across the Everglades, Florida, USA.

☐ Complete an indoor skydive.

☐ Land on and take off from an aircraft carrier.

☐ Raft the Colorado River, USA.
This is said to be one of the greatest

the number of people who raft the Canyon each year because of the popularity of the trip through the fragile environment.

If you want to raft along the 446 kilometres of river within the Grand Canyon then you had better get your application in soon. There is a long list of people waiting to raft the canyon, with it currently taking twelve years to receive a permit. It costs $100 just to get on the waiting list and new additions are only accepted during February each year. Once on the list, potential boaters must send a letter every year to keep them among the nearly 7,000 in line for a permit. If The National Park Service does not receive that letter each year by a certain date, then you lose your place on the list.

It takes around 18 days to navigate the entire length of the canyon, as the Colorado River flows west at a really nice pace. It is hard to imagine life getting much better than witnessing the Grand Canyon gradually change, whilst floating down the Colorado River.

Dive in a submarine

experiences on the planet, but there is a problem: its popularity. The experience of rafting through the Grand Canyon is one that I hope to experience in the future at some point, but unfortunately it is booked out for a ridiculous amount of time. I am talking about a waiting list that is measured in decades. The National Park Service limits

Patrick Hamilton Walsh

Underwater Exploration

"Between the air and the water a steel wave quivers. What people call the surface is also a ceiling. A looking glass above, watered silk below. Nothing is torn on the way through. Only a few bubbles mark the diver's channel and behind him the frontier soon closes. But once the threshold is crossed you can turn back slowly and look up: that dazzling screen is the border between two worlds, as clear to the one as to the other. Behind the looking glass the sky is made of water."

~ Philippe Dipole (Author and underwater explorer)

☑ **The Aegean Sea, Turkey.** *This was the first dive I ever completed. The training I received consisted of my Turkish guide informing me that the 'thumbs-up' signal meant 'everything is good'. Then he helped me to put on all my gear before telling me to put on my mask and dip my head under the water to get used to the sensation of the bubbles. Once he was happy that I had a good understanding of the 'thumbs-up' sign and the bubbles would not be too much of an issue for me, my scuba diving training was complete.*

My 'trainer' then led me into the water and off we went, exploring a completely new world. As we went further and further out he would come over to me every so often and point at the gauge on his watch, showing me the depth we had reached. I did not really care what the depth was; life underwater amazed me. He came over and pointed at the depth display on his watch notifying that we reached the 20 metres mark, then again after 30 metres and finally when we were at 40 metres. He seemed very impressed with himself at this stage and then signalled that it was now time to begin making our way back. It was an enthralling experience and it left me wanting more.

The following year I organised a holiday to Sharm el Sheik, Egypt so that I could dive the Red Sea. Upon booking myself onto a dive with a Padi registered instructor and completing a scuba diving refresher course, I realised that I was not an 'experienced diver'. In fact, as I relayed the events of my diving experience in Turkey to the diving instructors, the look of horror on their faces lead me to believe that maybe my prior dive did not fall under diving best practice.

In fact, I was to learn that the recreational diving limit for beginner divers was 12 metres and the average depth at which nitrogen narcosis symptoms begin to appear in adults is 30 metres. Ignorance really is bliss in some circumstances.

☑ **The Great Barrier Reef, Australia.** *This great location is known for its beauty worldwide and it attracts many tourists on a daily basis. Regrettably, so many visitors have no regard for the long-term* impact of their rash behaviour and, as a result, the Great Barrier Reef is in the process of permanent destruction. The saddest part of it all was that the tour operators (that I came across) that are making vast sums of money from the tourist trade could not seem to care less about the destructive behaviour of their customers. Let us hope that people that visit this great wonder begin to take more responsibility for their actions on an individual level before it gets to the point that this 'world wonder' is closed to divers.

☑ **The Red Sea, Egypt.** The Red Sea can be split into two regions: The North Red Sea and the South Red Sea. The North Red Sea takes in resort destinations such as Dahab, Sharm El Sheikh and Hurghada. This area is home to the most beautiful reef I have ever seen. It also has fantastic coral formations, lovely walls and is teeming with marine life. In addition to this, Dahab is famous worldwide for the Blue Hole, which is a wonder in itself.

The Red Sea is the best diving in the world, from what I have experienced. Nothing has ever come close – but, of the two, I have only dived in the North Red Sea. Recently I have been hearing that the less popular South Red Sea is even better. Consisting of much less crowded dive sites of pristine reefs and superb coral, apparently this is where experienced divers go when looking for world class scuba diving. These biblical waters just keep giving.

☑ **The Blue Hole, Dahab, Egypt.** This submarine sinkhole is one of the must-do dives. It is around 130 metres deep, yet rather outlandishly it is located right beside the road. Thus, it is very accessible. The Blue Hole has unfortunately earned the nickname "The Diver's Cemetery" due to the number of diving fatalities there. These fatalities are usually caused as a result of divers searching for 'The Arch', which is a tunnel at a depth of 52 metres under the water. I had no intention of searching for 'The Arch' at such depths hence I had a fantastic day.

☑ **The Belize Barrier Reef.** This was truly memorable for me as it was the first time that I experienced free swimming with sharks after many years of diving. It was quite surreal when, just as we had anchored at our second location on the reef, the captain of the boat shouted: "There is seven or eight large sharks swimming towards the boat right now – everyone get in the water quick!" As I stood there trying to figure out whether he was joking or not, two English girls had already jumped over the edge of the boat and were swimming towards the sharks. 'Ah well, when in Reef', I thought to myself as I grabbed my mask and jumped in amongst the sharks.

☑ **Scuba dive a shipwreck.** In 1942, a Japanese submarine torpedoed the U.S.A.T. LIBERTY, a US World War II freighter, while it was crossing the Lombok Strait.

The resulting shipwreck lay 70 kilometres away from the nearest safe harbour, until the astonishing events of 1963. As a result of the fatal eruption of the volcano Gunung Agung that year, the Liberty was pushed to her present location, where she now lays only 30 metres from Tulamben beach on the island of Bali, Indonesia.

I would consider this quite a stroke of luck for the local tourist trade. The story is nearly unbelievable. To get to the wreck we simply walked in from the beach. Whilst exploring the Liberty, I did some very impressive swim-throughs, however I always maintained an air of caution as the structure of the wreck is unstable, with parts collapsing regularly. If the wreck were in Europe, we would have been forbidden from attempting the dive due to health and safety precautions. Good job it is not then, as it was a fantastic experience.

☐ **Dean's Blue Hole, Long Island, Bahamas.** This is the deepest underwater sinkhole in the world. It plunges 200 metres into the ocean floor, making it vastly deeper than the Blue Hole in Egypt and Ambergris Caye in Belize. The best part about this is that there is very little tourist development and everything is low key, which allows for a perfect dive experience.

☐ **Experience a cave dive.** Practitioners of cave diving are small in number, due to it being one of the most challenging and potentially dangerous sports. However, the passion that my friend Xavi Miranda has for cave diving has really sparked my interest in this sport. Cave diving is a form of penetration diving, meaning that should an emergency occur, divers cannot swim vertically to the surface due to the cave's ceilings. Therefore, they must swim the entire way back to the mouth of the cave and then up when in an emergency situation. Nevertheless, it is not that simple.

When the divers enter the cave the water is naturally clear. However, as they progress along the cave, the air bubbles from the scuba gear will float towards the roof of the cave disturbing the silt. This causes the phenomenon of underwater rain, with the raindrops consisting of silt. This leads to a 'silt out' situation where underwater visibility is rapidly reduced to zero. It is a total blackout and the level of danger is significantly enhanced.

In order to return to the clear water at the edge of the cave, which may be a few hundred metres away, the divers have to enter what is similar to a meditative state and 'feel' their way back out. In addition to that, because the cave divers progress so far into the caves, they may be required to blindly search for back-up air tanks at drop spots just so they can have enough air to get them back to the surface.

☐ **Sistema Sac Actun, the Yucatan Peninsula, Mexico.**

Measuring 215 kilometres, this is the longest underwater cave system in the world. Whilst I was in the Yucatan Peninsula I was fortunate enough to visit some of the Cenote's around Tulúm and have a swim around. However, due to time constraints I never got to do what I really wanted, which was dive under and do a little bit of exploring.

☐ **The Fiji Islands.** *With unrivalled visibility year-round in this "Soft Coral Capital of the World," the waters around the Fiji islands offer some great diving experiences. The area is home to 'the Yellow Tunnel,' 'the Great White Wall' and many other underwater wonders. This is a fantastic place for diving, so why did I not experience any diving when I visited?*

Patrick Hamilton Walsh

S w i m

"The water is your friend. You don't have to fight with water, just share the same spirit as the water, and it will help you move."
~ Aleksandr Popov (Olympic swimmer)

Lake Malawi

☑ **The Dead Sea, Israel, Palestinian Authority.** *The shores of the Dead Sea are the lowest land point on the surface of the Earth. Resting 425 metres below sea level, the Dead Sea is one of the saltiest bodies of water on the planet. As a result, the water burns your eyes and tastes terrible, but there is one good thing: the salinity provides exceptional levels of buoyancy. This provides an unbelievable sensation that must be experienced.*

The water in the Dead Sea is so dense that you are forced to float on top of the water – whether you want to or not. Thus, the usual tourist photograph consists of the person sitting back in a reclined position reading a newspaper whilst floating on the water. I did not do that. Instead, I opted to spend the time trying to get as much of my body under the water as possible, before covering my entire body in the magical Dead Sea mud and baking under the hot sun.

☑ **Arctic Ocean, Norway.** *I swam in these coldest of waters with an elderly German lady. The fact that she was 83 years old sort of forced*

me to man-up and not complain too much about the cold, despite my chattering teeth and blue lips.

☑ **Lake Baikal, Siberia, Russia.** *It is so large that Siberians refer to Lake Baikal not as a lake, but as a sea. Its soft-turquoise water is unusually transparent and the mountains that surround it make for pleasant vistas no matter which way you look. I felt a sense of being well off the beaten track here as the natural barriers of Siberia protect*

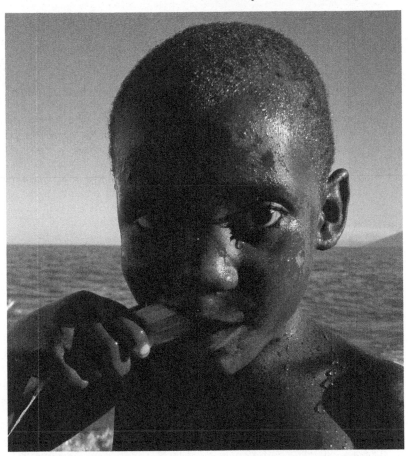

the area from everything, including electricity and running water. It is not often that I am afforded the opportunity to swim in waters so clean and pure.

☑ **Lake Mead, USA.** *Lake Mead is an artificial lake that formed due to the Hoover Dam, creating the largest reservoir in the United States. It is located on the Colorado River, about 50 kilometres outside Las Vegas. I crossed this part of the country in the peak of the summer*

and it was so hot that I could hardly function. Then we came across Lake Mead. I know that it was not built to save pasty white Irish boys from overheating in this seriously hot part of the world, but it certainly served that purpose fantastically.

☑ **Lake Malawi, Malawi.** *When the explorer Dr. David Livingstone first encountered Lake Malawi, he described it as the "lake of the stars." Also known as Lake Nyasa, the geographic name of the lake* itself is disputed. Malawi claims that this lake is named "Lake Malawi," whereas most other countries state the name as "Lake Nyasa".

The origin of the dispute over the name of the lake has its background in Dr. Livingstone's misunderstanding of the local language of the area. When Livingstone enquired to his colleagues, who were not from the area of the lake, to state its name for him, they said the word "nyasa." As a result, he named it Lake Nyasa not realising that "nyasa" was the local word for any large body of water. In effect, "Lake Nyasa" translates to mean "Lake Lake," thus the reason why I follow the Malawians and insist on calling it Lake Malawi.

The country of Malawi in central Africa is known as the "warm heart of Africa" due to the friendliness of the Malawians. The way of life around Lake Malawi today, remains similar to that which Dr. Livingstone would have encountered nearly 150 years ago. The people living on the shores of Lake Malawi have always relied on the lake for food, water, transport, recreation, washing and their other daily needs. The lake is their life.

Whilst I sat on the shore of the great lake, a group of eight children jumped on a large piece of driftwood that had come close to the shore, getting hours of fun out of it. An older girl played with a dead dog, swinging it by its tail as she spun happily in the sand. They all could swim, some of them had clothes,

none of them had shoes. None of them complained. They smiled and waved. The lake is their world, they care not for its name.

☑ **Lake Bunyoni, Uganda.** Located high in the hills and enclosed by steep sided, deeply cultivated, mountainous countryside, this is an African paradise. It is one of the deepest lakes in Africa, which, despite the country straddling the equator, means that the water is very cold. On offer is a breathtaking view from between the banana trees and mangoes of the 29 islands that polka dot its centre. Each island cradles a story of its colourful past. However, as it is one of the very few lakes in the region that was free of the tropical disease bilharzia, I was willing to overlook the dodgiest of diving boards on the shore and make a big splash into the cold water.

☑ **Fiji islands, Fiji.** Fiji is a paradise scattered across 500,000 kilometres^2 of ocean and consists of 322 pieces of land that are just about big enough to be called islands. Flying in, it is hard not to be struck by the beauty of the hundreds of islands below. Small islands, made up of blue-green lagoons, flourishing rainforests and mountains that are totally locked in by kilometres of the white, sandy beaches and their surrounding coral reefs. To go to Fiji and not swim would be unthinkable.

☑ **Swim off the coast of every continent.** I am one of the few people on the planet that has achieved this – if not the only one. I completed the continents in this order: Europe, Asia, Africa, North America, South America, Australia and Antarctica. It will not be of much surprise to anyone to notice that I swam off the coast of Antarctica last. It is obviously the hardest one to achieve for many reasons.

As I set off across the Drake Passage from Ushuaia towards Antarctica, I knew that I was going to have to go for a swim in the icy waters, I just did not know when, where, how, or even why. The first few stops that we had on the trip were at islands along the Antarctic Peninsula, which did not meet the criteria for me, as I wanted to swim directly off the coast of the continent.

Half way through the trip, I found myself standing on the beach, upon returning from a hike, talking to a fellow traveller, when she mentioned how cold the water looked. As I turned around, the waters edge was covered in small icebergs that had calved from the massive glaciers on two sides of us. The water looked so dark and, as it was March, it had a shine on it, as the summer was coming to an end. Within weeks, this water would be frozen solid for many kilometres out into the ocean as the winter bit hard.

Without saying a word, I started to unzip my jacket, before tossing it on the beach. I pulled off my hat, scarf and gloves, placing them on top of my jacket. Then my fleece and t-shirt followed. Next my wellington boots and the many layers of socks were discarded, followed by my trousers. As I stood there in my thermals I had noticed that the people around me had gone quiet and were looking at me silently, all wondering, "is he really going to do this?" They got their answer as I stripped off my upper and lower thermals and nonchalantly walked down the beach towards the water like I had done hundreds of times before, in my boxer shorts.

I did not dare to dip my toe in the water to test the temperature, as I did not wish to confront the indecision arising from the 'Hhhmm, maybe, maybe not' thoughts in my head which would ultimately have ended with a 'not'. I just looked out between the two icebergs that I aimed to swim between with the plan of walking into the icy waters until I got to waist height, at which point I would dive forward. I swear that even the penguins were looking at me as my feet entered the cold water. In my mind, I just kept telling myself that it was nice and warm. Soon I was in up to my knees... nice and warm Patrick, nice and warm.

Before I knew it, I was wading and the seawater was above my mid-thigh... nice and warm Patrick, nice and waaaaahhhhh! As the water got testicle deep, my body told my mind to shut up. It was freezing! There was nothing left to do, but dive forward and immerse myself in the water of Antarctica. As soon as I dived in, my skin was absolutely burning with the cold, not to mention the experience of massive hyperventilation. I felt a deep cold pain all over my body as I swam out into the salty Antarctic water. After a few stokes I felt the loss of feeling in my arms and legs as the blood rushed towards the core of my body to prevent the onslaught of hypothermia. After ten metres, with the feeling of a miserable, aching cold, deep inside me I felt that maybe this was not such a good idea. I turned and swam back towards the beach.

My mind was telling my arms to pull against the water, but they were barely moving. I put my feet down and relief swept over me when my feet touched the seabed. Pulling against the cold water with my dead arms and pushing against the seabed with my dead legs was a real struggle. As I got closer to the shore and the water got shallower, I found it really difficult to stand. I stumbled up onto the beach towards my clothes as our guide screamed all sorts of expletives at me, with the phrase "dumbass" and the word "dangerous" being mentioned once or twice. My teeth were chattering so loudly that I could not really hear him.

After great difficulty, I managed to get my clothes back on and I was then ordered onto the Zodiac with the instructions to get back on the ship and have a long hot shower immediately. I clumsily threw myself onto the zodiac and we sped towards the ship. The journey would not have taken any more than two minutes, I am not really sure, but by the time I got to the ship I was burning up. I felt all the blood rush around my body again and I was soon pulling off my hat and unzipping my jacket to cool down as I jumped from the zodiac onto the ship. Just to be sure, I did go for a warm shower as directed and as I stood in the shower with that hot water rushing all over me, I had a massive smile on my face, as, I have to admit, I felt a great sense of achievement.

☐ **Ongeim'l Tketau, Palau.** Around 15,000 years ago, a marine lake was created when one of the limestone rock islands was sealed off from the ocean. When this happened a small number of jellyfish were sealed inside, without any of their natural predators. As the Jellyfish multiplied over time, their sting evolved to the point that it became useless, culminating in jellyfish that are completely harmless to humans. Today there is estimated to be more than 10 million jellyfish in the lake, creating an unbelievably serene swimming experience.

☐ **The Devil's Armchair, Victoria Falls, Zimbabwe and Zambia.** This looks like the craziest thing you could possibly do. The Devil's Armchair consists of a naturally formed infinity pool at the very top of Victoria Falls, resting 130 metres above the raging Zambezi River below. They say it is perfectly safe in the dry season. They say! I was there in wet season *when the falls were raging, so it stays on the list. However, I have a question and it is an obvious one: Who was the first person to try this?*

☐ **Zacatón Cenote, Tamaulipas, Mexico.** *There are five interconnected sinkholes in northeastern Mexico, with Zacatón, at a depth of 335 metres, being the deepest water-filled sinkhole in the world. The name Zacatón comes from the free-floating islands of zacate grass, which move about on the surface of the water. As the zacate grass islands are unconnected to the lakebed, they float around the sinkhole moved by the wind. This provides the opportunity for people to swim to these floating islands to suntan and chill out as the islands gently drift around on the surface of the sinkhole.*

☐ **Bioluminescent Bay, Vieques Island, Puerto Rico.** *Located in a shallow body of water in a narrow inlet known as Mosquito Bay you will find what is probably the world's greatest swimming experience. In every gallon of water in the bay there are estimated to be over 725,000 phosphorescent single-celled organisms that, as a defence mechanism, glow when they are agitated. Apparently, when you swim in Mosquito Bay at night the glow from the organisms' bathes your limbs in blue-green light. The best part is that it is very hard to capture on camera, which means that you have to go there to experience it.*

Animal Adventures

"Guns have metamorphosed into cameras in this earnest comedy, the ecology safari, because nature has ceased to be what it always had been - what people needed protection from. Now nature tamed, endangered, mortal - needs to be protected from people."

~ Susan Sontag (Essayist and cultural theorist)

☑ **Witness the Great Migration.**
Imagine a migration of animals so colossal that it is known worldwide as the Great Migration. In July of each year something triggers inside the mind of over two million animals, sending them north from the Serengeti plains and the Loita plains into the Maasai Mara reserve, in search of fresh pasture. Zebra, topi, Thompson's gazelle, elands and wildebeest are all involved in this Great Migration.

For the wildebeest to reach their destination, they must travel across the bottleneck that is the Grumeti River. This is the major obstacle that must be overcome in order for them to reach their destination. I witnessed first hand the gigantic crocodiles that lie in wait for the wildebeest. The plume of dust from the mass of grunting wildebeest as they hesitantly stumble across the river is one of the most iconic wildlife sights on the planet. For the

crocodiles, it is their equivalent of pizza delivery. However, the danger does not end there for the migrants, as they are preyed on along their entire circular route by hungry predators, most notably lions, cheetahs, leopards and hyena.

The Great Migration is one of the most impressive natural events worldwide, as it is estimated to involve some 18,000 elands, 97,000 topi, 200,000 zebras, 500,000 Thompson's gazelle and an astonishing 1,300,000 white-bearded wildebeest. These lumbering animals will graze on the Maasai Mara reserve until October or November as the storm clouds gather in the south. As they graze, the storms replenish the ground they left behind, allowing the vast herds

to return to breeding grounds, which are once again green and lush. The cycle then begins again the following year. Nature is the omnipotent mother.

☑ **Cage dive with great white sharks, off Dyer Island, South Africa.** As I was climbing into my well-worn wetsuit, the crew were emptying buckets of blood and guts into the water along the side of the boat. Within minutes, the hungry sharks had the scent and were aggressively circling and patrolling the boat. When I was ready, they lowered the cage (which bore resemblance to a large shopping trolley) in amongst the school of hungry sharks, and then causally said, "In ya go, bro!"

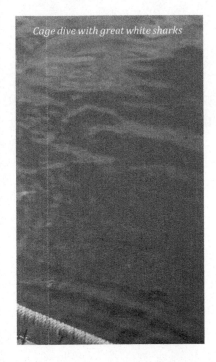
Cage dive with great white sharks

We were situated between Dyer Island and Geyser Rock and the cold water I was entering was known as "Shark Alley." The area is home to thousands of Cape fur seals that dash between the islands in search of food, whilst trying to avoid the patrolling 'great whites'. The seals are natural bait to the great white sharks, but being the predators they are, the 'great whites' would not hesitate to sink their teeth into a human as a starter.

Whilst in the cage, a gargled gasp rang out as the first 'shadow' zipped by and I pushed myself to the back of the cage. Then, after a few circles, the first shark came over to have a closer look at the menu. The teeth, pointing in every direction, were big, sharp and edgy. The effortless speed of the sharks was startling

and three metres seemed a lot bigger when I was in the water with them. This was their territory. When the beast started to aggressively bang against the cage and those dead black eyes were only centimetres from my face was when my heart started knocking on my rib cage.

Smaller sharks have been known to squeeze their way through the surprisingly big gaps in the cage bars. Each of my senses seemed to be on overdrive as the sharks inspected the cage, but thankfully the longer I stayed in the cage, the more I enjoyed what can only be explained as a staring competition with these great killers. Cowering in the cage as the 'great whites' aggressively banged against the bars gave a sense of the real hierarchy in those waters. With their supreme power and strength and those glistening white teeth I was well aware of the pecking order.

☑ **Ride horseback through the swamps of the Pantanal, Brazil.**

Argentina. *Whilst hiking through the hills of Patagonia I came across a large stud of wild horses as they played without restraint under the blue cloudless sky. These horses oozed freedom. They just seemed to be so happy, so free. After watching them as I hiked for a while I decided that this was not just something to admire as I continued down the valley. It was an experience that I must savour. Therefore, I plopped myself down on the side of the hill, keeping well back, to eat my lunch and look on at these magnificent creatures in their element. Some lay down and rubbed themselves on the grass, others munched at the vegetation whilst others galloped around. They were free from farmers and trainers. No one owned them; there were no fences or wire. They were free and watching them, I too felt free.*

☑ **Explore Corbett Tiger Reserve, India.** *In all the time we were in the reserve, we managed to see a grand total of one tiger's footprint. No, not a tiger – a footprint! In fact, we were so convinced that there were no tigers in the reserve, that when our pickup ran out of petrol and stopped amongst the foliage, we jumped out, leaving our armed guard behind and walked the five kilometres back to the main gate. Thinking back, maybe we acted a little irrationally.*

☑ **Admire the Andean Condor of Colca Canyon, Peru gliding in the wind.** *With wingspans of up to three metres, these birds are a joy to watch as they glide high*

The wild dolphins of Monkey Mia

The name 'Pantanal' derives from the Portuguese word for 'swamp' or 'marsh'. This is exactly what you get, the world's largest wetland of any kind, teaming with wildlife. Riding horseback is always a great experience, but having the opportunity to ride through the crocodile infested waters of this great wilderness during dry season was really something special.

☑ **Observe the wild horses of the Patagonian grasslands,**

in the sky and play in the winds. With this image in my mind, I was at a zoo in Australia a year later and to my disgust, they had a large condor locked in a small cage. It still saddens me when I think about it. No bird should ever be kept in a cage.

☑ **Meet the wild dolphins of Monkey Mia, Western Australia.** Imagine a place were you can take two steps into the sea only to be greeted by wild dolphins joyfully playing around your feet. No, I am not in the middle of some dusty desert creating vivid daydreams – such a place does exist. On the coast of Western Australia, there is a small body of water sheltered from the Indian Ocean called Monkey Mia. It is here that you will come eye to eye with these fantastically intelligent Bottlenose Dolphins.

It is a place where you can experience the mystical world of wild dolphins as they come up and swim around your feet in barely enough water to cover them. For the past 40 years the dolphins have been visiting the tranquil shores of Monkey Mia on a daily basis to come in and interact with humans before swimming back out to play in the waves. There is no payment and no opening times, this is nature at its purest and this is an exceptional experience. This is a must see. Put the words 'Monkey Mia Dolphins' on your Carrot list right now.

☑ **Watch orca (Killer) whales play in the sea.** A mother and son played along side our ship as we crossed the Drake Passage returning from Antarctica. It was one of those times when you do not even bother with the camera, but just admire nature in all its beauty.

☑ **Sit with the penguins of South Georgia Island.** My approach to the penguins on this sub Antarctic island was to sit in a clearing and just admire them. If they wanted to come over for a look at me, then that would be great, but I did not want to encroach on them and cause stress. Therefore, I found a clearing about ten metres from the penguins so I could observe without disturbing. I was sitting there for just a few minutes when a few of them turned and looked at me before making their way over. I sat still as they 'explored' me, pecking at my wellington boots and trousers. It was so unreal, all I could do was laugh as they investigated me in the way a human would treat an Extra Terrestrial.

The Macaroni penguins were my favourite of them all, as they have what looks like bright yellow feathers coming out of their brow. They are named after the young dandies who considered themselves the leaders of style in 18th century London. The dandies were young men who had returned from their 'grand tour' through Europe to Italy and they wanted everyone to know it. Accordingly, they dressed in the exaggerated fashions of the upper echelons of European society, consisting of outrageous colours and stripes. In addition, they set up the Macaroni Club where members were required to wear hats with feathers stuck in them. Thus, this is how the elaborately decorated Macaroni penguins got their name.

☑ **Watch elephant seals battle for supremacy on South Georgia Island.** *This was a very violent fight with an abundance of bloodshed throughout the battleground. The battle lasted for hours, with the seals taking breaks in between. I gave up watching before either of the elephant seals gave up the battle.*

☑ **Watch elephants battle for supremacy in Africa.** *When two bull elephants fight for the affection of the females in the herd, it can develop into quite a ferocious battle. Thankfully, on this occasion the young pretender quite quickly dropped the macho display. Despite his best efforts, he was sent packing. Although I suspect he returned again not long after.*

☑ **Get stood on by an elephant in Thailand.** *You know when you go to witness a show of some sort and they ask for volunteers from the audience to join in? Well my left arm has this habit of jumping into the air right at that moment. Therefore, despite the fact that I had just watched these exact elephants, on the BBC news, running in and killing a few members of the audience just a fortnight before landing in Thailand, I found myself lying on the ground with an elephant about to stand on me.*

She obviously was not going to stand on me and was trained to put her weight on the other three feet and just lightly stand on my chest, giving the illusion that I was being stood on. I am not sure if I would recommend it, although it all worked out fine that day and my left arm got the massive round of applause that it desperately craved.

☑ **Witness the nightly exodus of bats from Carlsbad Caverns, New Mexico, USA.** *Carlsbad Caverns is home to an estimated one million Mexican Freetail bats. During daylight, the bats crowd together on the ceiling of the cave, but it is at dusk when they really come alive. The bats leave the cave in swarms which, when silhouetted against the darkening sky, creates the most dramatic display. They make full use of their individual natural sonar systems to avoid each other, whilst unintentionally creating a living work of art.*

☑ **Get close to the black caiman crocodiles in the Amazon basin.** *I was fortunate enough to visit this area in the dry season, meaning the black caiman were plentiful as they huddled around pools of water. This meant that we could easily get close to them – maybe a little too close on a few occasions. However, things all changed beyond comprehension one fine evening. An Australian friend of mine, who shall remain nameless, seemed to have no respect for the Amazon at all. He would do things like jump out of the boat and hide under the murky brown water just* to frighten people coming behind in another boat.

One day he, matter-of-factly, declared that he was going to catch a black caiman crocodile, but we never really though anything of it and continued on with our day. That night after dinner, as we were all sitting around talking, he bound in with a baby caiman crocodile in his hands and a big smile on his face. He had gone down to the bank of the river, which was absolutely crawling with large caiman and managed to creep up on a baby and kidnap it. As he stood there proudly admiring his new catch, I could hardly believe what he had just done. What was in essence a little baby dinosaur was frightened for its life and obviously distraught. When he was finished playing around he returned the baby caiman to the exact spot where he found it on the riverbank. Surprisingly, he came back alive.

☑ **Witness a brown bear in its natural habitat.** *Whilst visiting northern Sweden I was out and about just after sunrise, when I unexpectedly witnessed a baby bear run across the road in front of us. It seemed so cute and fluffy, despite its obvious physical power. The entire experience lasted not more than 30 seconds before 'baby bear' had disappeared into the woods and out of sight. When we got back to our lodgings and excitedly told everyone the story of what we had seen, one responded by asking: "Are you sure it wasn't a fox?"*

☑ **Swim with manatees, Caye Caulker, Belize.** *These beautiful, friendly creatures are also known as Sea Cows due to their looks and their docile nature. As I was snorkelling along the reef, I had not even noticed a large male manatee, until he swam towards me and up to my level. Then he just hung around, a few metres away from me with a look on his face that said, "Hurry up and take the stupid photo!" before calmly turning and going back down to chill at the side of the reef. Fortunately, I did not have an underwater camera with me, as some experiences are best stored only in the memory.*

☑ **Ride horseback through the Mongolian steppes with Nomads.** *Sitting back on the worst saddle ever made, riding a beautiful stallion through the Mongolian steppes with Nomads, and their eager dogs running along side, is as close to the definition of freedom as it gets. My bum has never been the same since, but if I am honest, the uncomfortable saddle was all part of the experience.*

☑ **Visit the snake charmers of Djemaa el Fna, Marrakech, Morocco.** *A city of heritage and history, filled with colour, Marrakech is a city like no other. The city is a mish-mash of Berber, Arab, African, and European influences and it is perfectly summed up by Djemaa el Fna, the country's largest traditional souk in the city's medina quarter. The name "Djemaa el Fna" rather ironically translates* to "Assembly of the dead," as this is anything but!

Every day the square comes alive with acrobats, dancers, musicians, storytellers, magicians, fruit sellers and henna artists. Not to mention every small animal on a chain that you would never wish to have your photograph taken with. Then there are the infamous snake charmers. It always looked so foreign and exotic on the television and in photographs, but the reality is that the snakes are treated very badly. I should not have been surprised, but these unscrupulous men make a lot of money from the suffering of the snakes. To quote Mohandas Gandhi, "The greatness of a nation and its moral progress can be judged by the way its animals are treated."

☑ **Witness the jumping crocodiles of the Adelaide River, Australia.** There I was hanging over the side of the boat watching these prehistoric creatures slowly saddling up to us without making a ripple. The captain of the boat then started dangling some meat over their heads and, seemingly uninterested, they just drifted along side us in the most log-esque fashion. Then suddenly, in the blink of an eye this massive reptile rocketed out of the water with its mouth open and snatched the lump of meat before the captain could whip it away.

I was left shocked and speechless. You would never believe this until you see it. Crocodiles weighing 1,300 kilograms or more and measuring up to six metres can propel their entire bodies out of the water and snap food from the sky. Using the explosive power of their tails to effortlessly propel them to great heights, they go from being perfectly horizontal and still in the water to being entirely out of the water and vertical faster than you can say 'G'day mate'. After witnessing what these crocodiles were capable of, I quit hanging over the side.

☑ **Snorkel with anacondas, Bonito, Brazil.** Four syllables could hardly strike more fear into the heart of a man than the word anaconda, yet in some strange way it was one of the best wildlife experiences I have ever had. Although thinking back to it now I must have been out of my mind to go snorkelling in water that is frequented by anacondas.

Anacondas have been measured at up to nine metres long, but historical reports from native peoples and early European explorers to the area claim that they can grow up to 30 metres in length. In case you are in any doubt as to why it was maybe not such a good idea, consider that the word anaconda comes from the Tamil word 'anaikolra', which means 'elephant killer'.

☑ **Stand face-to-face with a silverback gorilla in the mountains of Uganda.** There are less than 700 mountain gorillas left on the planet and they all live in the forested mountains on the

The jumping crocodiles of the Adelaide River

green, volcanic slopes of central Africa. In order to catch a glimpse of these remarkable creatures, I found myself entering the Impenetrable Forest, which, as its name suggests, was not that easy. The vegetation was incredibly closely packed and the landscape steep and hilly. The forest floor was damp and heavy due to fallen vines, decomposing leaves and tangled vegetation.

All had to be overcome as we scrambled up and down the slippery slopes in pursuit of a glimpse of the elusive mountain gorillas. This was not so easy, as hiking in the muggy forest at altitudes of 2,000 metres was quite exhausting. Nevertheless, all the struggles were forgotten with the first glimpse of a blackback gorilla – an adult male, not yet of silver status – nestled amongst the foliage.

Soon we came across the rest of the group, mostly female, before the big boss arrived to see who was taking pictures of his girls. The silverback had arrived and this was his mountain kingdom, his world and we were his privileged guests. At the briefing they said that if the big male silverback charges at you, you should remain exactly were you are in a submissive pose looking down at the ground. These great words of wisdom were the polar opposite to what my natural instincts may dictate.

The clicking of cameras soon stopped when the big boss came over to see what all the fuss was about. No one was going to upstage

him in front of his girls so he let everyone within earshot know exactly who the boss was. He stood up tall and made a sort of cupping noise as he pounded his chest. He then let out a roar and ran towards me, of all people. The combination of the silverback pounding his chest a la King Kong and the ferocious mock charge was enough to make my heart miss a beat. As, although he may have the face of a saint, his puppy-dog eyes were combined with shoulders that regularly break trees in half, so there was no doubting whom the boss was.

Once the alpha male had established the hierarchy, he settled down and almost invited us to join with his group. Whilst we were there, we witnessed around fifteen gorillas, including the silverback, three blackbacks and two babies. Watching them play, eat, sleep and breastfeeding, it was striking how many similarities there are between them and us. Surprisingly it is the more undesirable traits that they share with humans such as picking their nose, farting and snoring that make them so endearing.

These magnificent creatures humbled me greatly. I never felt threatened or vulnerable in front of the silverback or any of his troop, despite the mock charges, the thumping on the chest and the loud roars. Seeing the gorillas in their habitat is one of the most emotional wildlife encounters I have ever experienced. Unfortunately, with just one mountain gorilla

Cheetah Park

now remaining for every 10 million people, it is an experience that our children may never get to appreciate.

☑ **Visit a Cheetah Park in Africa.** *They say that the leopard is cunning and ferocious, that the lion is powerful and noble and that the cheetah is refined and elegant. Despite being the smallest of the three cats, the cheetah is easily the most lethal on the attack. It is able to employ breathtaking acceleration to achieve speeds of up to 110 kilometres per hour within five seconds. This makes the cheetah the fastest land mammal on the planet. However, it can only run at such high speed for a short period, otherwise the cheetah faces the risk of overheating.*

Developed for speed, the cheetah has a small, round head with high-set eyes positioned on a long neck. It has short spotted fur, a deep chest, narrow waist and an adaptable spine. With that come semi-retractable

☐ **Get close to the dragons of Komodo Island, Indonesia.** *However, not too close, as these massive lizards have the capacity to run up to speeds of 20 kilometres per hour over a short distance before diving to catch prey, such as deer.*

☐ **Swim with bull sharks, without a cage, in Fiji.** *Considering the intensity of my experience cage diving with 'great whites' in South Africa, I was quite surprised to hear about the experience to be gained with sharks in Beqa Lagoon, Fiji. No cage, no chain-mail suit, no body armour and certainly no harpoon guns – just you, the water and the sharks. Beqa Lagoon is the only place in the world where you can get close to eight species of shark in their natural surroundings without a cage. It may come as a surprise to hear that no one has been bitten or eaten in the 15 years since the tours started.*

Listening to stories from travellers that have experienced the dive, the difference between life and death comes down to how you treat the sharks. Throwing bloodied lumps of meat into the water and snatching it away at the last minute, like they do off Dyer Island, is only going to make the sharks agitated and angry. This encourages the sharks to lash out with the only weapons they have – their teeth. In Beqa Lagoon, they go for the opposite approach, keeping calm and being gentle, petting the sharks and being zen-like. So there you have it, respect and humility towards the locals, seems like

claws with distinctive pads on its feet for traction and a tail as long as its trunk for balance. This, combined with the cheetah's slender, muscular legs, makes it a flawless speed machine. It has evolved into the perfect hunter. Therefore, when I found myself looking into the eyes of a purring cheetah as she happily licked my kneecap it was quite a surreal moment. Shouldn't she jump on me and bite at my face whilst ripping out my guts with the razor-like claws on her hind feet?

the best approach no matter the circumstance.

☐ **Mush a dog sled in the Arctic.**

☐ **Work at the Elephant Village, Nam Khan River, Xieng Lom, Laos.**

☐ **Dive with a whale shark, the world's largest fish.**

☐ **Witness polar bears in the Arctic.**

☐ **Observe a snow leopard in the mountains of Pakistan.**

☐ **Experience Denmark's 'Black Sun'.** *During springtime at around half an hour before sunset, flocks consisting of more than one million European starlings gather over the marshlands of western Denmark to create incredible formations in the sky. This phenomenon is known to the locals as the 'Black Sun' and can be witnessed from March through to the middle of April. They say that this sight is truly remarkable.*

H i k i n g

"Not all those who wander are lost."
~ J. R. R. Tolkien (Writer, poet
and philologist)

☑ **The Inca Trail, Peru.** *This hike is marketed as the trail that leads to Machu Picchu, the Lost City of the Incas, high up in the Andes. However, for me the best part of this trail was the trail itself and not where it led.*

The trail links a range of remarkably well preserved Inca ruins as it winds up through snow-capped mountains and the lush cloud forest over four days. This culminated in the fact that we were the first people into the great site of Machu Picchu in time for sunrise. More importantly, we had a few hours on site before the 'day trip tourists' arrived. Yes, Machu Picchu is as mythical a place as you are bound to find, but that is just like finding the pot of gold at the end of the rainbow. Gold is great, but it is not everyday that you get to travel along a rainbow.

☑ **FitzRoy Grand Tour, Patagonia, Argentina.** *Cerro FitzRoy is located near the village of El Chaltén, in the Southern Patagonian Ice Field on the border straddling Chile and Argentina. Chaltén comes from the local dialect of Tehuelche meaning, "Smoking Mountain" due to a cloud that usually forms around the mountain's peak.*

To reach Cerro FitzRoy on that nippy Sunday morning I had to set off on foot and complete what is a truly magnificent trek around pale blue lakes and roaring waterfalls, through beautiful woodlands, bogs and heath, past grazing lama and open plains to glaciers. This trek was in itself worth the trip to Patagonia. At the end of the trail, I was afforded the most spectacular views of FitzRoy and its surrounding peaks. This perfectly capped off what had already been the most satisfying of days. As even without the stunning views on offer at the end of the trail, this is one of the great hikes.

However, make sure you bring a camera for this one, as the vistas along the route are stunning, as you would expect in Patagonia. For those with a vivid interest in photography, you will be satisfied to catch the 'money shot' at the end of the trail. Sitting at the edge of the lake, you will be afforded a perfect view to capture snow blowing off the top of the peak, in ever-changing formations. This iconic Argentinean ridge provides a close up of the peaks of St. Exupery, Poincenot and FitzRoy as they tower out of the steppes of Patagonia like great oaks in a bonsai garden.

☑ **South Kaibab Trail, Grand Canyon, USA.** *After researching the various trails on offer at the Grand Canyon National Park, I settled on the South Kaibab Trail as my chosen hike. It is the only trail that so dramatically holds true to* a ridgeline descent and for most of its 10.5 kilometre length, the path offers extensive views of the Canyon in both directions. I knew that this was the hike I had to complete. It was a great choice, as throughout the entire hike into the Canyon I was afforded unparalleled panoramic views.

However, this exhilarating sense of exposure to the vastness of this 'Wonder of the World' came at a cost. There was very little shade available and there was no access to water throughout the length of this trail, which was not ideal as I was hiking in the middle of June. As I had travelled to the Grand Canyon within the first month of my travels, I had no real hiking experience as I set off into this great expanse. The trail descends 1,470 metres in total and as I set off at 6am, the heat was not much of an issue and the hike down was spectacular.

When you consider that it gets hotter and hotter the further down into the canyon you get, you can begin to see how issues may arise. The major problem for me was that it was mid June, the sun was high in the sky and I had spent the previous six years sitting on a comfortable chair in an office. Then, I had to hike back up in the brutal midday heat. Alone.

The others had sensibly turned back half way down because of the heat. I struggled up every step of the way treating my limited water supply as the precious commodity it had become. Because of the steepness, the lack of water and exposure to the sun, the hike back up the South Kaibab was very difficult and strenuous. This is a hike that I would recommend doing in the autumn, as in the summer it is just too dangerous for casual enthusiasts. However, do not be put off, as it is still definitely something that I would recommend.

☑ **Torres del Paine Circuit, Patagonia, Chile.** *Jutting out some 2,800 metres above the Patagonian Ice Cap on the Paine Massif are the Torres del Paine, meaning the "Blue Towers". Situated in a transition area between the Magellanic subpolar forests and the Patagonian Steppes, these spectacular granite pillars dominate the landscape of what must be South America's finest national park. Yes, these are the famous Patagonian mountains that you see on posters and book covers all over the world.*

However, despite their natural beauty, the great mountains of the park are not the main attraction. For the hikers of the world, this 2,400 kilometre^2 park is in itself the must-see destination, leaving even the Himalayas in the shade. The treks are named based on the shape of the route, with it being possible to trek the full circle, the "O", in eight-to-nine days, keeping the Torres to your left at all times. The more popular "W" route, takes around five days, with hikers starting and finishing at either of the five base points of the "W".

South Kaibab Trail

With all the varying colours of the many lakes in this mountainous area, it is doubtful that even two look remotely similar. Each lake in the park has been coloured by crushed rock, algae and sediment in the water. The result is the intense colours of the lakes, which range from a milky, almost grey colour, to intense blues, yellows and greens. To increase the surrealness of the area, the lakes will usually have a huge iceberg meandering past in them. This hike through the earth's wildest mountain range has been my favourite hike to date.

On offer is a marvellous path that leads through Magellenic forest, rocky gullies, muddy bogs, glacial lakes, glaciers and makeshift bridges. The trails go up and down steep hills, alongside and over roaring rivers, into the vast openness of the steppe, past groups of grazing wild horses and up to jaw-dropping lookouts. Throughout all of this, to my left hand, were towers of pinkish granite peaking almost impossibly out of the flat Patagonian scrub to create a constantly evolving scenic backdrop throughout my hike. It also provided fresh running water where

I could fill my bottle straight from the stream as I went. It does not get better than that.

☐ **Annapurna Circuit, Nepal.** *This 206 Kilometre 'U' shaped circuit will someday take me through Nepal's Annapurna range and the glorious snow-capped peaks. In addition to this, the route offers terraced rice paddies, deep canyons, jungle, pines and flowing water. My friends that have completed the trek tell me that the best part of this circuit is not the trekking, as good as it is, but the characters that they met along the way in the teahouses-cum-hostels selling yak cheese and yak-butter candles at night. It sounds fantastic.*

☐ **Zion Narrows, Utah, USA.** *I went into the park in June to attempt this hike. The heat was unbearable and so for my own safety I turned around and went back. I was disappointed to be in the park and not be able to fulfil a dream when I had travelled so far, but it was the correct decision. I just could not cope with the extreme temperatures. The Zion Narrows stay on the list until I get some free time to go back during the cooler months.*

☐ **Follow in The Way of Saint James, by completing the Camino de Santiago de Compostela pilgrimage.** *For more than 1,000 years, pilgrims have been walking along the Camino de Santiago. The pilgrimage is actually a collection of old pilgrimage routes, which* cover all of Europe with their final destination at Santiago de Compostela in northwest Spain. The Camino de Santiago is a 780 kilometre hike that traditionally starts in St Jean Pied de Port and finishes in Santiago de Compostela. Many people continue past Santiago to the sea at Finisterre, as in medieval times this was believed to be the end of the world.

☐ **Kungsleden, Sweden.** *160 kilometres inside the Arctic Circle, hides the "King of Trails." Kungsleden runs through four national parks and a nature reserve over its 443 kilometre path. Hiking the entire length in one go would take me at least three weeks as the route runs through an expansive landscape of birch forests, powerful rivers, looming glaciers and Sweden's highest mountains. This is a hike that I have pencilled in for completing in various sections over my lifetime.*

☐ **West Coast Trail, Vancouver Island, B.C., Canada.** *Originally known as the "Dominion Lifesaving Trail," it was built in 1907 to facilitate the rescue of survivors of shipwrecks along this treacherous part of coast. The trail is open from 1 May until 30 September each year and it consists of climbing steep ladders, wading through mud bogs, scrambling over slippery ocean boulders, walking over drift logs, racing the tide at the sandstone shelf, being hauled up rocky cliffs via pull ropes and even riding in cable cars. The beaches, bays, caves,* *coves, creeks, cliffs and waterfalls provide the scenic splendour, appropriate for such an adventure.*

☐ **Mount Everest Base Camp, Nepal.** *If you want to spend 16 days walking through the Himalayas to the foot of the world's highest mountain, then this is the trail to follow. Mount Everest Base Camp has been a popular destination for trekkers since the first expeditions to the Nepalese side of Everest in 1953 and after doing a number of small hikes in Nepal, I can only imagine how good this is.*

☐ **Mont Blanc, France, Italy, Switzerland.** *This multi-cultural Euro-hike is one that I would like to complete with my children when they get to the appropriate age. The route is very accessible within Europe and it is possible to sleep in little huts each night as we complete the 170 kilometre circle through the Alps of three European countries over a two-week period. Just picture the fabulous sight of green meadows, blue glaciers and white peaks as you hike through this wonderful part of Europe. Sure, it would be wrong not to share that with my family.*

VI

Fun is

a path to happiness

One of the great secrets of life is that happiness does not come as a gift or inheritance and it cannot be purchased. It is not something that we receive when certain conditions are met in our lives. Too many of us assume that we will be happier when we are rich or when we meet the man or woman of our dreams or get the perfect job/ car/house or whatever. Many people with great material wealth are sorrowful. Many healthy people are depressed. Many people in "perfect" relationships are miserable.

Happiness is a choice. When we wake up in the morning we can choose to be happy. We can choose to be grateful for all that we have. Many of the world's poorest people are the happiest people I have ever met. I am always humbled by the happiness of the people that I meet in the poorest parts of Africa, Asia and South America.

These people have nothing compared to what the people in Europe, Australia and North America possess, but yet they are constantly smiling from ear to ear. They are filled with gratitude for the meagre possessions that they have, if they have anything at all. The happiest of people do not necessarily have the best of everything; they just seem to make the most of whatever comes their way.

With this in mind, I now make a choice to be happy every morning when I wake up. I do this because the alternative is to be angry, frustrated, annoyed and sad. Every minute that I spend feeling any of these emotions is 60 seconds of happiness that I have wasted. It is important to identify the things in life that make us happy and make more time for those activities, people, pastimes and events.

This will be different for everyone, as what may seem to be mundane or boring to others will be neither of those if it creates happiness for us as individuals. Often it is the simplest things in our lives that bring us the most pleasure. It is the small things that make us smile inside. It is those with whom we are most familiar that bring the loudest laughs.

After coming to this realisation a few years ago I made a pledge, that from that day forth, I would take too many photographs, cheer louder for my team, talk to the stranger on the bus, laugh too loud, spend too much time in the museum and see the good in everything and everyone. I want to watch the sun rise and set again. I want to stroll leisurely through the lashing rain with a smile on my face and I want to stand on a bridge and watch the water flow past without consideration of the time.

I have made an effort to spend more time having fun because that is what fills my life with joy and creates happiness in my world. If you are having doubts on whether this is really the way to proceed, then take a few minutes to ponder on the answer to this question;

"What would the child that I was, think about the person that I have become?"

If you do not like the answer then maybe it is time to make some changes. A good place to start would be by having some fun.

The cars of Havana

Phoneography

I have come to believe that life is like a camera. We should always aim to show ourselves in good light and focus only on what is important in order to capture what is best. When we face the negatives we must develop from them and if things do not work out as we had desired, then we can always take another shot until we capture perfection. *('Phoneography' is photography using a mobile phone.)*

"Photography records the gamut of feelings written on the human face, the beauty of the earth and skies that man has inherited, and the wealth and confusion man has created. It is a major force in explaining man to man."

~ Edward Steichen (Photographer and painter)

☑ **The cars of Havana, Cuba.** *Havana, and Cuba in general, has been stuck in a time warp, with nothing being done to maintain the beautiful architecture of this once great city. In effect, the country has stood still for half a century, and all of its once beautiful streets, buildings, homes and businesses are sorely in need of revitalisation and maintenance.*

It is quite sad to see a once-great town reduced to this state, but the

make their own parts or take them from other cars or even tractors. Quite ironically, as the automakers of Detroit fight for their survival, their vintage cars in Havana threaten to outlive them.

☑ **Africa's 'Big Five':** *Lion, African elephant, Cape buffalo, leopard and rhinoceros. Despite what many believe, the members of the 'Big Five' were not chosen based on their size. The 'Big Five' is based on the difficulty involved in hunting them and the degree of danger involved in bringing back the trophy. The only shots that I wanted to take at the 'Big Five' was on my Nokia camera-phone, as I was more than happy to settle for photo-trophies.*

☑ **Mount Everest, Nepal.** *Many will never be able to commit the time, money and energy required to conquer this greatest of mountains' and climb to its peak. However, the flight around Mount Everest is the next best thing. It offers jaw-dropping views and a unique experience, but just as the hike to the summit has its dangers, there are also great risks associated with the flight.*

one benefit of this is the abundance of classic American cars plying the streets. As a result of Castro taking over in the late 1950s and the American trade embargo being introduced in 1960, it has been illegal to import U.S. made cars to what was one of Detroit's most enthusiastic customers.

This has forced Cubans to maintain the cars they had possessed prior to the revolution. This has turned Havana into a classic car fanatic's paradise. On every street and around every corner there are classic Buick, Chevrolet, Cadillac, Chrysler, Dodge, Ford, Mercury and Oldsmobile's chugging along. As they are prevented from accessing original spare parts, Cubans are forced to

Tenzing-Hillary airport provides the main access to the Mount Everest region of Nepal and, being based deep in the Himalayas, it provides a notoriously difficult landing. To fly into the region airplanes have to land within a meagre 550 metres of a steeply sloped runway that is less than 20 metres wide. On top of this, it has an obstructed approach path and the weather does not provide ideal visibility at the best of times.

I was fortunate enough to take a flight around Mount Everest on a very clear day and capture some nice pictures. Although my phoneographs did not turn out to be as good as I had hoped, the experience itself was astonishing. However, on 8 October 2008, not long after completing my 'flight around Everest', Yeti Airlines Flight 103 was returning to Tenzing-Hillary airport with the latest batch of happy snapping tourists, with their cameras filled with the same photographs I had captured.

Unfortunately, due to the weather conditions and heavy fog the pilot could not see the landing strip. Yet, under pressure to get the airplane on the ground to be filled with the next group of tourists he still attempted to land the plane. The pilot came in too low and too far left, which ultimately caused the plane to crash into the mountainside. There was only a single survivor that day. Eighteen people died in the same airplane that I had sat in only months earlier. This makes me more appreciative of the phoneographs that I was able to capture on my Nokia N95 and the fact that I have the opportunity to show these to the world.

☑ **The Mud City of Bam, Iran.** In southeastern Iran, the city of Bam has stood since the third century. The city was made entirely of mud bricks, clay, straw and the trunks of palm trees. It was because of its location as a commercial and trading centre on the famous Silk Road, that the city thrived. Upon learning of this unique city, I could not wait to visit. However, picture the look on my face as I stood in the Iranian Embassy in Dublin gazing up at a splendid photograph of this great city, waiting to obtain my visa to visit Bam, only to be told the devastating news.

On 26 December 2003, an earthquake with a magnitude of 6.6 devastated the city resulting in the death of more than 26,000 people and the almost total destruction of Bam. I was so disappointed. However, they are rebuilding the city and whilst I was in Iran, I still went to the site of the disaster and had a look around. It was so sad to witness this great city in ruins. Nevertheless, I went and visited other smaller towns made from mud in the region, but it was not quite the same.

☑ **Chernobyl Exclusion Zone graffiti, Ukraine.** Chernobyl, the name synonymous with the largest civil nuclear disaster in history, has always been of great interest to me. Following the mass evacuations, the nearby city of Pripyat was totally abandoned. A 30 kilometre radius "exclusion zone" was established due to the radiation contamination that resulted in long-term health, agricultural and economic distress. The term 'ghost town' has never been more appropriate.

When I learned that a group of Belgian graffiti artists had gone in and tried to bring the desolate landscape back to life, in the run up to the 25th anniversary of the disaster, it brought mixed emotions. I wanted to go over and explore this unoccupied land to see with my own eyes what the outcome of this disaster was. I felt that I needed to go soon after the graffiti had appeared, as one thing that we all know about graffiti is that is spreads. Fast. I brought my Nokia N95 with me, so I could capture 'phoneographs' of what the area had become, as well as the message the graffiti artists were trying to convey.

Upon arriving in the Exclusion Zone, I realised that, for some, the images of abandoned, silhouetted children and imperishable roaches, reflected the scene and may have a part to play in its future. The graffiti artists decided that the time was right to start reshaping the area. Yet, it was only one of many perspectives as to how a damaged landscape can be regenerated and reshaped. Some of the people that I toured the site with were delighted with the artists' impressions.

Nevertheless, I felt that the deserted buildings were better left alone. I was no longer interested in the message of the graffiti artists. I became more interested in photographing the essence of the area. This forgotten landscape is unique in this world. In my opinion, it should be left alone. Images of a young girl bouncing along in her bright yellow dress do not belong here, amongst the death and suffering.

Chernobyl is a wasteland that will forever be uninhabitable. It is a reminder of the unpredictability of our future. Indeed, it is a reminder of our ignorance towards nuclear power and the unsustainability of its use. The fact that another disaster, that is believed to be 33 times worse, has recently happened in Japan is a travesty for mankind. Whether graffiti artists should 'brighten up' a wasteland is not the major issue here.

☑ **The Island of Santorini, Greece.** Santorini has one of the most spectacular landscapes in Greece with traditional villages built into tall cliffs, offering a breathtaking view over the submerged volcano below. The village of Oia is the picture perfect village consisting of little white houses with rounded sky-blue roofs providing the perfect vantage point to one of the most famous and stunning sunsets to be found anywhere. It is very difficult to take a bad photograph here.

☑ **The street children of Kolkata, India.** Exposed to constant hardship and abuse, there is estimated to be around 65,000 street children in Kolkata. Typically, they have run away from abusive families that had beaten and tortured them and felt it better to escape to a life of uncertainty and struggle on the streets. They live anywhere and everywhere and can be found asleep on railway platforms, under bridges, under shop entrances and even inside *sewage pipes. They complete any work that will allow them to survive another day, ranging from begging to picking through huge piles of garbage for items to be recycled. They exist in a harsh environment that many adults would struggle in, with many children physically and sexually abused by the most sinister elements of Kolkata's vast underworld.*

☑ **Young Israeli soldiers climbing Mount Masada at sunrise.** *Mount Masada was the last Jewish stronghold to fall to into the hands of the Romans in the first century. The Zealots held the fort for seven years before it finally fell into the hands of the Roman army in A.D. 73 after they built an enormous ramp up the mountain. However, rather than be killed or enslaved, the Jewish people chose to commit a mass suicide, a deed which forever enshrined them in the annals of Jewish history. Today Mount Masada is held as a symbol of the exile of the Jewish nation from the Holy Land,* with many young Israeli soldiers, sworn in atop Masada as they emotionally chant, "Ma-sa-da, never again."

☑ **Salar de Uyuní, Bolivia.** *Using the vast expanse of white at the Salar de Uyuní, Bolivia to bend light is without doubt the most fun that any person can have with a camera, despite their level of interest in photography. These flats are located in southwest Bolivia, at the crest of the Andes. Covering an expanse of 10,582 kilometres^2, Salar de Uyuni is the largest salt lake in the world. It looks like a vast snow-covered frozen lake like you might find in northern Finland, yet this white surface stretching to the horizon in every direction is salt, not snow.*

As I stood in the middle of Salar de Uyuní, the world's greatest salt desert, the first descriptive word that sprang to my mind was: 'Nothing'. For as far as the eye can see, there is absolutely nothing. Not a shrub nor a tree, not a hill nor a valley, just an

Salar de Uyuní

endless hexagonal carpet of white. The Salar de Uyuní is the kind of place I did not just visit. Instead, I inhaled the vastness and colours of the salt desert with every fibre of my being. This bed of white offers the most fun that I have ever had with a camera. It is so mind-blowing that it almost appears as if Salvador Dali had painted this landscape himself.

☑ **The Buses of Malta.** What will forever remain in my memories of Malta are the buses. What most would consider a road worthy bus are few and far between and what would come screeching around the corner (possibly up on two wheel's) was a slice of nostalgia. Each bus is an individually created piece of moving art, colourfully painted, covered in chrome and with an allotment of friendly phrases painted throughout to welcome the passengers.

The uniqueness of the Maltese bus fleet derives from the ownership of the buses by the drivers themselves, and their tradition of customising and decorating them. This practice has been going on long before MTV's 'Pimp My Ride' came along, and in fact goes back over 100 years. This has lead to the incredible diversity of the fleet and is the reason why the buses have been maintained for so long. Astonishing really considering that nearly all models date from the 1970s and are from the traditional British manufacturers, such as AEC, Bedford, Ford and Leyland.

The only consistency with the buses seemed to be that anything displayed in the interiors had to be elaborately decorated, religious or charming. Welcoming messages ranged from, "I Love Jesus Christ" to "I Love Sexy Girls." Each Maltese bus journey I went on was filled with humour, adventure, colour, laughing, shouting, conversation, screaming tyres, charming drivers, blaring music and being bumped off seats. The Maltese bus journey is more about the bus itself and the goings-on within it than the journey or the destination.

For each journey, I would battle my way onto the bus to be greeted by the Bus Driver, the man that held the power of life or death in his hands. He (this is no job for a woman) had that one brown arm and one white arm that Maltese bus drivers typically have from hanging one arm out the window as they zoomed around the island. With a big smile and his white arm outstretched he would ask for the €0.47 that is required to go on the ride of a lifetime to anywhere on the island. As the door behind me slammed shut, we would speed off into the unknown. Each journey was pretty much summed it up by the Maltese saying that "The Italians drive on the right, the British on the left and the Maltese in the shade."

☑ **A forgotten Communist town.** The little villages on Olkhon Island, Lake Baikal certainly meet this criterion, but it was in Central Russia and the town of Yekaterinburg that I unexpectedly came across what I was looking for. The region was closed to visiting foreigners for decades due to secretive military enterprises in the area. The town, with its rows of apartment blocks, is the very definition of 'Communist', as it is grey, cold and desolate, but still beautiful and so picturesque in so many ways.

☑ **The Moscow Metro stations, Russia.** *The building of the Moscow Metro was one of the USSR's most extravagant architectural projects. It was Stalin who started the project, with the instructions that the architects design a structure that embodied the brilliance of the USSR, depicting a radiant future. With marble walls, high ceilings and grandiose chandeliers, the Metro stations are an underground communist paradise. The rationale behind this was to remind commuters that Stalin and the Communist Party were delivering something substantial to the people in return for their labour and sacrifices. The stations really are striking and I spent a full day dedicated to exploring and 'phoneographing' as many of them as possible.*

☑ **Stockholm's Tunnelbana stations, Sweden.** *Works of art have been integrated into almost every metro station in Stockholm since the 1950s, leading to the Tunnelbana being referred to as the world's longest art gallery, at 110 kilometres long. More than €1 million is invested each year in safeguarding and developing artwork in 90 of the 100 stations. What is unique about the*

Tunnelbana is that many stations have been left as rock caverns, giving them an outstanding, unique atmosphere and allowing for a unique setting in which to capture some great photographs.

☑ **Sunrise at Dune 54, Namibia.** *The winds coming in off the Atlantic Ocean have helped create the world's largest sand dunes, deep in the desert that geologists believe is the oldest on the planet. They say that the darkest hour is just before*

The trees of Dead Vlei

dawn and yet the feminine curves of these great sand mountains still seemed silently enticing, even in the black of night. As I began my ascent up the dunes in the dark of the desert, I soon realised that they are also deceptively enormous, rising alluringly to almost 325 metres in height.

Throwing off my boots and socks and attacking the cold soft sand of the dune with a smile on my face was the most fun way to scramble

to the top, albeit the least efficient. Each large step only carried me a few centimetres further due to the ultra-fine, almost liquid, nature of the sand. Taking a breather and looking back on the distance covered reminded me of looking at an insect trail, as footprints were dwarfed by the enormity of the dunes.

The stunning vistas from the top of Dune 45 made the torturous climb all the more special, as the view seemed to change with a liquidity

I have never before been witness to. As the morning sun moved up and across the desert sky and the shadows lengthened, the dunes threw an array of colours into the environment. Sitting on top, it was spectacular to watch as the dunes metamorphosed from bright amber through a spectrum of reds to electric violet. It was almost impossible to take the same photograph twice, due to the fast pace of change. This was one of those areas on the planet that made me feel so small and humble.

The mind is opened to lots of new possibilities whilst sitting on top of that biggest of sand castles with encroachment all around. To the sound of the most deafening silence, strange thoughts can drift through the minds of men on top of Dune 45. It was up there that I came to realise that our fancy towns and cities are temporary measures, remaining only until Mother Nature decides to take the land back. In these areas, you begin to realise that the pecking order on this earth is not as we wish to believe. Maybe this is just 'our turn'?

☑ **The trees of Dead Vlei, Namib-Naukluft National Park, Namibia.** *Located near the highest sand dunes in the world at Sossusvlei, is the Namib-Naukluft National Park with its white clay pan known as Dead Vlei. This fascinating clay pan formed in the first millennium as a result of the Tsauchab River that flowed through the area. During one wet season the river flooded and swelled to such*

an extent, that it created shallow pools that remained long after the floodwaters had receded.

In fact, the pools remained for such an extended period that they facilitated the growth of Camel Thorn trees to full height and the area thrived. But Mother Nature had other plans for this area and she served up a double whammy, with the combination that has landed many a man in trouble, her deadly desert 'Double D's' – That's drought and dunes! Obviously.

If the sustained drought that hit the area was not severe enough, then the encroaching sand dunes surely provided the killer blow to the area. What now stands as the highest dunes in the world blocked the river from feeding the area with much-needed water supplies and the trees ultimately died. What remain today are the dead skeletons of the trees, believed to be about 900 years old. The trees are not petrified; they have turned black due to the intense sun scorching them over a prolonged period. The trees died due to there being insufficient water to maintain them and with every drop of water sucked from them, they are so dry that the wood will not decompose.

☑ **Hong Kong's lightshow.** *The 'World's Largest Permanent Light and Sound Show' as named by Guinness World Records, is a spectacular multimedia display that uses coloured search lights and laser beams to perform a striking spectacle of light, synchronised* to music and narration that apparently celebrates the spirit, energy and diversity of Hong Kong. I just love that someone came up with an idea to light up the entire harbour every night at 8:00pm in the name of entertainment and others supported that person until it became a reality. However, this is one of those occasions when I noticed that none of the 'phoneographs' that I was capturing were any good, so I just put my camera-phone away and enjoyed the celebration.

☑ **The midnight sun, above the Arctic Circle.** *On 21 June every year the sun is at its lowest point in the sky at 12:50am before, without ever dropping below the horizon, it starts to rise again. I was sitting on top of a mountain in northern Norway with a local guy who looked like the very definition of a 'train spotter', but who also happened to know every fact and figure possible about the midnight sun. Therefore, to sit up there and have him relay fact after fact to me as I snapped great phoneographs whilst enjoying the view culminated in this being a wonderful night.*

☑ **Hoxha's Bunkers, Albania.** *Some dictators leave behind ghastly monuments, some leave great engineering feats, Enver Hoxha left bunkers. Enver Hoxha was the iron-fisted ruler of Albania from 1945 to 1981 and he certainly knew how to lose friends and alienate people. During his dictatorship not only did he alienate the country from the Western world, but he also broke off relations with China, the Soviet Union and every other socialist and communist country on this planet.*

The xenophobic leader proceeded to completely seal Albania off from the rest of the world. Hoxha was certain that his newly sworn enemies would invade Albania any day; he was just unsure what side would invade: the communists or the capitalists. To counteract this imminent invasion, the paranoid leader ordered that a line of defence be set up to protect the country, by way of up to a million bunkers. It is estimated that more than 750,000 of them were eventually built to polka dot the fabric of Albania.

The bunkers were built based on the idea that if an invasion occurred, every Albanian resident capable of carrying a gun would retreat to the nearest bunker and protect the motherland. Considering that Albania had a population of less than three million at the time, there was one bunker built for every four people in the country. They were strategically located on hillsides, fields, mountains, as well as along beaches, railway lines and roads. Not to mention, along every horizon, which becomes less of an eyesore the longer you spend in the country.

Sometimes I witnessed many concentrated together in a single field, which remained an eyesore despite familiarity. Hoxha's bunkers were built to last and they have proven very expensive to remove, with insufficient funds available to

dispose of these destitute reminders of a fallen political regime. So, from what I could see, the people just integrated them into their lives, using bunkers on their property as refrigerators or storage spaces to hold sheep or cattle.

In public spaces, the local artists had brightened up the cold, grey bunkers by decorating them with great imagination. In addition to this, I learned that the bunkers tend to get used as handy public toilets and one local I talked to even admitted to having lost his virginity in a bunker, which apparently is not that unusual. It is estimated to cost around €7,500 to breakdown and remove a bunker, but I got the feeling that not only are the bunkers built securely into the Albanian countryside, they are also built firmly into the Albanian psyche.

☑ **The circumhorizontal arc.** This is an ice-halo formed by sunlight entering horizontally oriented flat hexagon-shaped ice crystals through the vertical side face. The magic happens when the light departs

Africa's child labour

that the sun be very high in the sky and for the cirrus cloud or haze to contain plate-shaped ice crystals. The sun's altitude determines the visibility of the halo. The higher it is, the clearer it will appear and the better the photo opportunity.

☑ **Watering holes at Etosha National Park, Namibia.** *You may have read this far and think, surely this guy has been to enough safari parks. However, you would be wrong, as there is no such thing as too much safari. Even the guides that work in the parks are constantly amazed by what each day presents. No one gets bored of safari in Africa. Etosha is one of Africa's better wildlife sanctuaries, offering excellent game viewing of many endangered species. This is a result of the park having one of the richest ecosystems in Africa, providing habitat for many species of mammals and birds.*

It was here that I went in search of the many easily accessible waterholes that animals concentrate around, which enhanced viewing prospects and allowed me to get some great close up phoneographs on my Nokia. One may ask why I would want to set off into the centre of Africa on such quests as to sit around a waterhole and wait on animals, but to answer, I need to use the words of Brian Jackman; "Everything in Africa bites, but the safari bug is worst of all."

☑ **A village celebration in Fiji.** *It may be hard to believe, but the best part of Fiji is not the picture perfect*

through the near horizontal bottom, to create an optical phenomenon in high-level cirrus clouds known as a "fire rainbow", despite it being neither fire nor a rainbow.

I unexpectedly experienced a circumhorizontal arc whilst in Kenya, when a travel companion pointed it out. I got very excited, much to my colleague's amusement. The halo was a huge, multi-coloured band running parallel to the horizon with its centre beneath the sun. Formation of the halo requires *natural beauty that is all around. It is the overwhelming sense of community that welcomed me whilst I casually wandered around the islands as the locals called out the greeting "Bula." Fiji is a rich cultural surprise, a place where the Fijian people with their great smiles captivated my heart. They had me instinctively shouting "Bula" as I wandered the sandy roads and it soon became evident as to why they are known as the friendliest people on Earth.*

However, to be here at a time when I got to attend a village celebration made a good experience great. What I really love about local celebrations is the effort that the locals put in, to show their locality in the best possible light with a multitude of colours on offer. The song, dance, costumes, customs, fire and hospitality make for a great occasion and provide a great backdrop for any budding photographer.

☑ **Africa's child labour.** *Africa has the highest incidence of child labour in the world. According to an ILO report, 41 percent of all African children between the ages of five and fourteen are involved in some form of economic activity. Whilst in Uganda, I photographed children as young as five years old sitting on a hillside from morning to night charged with the task of breaking large rocks into smaller rocks. Nothing is as heart breaking to witness as that.*

☐ **Africa's child soldiers.** *In contravention of international law, there is estimated to be around 350,000 children, some as young as seven years old, being used as soldiers in conflicts around the world. Of these, some 120,000 child soldiers are believed to be used as soldiers across the continent of Africa. Can any face tell a story better than that of an African child solider?*

☐ **The Stilt Fishermen of Kathaluwa, Sri Lanka.** *Stilt fishing is a tradition in the district of Galle were the fishermen sit on a cross bar, known as a Petta, tied to a vertical pole planted into the coral reef. The fishermen hold the stilt with one hand while fishing with a rod in the other. Their hope is to catch spotted herrings or small mackerels, which they store in a bag tied around their waist. Whether they can place food on their table that night will be determined by what they catch that morning. The poles measuring up to five metres long are driven into the reef, allowing the fishermen to sit two metres above the water and avoid the waves. This truly is a unique sight and one I want to phoneograph soon.*

☐ **Morocco's Climbing Goats.** *Everyone knows that goats are capable of navigating extreme terrain, but not many know that they can climb trees and hop gracefully from branch to branch. In Morocco, the native Tamri goats have become adept at climbing the branches of Argan trees to feed on the berries that the trees produce. The trees are not that big, but there can be up to 20 goats balancing precariously on the branches.*

The goats' cannot digest the kernels from the berries, so to make this even more unbelievable; the local farmers follow the goats around collecting their droppings. The farmers then grind the kernels into oil and use it for cooking and in cosmetics, which women all over the world then rub on their face. I was on holiday in Morocco when I first learned of these goats from images on postcards but dismissed them as being 'photoshopped'. I was only convinced that the goats existed after I went and searched for evidence online. Now, I must return and experience this spectacle for myself.

☐ **Go into space to photograph the Earth using a mobile phone.** *I want to be the first person travelling onboard Virgin Galactic that uses a Nokia device and nothing else to take photos of our beautiful blue planet from outer space.*

☐ **People and culture of Papua New Guinea.** *More than a third of the five million population of Papua New Guinea live in the rugged Highlands, were more than 60 separate languages, cultures and traditions have been identified. Papua New Guinea's culture is extremely diverse with each region, hosting a rich variety of traditional customs. The traditional cultures of the region are kept alive in elaborate rituals involving initiation rites, feasts, marriages, compensation ceremonies and even deaths. The Goroka and Mount Hagen Cultural Shows provide such good photo opportunities that accommodation must be booked a year in advance.*

☐ **Venezuela's Everlasting Storm.** *The mysterious "Relámpago del Catatumbo" (Catatumbo lightning) is an atmospheric phenomenon that occurs strictly in the area over the mouth of the Catatumbo River where it empties into Lake Maracaibo. The phenomenon is cloud-to-cloud lightning that forms a voltage arc measuring over five kilometres for ten hours a night and up to 280 times an hour. This almost permanent storm can occur up to 170 nights per year, giving me many opportunities to work some magic on my new Nokia Lumia 920.*

☐ **The cherry blossom season in Japan.** *The cherry blossom season is so beautiful that it is known as 'Hanami' and has developed into an important Japanese custom, held all over the country each spring. 'Hanami' literally means 'viewing flowers'. It is said that the origin of Hanami dates back a millennium to a time when aristocrats wrote poems whilst admiring the beautiful cherry blossoms. Bright pinks and whites against a perfect blue sky in Japanese spring time equates to beautiful phoneographs.*

☐ **The Architecture of Oman.** *Architecture can be used as a measure of the evolution of a nation's civilisation and nowhere is this more evident that in Oman. Diligent effort has been exercised to preserve the ancient and traditional architecture of the region, which radiates beauty through the use of simple lines. There are no high rises as they have maintained the* *understated elegance of the regions history with many buildings now listed as World Heritage Sites.*

☐ **Lluvia de Peces, Yoro, Honduras.** *This phenomenon is also known as the 'Rain of Fish' due to fish falling from the sky. This has been occurring in the city of Yoro on a yearly basis, between the months of May and July, for more than a century. The locals are quite open to it as for them their dinner literally falls out of the sky and then they go around collecting the fish, which they will later cook and eat. Imagine how good it would be to witness this event and capture it on camera.*

Waterfalls:

☑ **Victoria Falls, Zimbabwe/ Zambia.** *Known as Mosi-oa-Tunya, (meaning "the Smoke that Thunders") by the Kololo tribe in the area, this is the greatest curtain of falling water that I have ever visited. The sheer noise of the water as it falls 111 metres across a width of 1.7 kilometres is an experience to behold. Columns of spray can rise to over 600 metres above the falls with the spray visible from up to 50 kilometres away. However, what goes up must come down and I recommend wearing as little as possible when you get close to the falls, as no raincoat can keep out this amount of falling water.*

☑ **Iguaçu Falls, Brazil/Argentina.** *Stunning.*

☑ **Niagara Falls, USA/Canada.** *Commercialised*

☑ **De Tain Falls, China/Vietnam.** *Picturesque.*

☑ **Gullfoss, Iceland.** *Jagged.*

☑ **La Fortuna Waterfall, Costa Rica.** *Spectacular.*

☑ **Mitchell Falls, Kimberley, Western Australia.** *This 80 metre four-tiered waterfall is found deep in the remote Kimberley region of Western Australia. The stunning backdrop of the water rushing over the red rock of the Mitchell Plateau provides an oasis feel to allow the falls to really stand out, providing an opportunity to capture wonderful phoneographs.*

☐ **Ángel Falls, Canaima, Venezuela.**

☐ **Sutherland Falls, Fjordland, New Zealand.**

☐ **Kaieteur Falls, Potaro River, Guyana.**

☐ **Sivasamudram Falls, India.**

☐ **Jim Jim Falls, Kakadu National Park, Australia.** *This is another example of an adventure to a potential 'once in a lifetime' destination that just was not meant to be, due to a combination of nature and bad timing. When we ventured out to this desolate part of the world, there had been heavy rainfall in the days prior that had caused flooding, making the track to the falls impassable. I never got to phoneograph Jim Jim Falls.*

Museums

"Too often in the past, we have thought of the artist as an idler and dilettante and of the lover of arts as somehow sissy and effete. We have done both an injustice. The life of the artist is, in relation to his work, stern and lonely. He has laboured hard, often amid deprivation, to perfect his skill. He has turned aside from quick success in order to strip his vision of everything secondary or cheapening. His working life is marked by intense application and intense discipline."

~ John F. Kennedy (President of the U.S.A.)

☑ **The War Remnants Museum, Ho Chi Minh City, Vietnam.** *Outside the museum, posters read, "Vietnam is not a war, it is a country!" Sometimes it is hard for people in the West to understand this, but this museum certainly helps clarify any misconceptions. Up until 1993, it was known as the 'Museum of American War Crimes' as that is what this museum is primarily concerned with. Throughout the museum, tourists, with a horrified look on their faces, will usually have their hand over their mouth as they study the photographs and read accounts of the terrible events that unfolded during this infamous war.*

☑ **The Egyptian Museum in Cairo, Egypt.** *I was rather disappointed by this museum the first time I visited Cairo, so I went again for a second visit a few years later. I left disappointed again. Is it just me or is this museum too messy and disorganised? Thankfully, they are now building a massive new underground museum to house the many artefacts, beside the Pyramids in Giza. I look forward to going back for a third time.*

☑ **Stokes Croft, Bristol, England.** *Not a museum in the traditional sense, but as it is a location where many great artists present their work to the world it is very much an open-air museum. I went to Stokes Croft in search of some original Banksy's but what I found was some of the most fantastic street art imaginable, by an array of great artists. Bristol is a fantastic city and the neighbourhood of Stokes Croft provides the little bit of magic that all the great cities seem to possess.*

☑ **Muse Nacional de Antropología, Mexico City, Mexico.** *A gay barber in New Orleans recommended this one to me as he spent over two hours cutting my already short hair. My hair was destroyed, but that guy certainly knew a good museum when he saw one.*

☑ **The American Museum of Natural History, New York, U.S.A.** *What began as a museum and library in 1869 to foster the study of science is now a complex of 27 interconnected buildings covering 73,000 metres^2 in Manhattan. The collection now consists of more than 32 million specimens and artefacts.*

There are so many cool exhibits in this great museum that I could spend my entire holidays there every year and never get bored. My approach to this great building was to have a walk around all the buildings, then just settle in and enjoy what time was left learning about what ever caught my eye the most. Because of this approach the 29 metre long model of a blue whale, hanging from the roof attracted me in and I spend the remainder of my day there learning about Ocean Life.

The Hermitage

☑ **Aboriginal Art Museum, Darwin, Australia.** *What appears to be no more than "dot painting" is actually a quite amazing way of passing on their 'dreamings'. It really is phenomenal to learn about this ancient art and the wide range of media they used, including painting on leaves, rock carving, wood carving, ceremonial clothing and sculpture. The more I learn about the aboriginal people of Australia the more respect I have for them and their ways.*

☑ **Van Gogh Museum, Amsterdam, The Netherlands.** *It would be a bit strange if this museum did not house the largest collection of paintings, letters and drawings by Vincent van Gogh (1853-1890) in the world. Wandering through this museum, despite its vast floor space, provides only a glimpse of what went on within the mind of this unique man. It was a quote from "Vincent and the Doctor," a 2010 BBC Doctor Who episode, that I watched that I believe provides the* best description of what this man put into his art and indeed his life:

"To me, Van Gogh is the finest painter of them all. Certainly the most popular, great painter of all time – the most beloved. His command of colour, the most magnificent. He transformed the pain of his tormented life into ecstatic beauty. Pain is easy to portray, but to use your passion and pain to portray the ecstasy and joy and magnificence of our world… no one had ever done it before. Perhaps no one ever will again. To my mind, that strange, wild man who roamed the fields of Provence was not only the world's greatest artist, but also one of the greatest men who ever lived."

☑ **The Hermitage, St. Petersburg, Russia.** *This is one of those museums where the building itself is nearly as impressive as the contents it houses, if not more so. The museum consists of five buildings arranged side-by-side along the river embankment, one of which was originally the Winter Palace of Empress Elizabeth, the daughter of Peter the Great. This green-and-white three-storey palace is a marvel of Baroque architecture boasting over a thousand lavishly decorated rooms.*

The Hermitage was founded when Catherine the Great purchased a collection of 255 paintings from Berlin in 1764. That number has now risen to over 2.7 million exhibits with

The Hermitage displaying a diverse range of art and artefacts from all over the world. The Hermitage's collections include works by Michelangelo, Raphael, Leonardo da Vinci, Titian, Renoir, Cezanne, Manet, Monet Pissarro, Rembrandt, Ruben, as well as numerous canvasses by Gaugin, Van Gogh and Matisse. It also houses several sculptures by Rodin.

The collection is both enormous and diverse and is a must see no matter how deep your interest in art and history. The collection is so large that it is said that if you were to spend a minute looking at each exhibit on display in The Hermitage, then eleven years would pass before you had seen them all. It may take me a lot longer, based on the fact that I spent 30 minutes in the entrance alone, just admiring the work that went into the architecture there.

☑ **Spy Museum, Washington D.C., U.S.A.** *Of all the museums that I have visited, this has probably been the most fun. A great feature of the Spy Museum is its controlled entry. I was given five minutes to memorise details of my new spy profile, consisting of name, age, birthplace, destination, et cetera before I was allowed into the exhibit area. During the tour, I was then tested on interactive displays, as well as being stopped by "police" and "questioned" about my cover identity. Great craic. Any boy that has grown up watching James Bond movies will love this day out.*

☑ **Suicide Bomber Museum, Tehran, Iran.** *There are some bizarre museums around the world, but this one, situated across the road from the old US Embassy in Tehran, is in a league of its own when it comes to weird subject matters. From what I could tell it was mostly dedicated to female suicide bombers, with photographs of the women standing in front of flags with guns in their hands pre-bombing. This museum is beyond strange.*

☑ **The Sex Museum, Amsterdam, The Netherlands.** *It is exactly how you would imagine a museum of sex in Amsterdam to be. Situated a short walk from the city's infamous Red Light District, the museum consists of a collection of erotic pictures, paintings, toys, objects, recordings, photographs and a bicycle. The people of the Netherlands have always been known for their deep love of bicycles, but someone has taken this love too far.*

☑ **Tate Modern, London, England.** *This is my number one favourite gallery on the planet. No other museum gets me thinking and inspires me as much as this old Power Station on the banks of the River Thames. Whilst here I find myself contemplating relocating to London just so that I could have easier access to the great facilities that most Londoners seem to take for granted, such as the Tate Modern.*

☑ **The Nobel Peace Centre, Oslo, Norway.** *Whilst visiting I was rather surprised to learn about the many controversies involved with the Nobel Peace Prize. The most recent recipient to 'raise a few eye brows' was 2009 winner Barack Obama, who received criticism due to the award being "undeserved, premature and politically motivated." Much of the surprise arose from the fact that nominations for the award were due by 1 February 2009; only twelve days after Obama took office. The centre is really interesting and certainly worth a visit when in Oslo.*

☑ **ArtScience Museum, Singapore.** *The world's first ArtScience museum is referred to as "The Welcoming Hand." This is due to the ten "finger"* extensions coming out from the round base in the middle of the building. The design concept for each of the fingers denotes various gallery spaces sporting skylights at the "fingertips" which are included as sustainable illumination for the dramatically curved interior walls. It really is a great building in a perfect location and compliments the wonderful Singaporean skyline perfectly.

☑ **The British Museum, London, England.** *This permanent collection is among the largest and most wide-ranging in existence, consisting of over eight million works. Derived from every continent, the range of works is largely a result of the ever-expanding British Empire over the past 300 years. Despite housing some remarkable objects, such as the Elgin Marbles, which have been 'borrowed' from the Parthenon, the one thing that continues to impress me most about this museum is the illustrious roof that covers the interior court. I am obviously quite a simple man.*

☑ **National Leprechaun Museum, Dublin, Ireland.** *If you want to experience the incredible Irish tradition of storytelling, then this is the place to go. Here you will get to experience the real passion that the people of Ireland bring to storytelling as you sit on oversized furniture (to make you feel small) whilst learning the "truth" about Leprechauns and other Irish folklore characters.*

☑ **The Guggenheim Museum, Bilbao, Basque Country.** *Regardless of the fabulous work inside, for me this museum is all about the building itself. This building was the very reason why I detoured across the country on my way from Paris to Madrid. Despite the fact that Gehry once appeared as himself in an episode of 'The Simpsons' suggesting that his idea for the museum derived from a piece of paper crumpled into a ball, it wasn't. It would appear that a lot more effort than that had went into the design.*

The building, a spectacular structure made of glass, limestone and titanium, consists of graceful, sensuous curves, reminiscent of the ships that once lined the banks of the river Nervion, on which the museum now sits. In addition to this, the spectacular twisting reflective titanium panels are designed to resemble fish scales. I could just sit and have tea in the sun outside and admire the work of architect Frank Gerry for hours on end. For every hour I spent inside, I spent two outside just admiring the building from many different distances and vantage points.

With over one million visitors a year passing through its doors, the Guggenheim Museum Bilbao has challenged the art world to reconsider the connections between architecture, art and collecting. However, more important than any thing else, this great work of contemporary architecture has changed the way that the general public thinks about museums. For me, to exhibit my work in this building would be a great honour.

☐ **The Guggenheim Abu Dhabi, U.A.E.** *It almost seems as if I have been waiting forever for this museum to open, despite the fact that its completion is not expected until 2017. The reason why I am so excited about this is because the rulers of Abu Dhabi have signed an agreement with the Solomon R. Guggenheim Foundation to build a 30,000 metre² Guggenheim Museum that reflects Islamic and middle-eastern culture. Maybe I should also mention that architect Frank Gehry has been commissioned to design this new museum. I suspect that the result will be the middle-eastern version of the perfect museum. What is there not to like about this?*

☐ **Le Louvre, Paris, France.** *I was in Paris with my fiancé one lovely summer morning and we were looking at the map wondering what to do that day. "How about we go to Le Louvre?" I ask. "Yeah, great idea, lets go" she responds. When we get to Le Louvre, we find that the mother of all queues is winding its way out of sight. We glance at the queue then glance back at each other with that same 'screw it' look on our faces.*

We concluded that Le Louvre is more of a winter attraction, as being stuck in a museum with thousands of tour groups was not the best way to spend a summer's

day in Paris. We instead decided to take off our shoes and sit on the side of a fountain with our feet in the water basking in the sun. I think Paris may be more beautiful in the snow anyway.

☐ **The MoMa (Museum of Modern Art), Manhattan, New York, U.S.A.** *I was so excited to go and visit the famous MoMa in New York. I had a week in NYC so I decided that I would wait until the final day of my time in the city and I would then spend all day at the great MoMa. I was up early and waiting outside the locked gate at 9:00am. However, I soon realised that the gate was never going to open that day. Was I the only person on the planet that did not realise that all museums are closed on Mondays? Yes I was. On the early hours of Tuesday morning, I left New York to begin my drive to California. I never did get to see the inside of New York's MoMa.*

Amusement Parks

"The world is like a ride in an amusement park, and when you choose to go on it you think it's real because that's how powerful our minds are. The ride goes up and down, around and around, it has thrills and chills, and it's very brightly coloured, and it's very loud, and it's fun for a while. Many people have been on the ride a long time, and they begin to wonder, "Hey, is this real, or is this just a ride?" And other people have remembered, and they come back to us and say, "Hey, don't worry; don't be afraid, ever, because this is just a ride."

~ Bill Hicks
(Stand-up comedian, social critic, satirist and musician)

☑ **Disneyland Resort, California, U.S.A.** *For me this was the major amusement park that I just had to visit. As soon as I arrived in Los Angeles, I booked into the campsite just up the road from the Disneyland Resort entrance so I did not have to walk too far. Before 8:00am the following morning I was standing outside Disneyland Resort holding onto the gates with my head pressed against the bars, eagerly gazing in. I was the first person to enter that day and literally the last person to leave that night following the 'Fantasmic' firework finale. No, I wasn't a 10 year old at the time. This was only five years ago.*

☑ **Jumeirah, Wild Wadi Water Park, Dubai, U.A.E.** *Situated in a great setting between the iconic Burj Al Arab and the Jumeriah Beach hotels, this is the best water park I have ever been to. What I remember most about it, apart from the great rides, was the extreme heat that carried on right into the night, with us sitting by the poolside in the dark, still trying to keep cool.*

☑ **Ferrari World, Abu Dhabi, U.A.E.** *I needed a flight out of Cairo to get back to Ireland and the cheapest two options available were via either France or Abu Dhabi. As I was searching for flights online, I had learned that an amusement park dedicated to all things Ferrari was about to open in Abu Dhabi. That settled it. I just had to attend Ferrari World. It would mean doubling the length of my journey, and maybe staying over for a night, but that was actually part of the appeal for me. I booked my flight via Abu Dhabi and before I knew it, I was strapping on my safety goggles as I sat beside the German Engineer of the Worlds Fastest rollercoaster, Formula Rossa, on its maiden voyage.*

As we talked about the engineering feats that went into making this ride possible, we were, without notice, shot out of the hub mid-sentence. As we accelerated up to 240 kilometres per hour, we were given the full effect of what 4.8Gs really feels like as we went from 0 to 100 kilometres per hour in less than two seconds. On that initial straight

Gröna Lund

the rollercoaster goes so fast, that it causes the machinery to heat up to such an extent that water must be sprayed on it to keep it cool. This is something you will only find out if you sit up front, as you feel a spray of water hitting you across the face (It's quite refreshing in the desert heat).

The chicanes on the 'track' are inspired by some of the most famous racetracks in the world. The Engineer told me many great facts, but the Formula Rossa ride was so good, they were blown out of my brain by the adrenaline by the time we had crossed the 'finish line.'

☑ **SeaWorld, Orlando, U.S.A.** *Watching Killer Whales doing back flips and waving to the crowd, among* many other tricks, is something that is not to be missed.

☑ **Vinpearl, Nha Trang, Vietnam.** *This is one of my all time favourite theme park experiences, possibly because my expectations were quite low. Vinpearl is based on an island and consists of water rides, ground based rides, shows, under water world, 4D cinemas and arcade games. The best part is that apart from food, absolutely everything is included in the ticket price. Yes, free arcade games until your arms fall off. Best thing ever.*

☑ **Gröna Lund, Stockholm, Sweden.** *Gröna Lund has been located on Djurgården Island since its inception in 1883. Due to the*

in the wild, in India, it was great to see Bengal and Sumatran tigers up close as they played, wrestled and swam with their handler's.

☑ **Australia Zoo, Queensland, Australia.** *Home of the Crocodile Hunter, but unfortunately I was there just a few months after Steve Irwin passed away and never got to see him feed the crocodiles. His wife Terri had stepped in to fill his role by then, but it just was not the same. Steve Irwin, what a legend!*

☐ **Europa Park, Germany.** *Home to eleven roller coasters, which should be enough to keep me occupied for a full day.*

☐ **Disneyland Paris, France.** *The most popular amusement park in Europe.*

limited amount of land available, the park is relatively small compared to other amusement parks around the world, but this, along with its 'old skool' feel, is what makes it so great. What I really love about Amusement Parks in Sweden is that they award prizes of massive one metre x fifty centimetre bars of chocolate for winning on the games. I rarely take my winnings home, as no one can eat that amount of chocolate, but the kids I pass my winnings to, certainly give it a good go.

☐ **Alton Towers, England.** *The home of 'Oblivion', the first roller coaster with a vertical (88.8°) drop.*

☐ **Legoland, Denmark.** *To see the skill that goes into recreating the world's iconic landmarks via the medium of Lego is an experience that I have been waiting to experience for as long as I can remember.*

☑ **Dreamworld, Australia.** *Despite all the effort that went into creating the rides and thrills, the best part of my time in Dreamworld was the remarkable Tiger Island. After failing to witness any Tigers*

Sports

"I've missed more than 9,000 shots in my career. I've lost almost 300 games. 26 times, I've been trusted to take the game winning shot and missed. I've failed over and over and over again in my life. And that is why I succeed."

~ Michael Jordan
(Professional basketball player and entrepreneur)

Football

☑ **Sing until I am hoarse at a Champions League Final.** *Juventus and AC Milan contested the 2003 UEFA Champions League Final. The match made history, as it was the first time two clubs from Italy had faced each other in the final. The game finished 0–0 after extra time with AC Milan going on to win the game 3–2 in the penalty shootout to claim their sixth European Cup. In the days before the game the Ultra supporters of each team had come to an agreement that there would be a truce between the fans for the game. Therefore, instead of fighting each other on the streets around the stadium, it was as if they had decided to battle it out through chanting for their team.*

The wall of sound was relentless due to the stadium being split in half so that the apposing fans where looking into each other. I sat behind the goal with the AC Milan fans, whilst my brother sat with the Juventus fans at the other side of the ground. We both met up after the game and the main topic of conversation was the wall of noise that the Italians generated for their teams. It must have been an awesome experience for the players to be in the middle of it all. Ticket price: £150 for two tickets.

☑ **Attend a Europa League Final.** *The 2011 UEFA Europa League Final was played in Dublin and once again, it was between two teams from the same country. Again, it made history as the first time there has been an all-Portuguese European final. As the game was between Porto and Braga, this final also broke the record for the smallest distance separating finalists of a UEFA competition with only 47 kilometres separating the cities. A great game of football ended with a 1–0 victory to Porto. I spent the entire game jumping around with the Porto Ultras bare backed waving my t-shirt around my head. I just got into the spirit of things, as these were not the type of boys that I wanted to have a disagreement with. Ticket price: €100 for two tickets.*

☑ **Support Manchester United at a FA Cup Final, Millennium Stadium, Cardiff.** *In a one-sided encounter, with Manchester United dominating the game, Arsenal surprisingly went on to become the first club to win the cup on penalties. It was the first goalless draw in an FA Cup final since 1912. That is all I* have to say about that. Ticket price: £120.

☑ **Support Manchester United at a Football League Final, Wembley, London.** The 2010 Football League Cup Final was the perfect way in which to celebrate the 50th season of the Football League Cup. It was played at the new Wembley Stadium and won 2-1 by Manchester United after falling behind to an Aston Villa penalty in the fifth minute. As I had been away travelling for an extended period and missed a lot of football, it was great for me to be back in a massive stadium surrounded by United fans and watch our team win the cup. Happy days. Ticket price: £100.

☑ **Sing my heart out at a Championship deciding match at Old Trafford.** I was privileged to own season tickets at Old Trafford for quite a few of the seasons that Manchester United was crowned as champions. However, the one game that sticks in my mind the most is the deciding game of the 2001/02 season when Arsenal strode into the enemy territory at Old Trafford and won 1-0 to seal victory and with it, the Premiership title. If you have ever seen a sporting event on television where there is that one boy sitting there with a look of distraught on his face an hour after the stadium has emptied, then it may just have been me after that game. I was gutted.

☑ **Watch River Plate play for the Championship in Buenos Aires, Argentina.** I actually spent more time watching the antics of the fans during this game than the actual game itself. I have been to many football games around the world and witnessed a lot of unruly behaviour, but this was different. There was something wrong within the minds of these 'fans'.

☑ **Chant along at a local derby in Estádio do Maracanã, Rio de Janeiro, Brazil.** During my time in Rio, I got to watch all the big local teams play, including two local derbies: Botafogo vs. Flamengo and Fluminense vs. Vasco da Gama. The skills are fantastic, but it is like watching an English Premier League game in slow motion.

☑ **Watch the A-League Football final.** I went to see Newcastle United Jets vs. Central Coast Mariners at the Olympic Stadium, Sydney, Australia in 2008. It was a decent game of football with Newcastle United Jets going on to win the cup by a single goal, scored by Mark Bridge.

☑ **Attend the FAI Cup final, Dublin.** 2012, Shelbourne FC vs. Sligo Rovers, 1–1 (a.e.t.). (1–4 after penalties). This was a fantastic day out, as despite going to watch football in many foreign countries, it pains me to say, I did not appreciate League of Ireland football until this day.

☑ **Survive an Old Firm derby at Ibrox, Glasgow, Scotland.** A lot of anger and not very nice words are spewed forth before, during and after the game. The "Old Firm" is the collective name for Rangers and Celtic football clubs, the two most successful clubs in Scotland. Between them they have won an astonishing 97 league championships, 68 Scottish Cups and 41 Scottish League Cups. In addition, Celtic won the European Cup once and Rangers have won the UEFA Cup Winners' Cup once, with each club holding many records.

☑ **Watch a big European Football derby in the Middle East.** I am fortunate enough to have experienced this a few times. The passion that the locals have for football teams that are from a culture so alien to theirs has always astonished me. However, the time I watched Barcelona vs. Real Madrid when I was in Aqaba, Jordon will never be equalled.

The game was due to kick-off at 9:00pm local time so I decided to wander up the town for some food and a look around before the game. As I got closer, I could hear a great noise coming from the town square. I went to investigate further and as I turned the corner, I was astonished by what I saw. The main square was heaving, with what seemed like every youth in the town crammed into it. They were waving flags and chanting. In front of them were three projector screens roughly attached to trees, showing the build-up to the game. This was <u>four hours</u> before kick-off yet it seemed like the square had been busy for quite a while.

Every time a Barcelona or Real Madrid player came up on screen, half the crowd would spontaneously cheer whilst the other half would boo and hiss. I joined in for a while, before going off to get some food. I came back to the square just before kick-off and now the locals were really going crazy. As the teams came out, they went wild, chanting for their team in Arabic. Then, quite bizarrely, when the game kicked off they all sat down and silently (nervously maybe?) watched the game.

When Xavi scored the first goal for Barcelona after 10 minutes, half of the square went wild, screaming right into the faces of the Real Madrid fans sat beside them. Things got worse for the Real Madrid fans in the crowd when, after 18 minutes, Barcelona went two up through Pedro. That was too much for the Real Madrid fans to handle and fights and scuffles broke out all over the square. They were really getting stuck into each other with full forced punches, leaving quite a few bloody noses. Now, remember that this is thousands of kilometres away, on a different continent from where the actual game was being played.

At half time, I had to leave to catch an overnight boat to Egypt, but I learned during the night that Barcelona had won the game 5–0 scoring the fifth goal in the final minute, to rub salt in the wounds of the Real Madrid fans. I can only imagine how the square looked by the end of the game, not to mention the bruised and battered faces of the young lads. As Sir Alex Ferguson once said, "Football, bloody hell!"

☐ **Support Ireland at the World Cup finals.**

☐ **Admire the talent on view at 'El Clasico' in Camp Nou, Barcelona, Catalonia.**

☐ **Watch Ajax play Feyenoord at the Amsterdam Arena.** *The fans of these clubs are not very friendly towards each other, so I know that the passion inside this great stadium would be something that would be fabulous to experience.*

Rugby

☑ **Urge on the boys at a British & Irish Lions game.** *Prior to The British & Irish Lions tour to New Zealand in 2005 I watched 'The Lions' play Argentina at the Millennium Stadium in Wales in May of that year. Despite the fact that Argentina were without 25 players who may have made their first-choice team if it was not for club commitments, the Lions were lucky to get a draw out of the game. It was only thanks to a penalty kick by Jonny Wilkinson in the eighth minute of stoppage time that the Lions salvaged a 25–25 draw.*

☑ **Attend the Rugby grudge match of Australia vs. New Zealand.** *Despite the high quality*

of the rugby on the pitch, the atmosphere was non-existent. Definitely one that I would advise is better watched on television.

☐ **Support Ireland at a Six Nations Rugby match.** *The 'Six Nations' is an annual international rugby union competition involving six European countries: Ireland, England, France, Italy, Scotland and Wales. From where I now live, I can see Lansdowne Road Stadium, the home of Irish Rugby, yet I have never attended a Six Nations game. It is just so difficult to get tickets. In fact, I used to have to complete the stock-take on the match programmes after every game, when I worked as an auditor, and I still could not get my hands on a ticket.*

American Sports

☑ **Enjoy the fireworks at Dodgers Stadium, Los Angeles on Independence Day.** *Crack! "It's going, going. GONE and the crowd goes wild." This is how I imagined baseball to be, but the reality was that it was a long day of sitting around with me not really knowing what was going on. Apparently, the game of baseball can infect anyone who watches long enough. I obviously need to spend more time with people that are passionate about the game so that I can get a feel for what is going on.*

☑ **Attend a Notre Dame American Football game.** *In sport,* no matter the competition, people can undertake some strange and desperate acts, as I have witnessed first hand on many occasions around the world. However, when I attended the Navy vs. Notre Dame college football game I soon realised that this was going to be a little different. The Navy vs. Notre Dame series is the longest uninterrupted intersectional series in college football, with it being played annually since 1914. This match-up has an intense rivalry that is fuelled by respect rather than revulsion.

It is this feature that distinguishes this rivalry, not just in terms of American football, but sport in general and it was quite refreshing. The levels of mutual respect are evidenced by the tradition of each team standing to attention during the playing of the other's alma mater at the end of each game. For the record Notre Dame ran out winners by 50 points to 10.

☐ **Watch Boston Red Sox against the New York Yankees at Fenway Park, Boston, U.S.A.**

☐ **Attend a basketball game at Madison Square Garden, New York, U.S.A.**

☐ **Watch the baseball from an inflatable boat outside the Stadium at AT&T Park San Francisco, U.S.A.**

☐ **Eat hotdogs and drink beers at the Super Bowl.**

☐ **Spend a big fight weekend in Las Vegas, U.S.A.**

Other Sports

☑ **Experience Tyrone winning an All Ireland Football Final.** *My county, Tyrone, had never won an All Ireland Football Final until 2003 and despite my best efforts, I was unable*

The Nomad Olympics

to obtain a ticket for that historic final. However, when Tyrone again reached the final in 2005 my boss at the time was a massive Gaelic football fan, and was generous enough to provide me with a ticket for the final. To be a part of local history like that is a great thing as it is something that I believe will grow in importance with time and be looked back on as a golden age for sport in the county.

☑ **Attend an All Ireland Hurling Final.** *I always believe that the tickets for big sporting events such as finals should go to the fans that are passionate about the teams playing. I have always appreciated hurling, but in my county, Tyrone, hurling is not very popular, simply because we are not very good at it. As a result, I had never been to a hurling final before.*

On the day of the All Ireland hurling final 2009, I was walking past a pub that was emptying out as the hurling fans made their way towards Croke Park. As I made my way through the crowd, a guy was selling tickets to the stand and I could not believe my ears when he said he would sell the pair for €20. As the face value of the tickets was closer to €80 each, I snapped them up. My girlfriend and I were then treated to a fantastic game, as the Kilkenny team created history by becoming the first team since Cork, in the 1940s, to win four All Ireland Finals in a row.

☑ **Attend the Formula One Australian Grand Prix, season opener at Melbourne.** *I decided to purchase the four-day ticket, so I could take in the entire events that surround a 'F1' season opener, from the warm-ups to the event itself. The cars were so fast that I do not have a single photograph of a full car. I have many pictures of the back half of the cars and some blurry shots of the front of the cars. I recommend sitting right up the front to feel the roar of the cars in your chest as they speed past. Earplugs are recommended.*

☑ **Attend Naadam, the Nomad Olympics in Ulaanbaatar, Mongolia.** *The biggest event of the Mongolian year draws the locals together from far and wide. Dating back 800 years, Naadam has its roots in the Nomad assemblies and hunting extravaganzas of the Mongol armies lead by the great warrior horseman, Genghis Khan. There are only three events on offer, with men that resemble grizzly bears involved in the wrestling, small boys participating in the horse racing and the 'inbetweeners' involved in the archery. It really is a remarkable sight. It is believed that Genghis Khan introduced the festival to keep his men in fighting form when they weren't conquering new lands and furthering an empire that stretched from Asia, to the Middle East and across to Europe.*

☑ **Attend a Handball game in Sweden.** *A fantastic game that is very popular in northern Europe due to the skills required in the high scoring games. The best way* that I can describe it to people that have never come across this sport is that it is like indoor football, played using only hands. The sports purists probably will not agree with that assessment, but it is certainly a game that I would like to get more involved in, either as a player or spectator.

☑ **Watch Cricket in Lahore, Pakistan.** *I attended the Pakistan vs. South Africa One Day International at the Gaddafi Stadium, Lahore, watching the home side win by 25 runs. In all honestly, I spent more time admiring the passion of the Pakistan fans than the events unfolding on the field.*

☑ **Watch Baseball in Havana, Cuba.** *After much confusion as to whether a foreigner should be allowed in to watch the game (read: how much I should pay), I eventually got through the turnstiles to support Habana Industriales. Historically this is the most successful team in the National Series, which has become the main domestic competition in post-revolutionary Cuban baseball.*

I do not know much about baseball, but from what I was told, Habana Industriales are the Cuban equivalent of the New York Yankees. They attract all the best players, will sell-out in any stadium, have fans all over the country and, of course, they are detested by all opposing fans. The passion inside the stadium was similar to what I experience at European football stadiums, making

it a more superior experience than watching the LA Dodgers.

☑ **Attend the FINA World Swimming Championships.** *I attended the final day of the 13th FINA World Championships in Rome, Italy in 2009, which turned out to be a spectacular occasion. On the day, four new World Records were established and 43 global marks were set in the Italian capital. This turned out to be a record in the history of FINA. It nearly got boring by the end, as if the competitors did not set a record or do something spectacular then we were almost disappointed.*

☑ **Attend the Opening Ceremony of the Special Olympics.** *The 2003 World Games were the first Special Olympics to be held outside of America. I attended the opening ceremony in Croke Park, Dublin as Nelson Mandela officially opened the games with the President of Ireland. I was one of the 75,000 spectators and athletes in attendance that watched performances by U2, The Corrs and the largest Riverdance troupe ever assembled on one stage. Also in attendance at the opening ceremony was a random selection of Irish and international celebrities such as Muhammad Ali, Roy Keane, Arnold Schwarzenegger and Jon Bon Jovi to name but a few. It was a proud day for Ireland, as the games went on to be a resounding success.*

☑ **Attend an 'Indoor Bandy' game in Sweden.** *Developed in Sweden in the 1970s the sport is* now commonly known as Floorball, a type of floor hockey played indoors. The game that I attended had Swedish football legend Henrik Larsson playing for his local side Helsingborg against VIK Västerås. He was unsurprisingly playing as a forward using the sport as a way to keep fit during the off-season, and scored his first ever goal to win the game in added time. I even had the pleasure of meeting him after the game, something that may not have been possible during his time playing for Celtic, Barcelona or Manchester United, due to his popularity.

☑ **Bet on the Horses at the Melbourne Cup, Australia.** *This one event brings Australia to a halt. Held on the first Tuesday in November each year, the Melbourne Cup is so important that 'Cup Day' has been made a public holiday in many parts of the country. As much of a fashion parade as it is a sports event, Australians everywhere will stop everything at 3:00pm AEST to listen in or watch the race on TV. In a strange way the party atmosphere from the trackside seems to spill out throughout this huge country as champagne, canapés and large feathered hats overshadow the business of horse racing.*

☐ **Watch the Formula One Monaco Grand Prix from a Yacht.**

☐ **Watch the Men's 100 metre final at the Summer Olympics.**

☐ **Attend the Winter Olympics.**

☐ **Watch the Men's tennis final at Wimbledon, England.**

☐ **Watch the Australian Open Women's tennis final at Rod Laver Arena, Melbourne.**

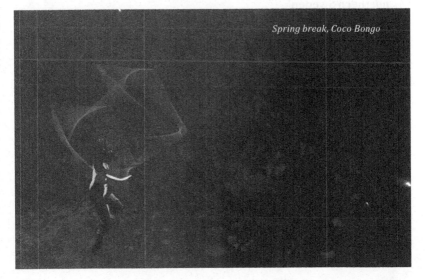

Spring break, Coco Bongo

Music

"And those who were seen dancing were thought to be insane by those who could not hear the music."
~ Friedrich Nietzsche
(Philosopher, composer and cultural critic)

Festivals

☑ **Camp over at Oxegen Festival, Co. Kildare, Ireland.** *Voted Best Major European Festival two years in a row now. It really is.*

☑ **Rezerection, Edinburgh, Scotland.**

☑ **Attend the Big Day Out festival, Sydney, Australia.**

☑ **Attend a Rockabilly gig in northern Sweden.**

☑ **Attend the NXNE (North By Northeast) Festival in Toronto, Canada.**

☐ **Party all night at Mardi Gras, New Orleans, USA.**

☐ **Feel the unique energy at a *Slane* gig, Ireland.**

☐ **Do Glastonbury. All of it.** *This is the big one, the mother of all parties.*

☐ **Chill out at Electric Picnic, Co. Laois, Ireland.**

☐ **Participate in Carnival, Rio de Janeiro, Brazil.**

☐ **Do whatever at The Burning Man festival, Black Rock Desert, Nevada, USA.** *They say that trying to explain The Burning Man festival to someone that has never been is like trying to explain colour to a blind person.*

Concerts

☑ **Play air-guitar in a field as Red Hot Chili Peppers drop the first strings of 'Scar Tissue'.**

☑ **Sit in the VIP section at a U2 gig.** *To make this occasion even better I was sitting beside the then-England football captain Alan Shearer and I got a kiss from, the then current, Miss World. The band was not too bad either.*

☑ **See the whites in the eyes of Marshall Mathers III at an Eminem gig.**

☑ **Attend a gig at the famous Fillmore Venue in San Francisco, USA.** *Black Crowes.*

☑ **Attend an intimate 'Album Release' gig.** *The Script, at the Guinness Storehouse, Dublin.*

☑ **Stand in a big crowd as Underworld unexpectedly drops the first few notes of 'Born Slippy'.**

☑ **Listen to Jesus Reina play a Stradivarius.** *I was fortunate enough to experience this in the front room of a friend's apartment in New York after I sat beside Jesus on a flight from Madrid. He was returning to New York following a sold out concert in Barcelona and as I did not know where I was going, he walked me to the apartment, came in for a drink and played us something by Bach.*

☑ **Attend 'The Cavern' in Liverpool on Beatles Day.**

☑ **Visit a real Jazz Bar in the French Quarter, New Orleans, USA.**

☑ **Line dance at a cowboy dance hall in Texas, USA.** *A group of us, from Britain and Ireland, that were staying in the same campsite, went out shopping that day in preparation for our big night at the cowboy dance hall. We did not want to stand out too much from the locals so we purchased cowboy hats, jeans, checked shirts, et cetera. It was a good idea, as we were all looking well and having a good time – apart from one guy. He thought it would be funny to wear a pink cowboy hat for the night. The super macho local boys did not find it quite a funny as he had hoped.*

☐ **Visit a bona fide Blues bar in Chicago, USA.**

☐ **Hear Andrea Bocelli and Sarah Brightman sing 'Time To Say Goodbye' in Milan.** *Leopold*

Stokowski was quoted as saying "A painter paints pictures on canvas. But musicians paint their pictures on silence." *This has never been more apt than when this pair gets together to sing.*

Parties

☑ **We Love Sundays @ Space, Ibiza.**

☑ **Cream, Liverpool, England.**

☑ **Basement Jaxx warehouse gig, Buenos Aires, Argentina.**

☑ **Sankeys Soap, Manchester, England.**

☑ **Gatecrasher @ The Republic, Sheffield, England.**

☑ **Coco Bongo, Cancun, Mexico.**

☐ **Love Parade, Berlin, Germany.**

S h o w s

"The word theatre comes from the Greeks. It means the seeing place. It is the place people come to see the truth about life and the social situation."

~ Stella Adler (Actress)

☑ **See a contortionist perform.** *I witnessed a small Mongolian girl in Ulaanbaatar do things that I cannot even describe. I had attempted to provide a description here, but it just makes it sound too unrealistic.*

☑ **David Copperfield, MGM Grand, Las Vegas, USA.**

☑ **Wicked at London's West End.**

☑ **Blood Brothers at London's West End.**

☑ **The Lord of the Rings stage show at London's West End.**

☑ **We Will Rock You at London's West End.**

☑ **Mamma Mia at London's West End.**

☑ **Cirque du Soleil, Point Depot, Dublin.** *Are these people some sort of alien race? What they are capable of is breathtaking.*

☑ **Billy Elliot at Sydney's Capitol Theatre.**

☑ **Priscilla Queen of the Desert at Star Casino, Sydney.**

☑ **Singin' In The Rain at London's West End.**

☑ **The Phantom of the Opera at London's West End.** *You would not want to be sitting behind me, beside me or in front of me at the Phantom of the Opera, as I attempt to 'sing' along. Strangely, no one has ever told me to keep quiet.*

☐ **Les Misérables at London's West End.**

☐ **The Nutcracker.**

☐ **The Russian State Ballet of Siberia.**

☐ **TED talk.**

☐ **Victoria's Secret Fashion Show.**

VII

Interaction is

what life is all about

For me it is vital that I spend time with people of all backgrounds, religions, races and social status. There is so much to learn from other people and for me to surround myself with people of one particular demographic would be like reading only the first page in the book of life.

The people that I like to be around most are the people that generate energy when they enter the room, as opposed to those who generate energy when they leave. Both types are to be found everywhere on this planet, no matter the social bracket that they are placed within.

It is said that as individuals we are the sum of the five people we spend the most time with. Being in the company of positive and accomplished individuals allows us to flourish and become more successful than if we were surrounded by individuals with a victim mentality. Reaching out and connecting with influential individuals that are successful in their field allows us the opportunity to see at first hand how they achieved their dreams and goals.

Although many of them are treated as idols throughout the world, they all started off at the bottom of the *Ladder*, exactly like the rest of us. Of the few that I have had the pleasure of meeting, I have found them to be open and honest about the skills and the mindset that propelled them to the top of their field. For most of them, their success came from hard work, determination, dedication and overcoming great difficulties. As a result, they reap the rewards and receive adulation around the world.

However, the paradox of this is that, despite all that I could learn from the successful people of the world, none of them can offer me what we all truly desire; harmony, balance, contentment. Ultimately, we desire happiness. The things that we are increasingly craving in this modern world are the traditional values that we have left behind.

Our modern world is the exact opposite of harmony and stability. Many of the world's most successful people are greatly troubled in mind. They are not at peace within themselves and many suffer from illness at a relatively early age. Sadly, many die of troubled minds long before their time.

Hence, more than the successful people of this world, given the choice, the people I wish to spend more time with is the indigenous people of our world. These people possess an inner spirit of contentment in abundant measures.

The belief systems and lifestyle of the indigenous people provide them with balance, an inner calmness and security. They are still at one with nature, with the utmost respect for Mother Earth below and the Gods above. Strange, that during better times, these were the values that we held in common and the rewards were shared and enjoyed in abundant measure.

Life is experienced through people and life is all about the people that we share our time with. The wise man knows this. He also recognises that the ones that we believe to have everything may not have very much at all. Those that seem to have nothing may hold the key to paradise just out of sight.

Much can be gained in our lives by learning from the people that have gone before us. By surrounding ourselves with people from all walks of life and studying them, we have a far greater chance of becoming a success. How you define success is up to you.

People to Meet

Any time I have been in the presence of the world's greatest people, I have always left feeling empowered. Meeting the people that have achieved so much in their chosen field is infinitely humbling, as they have 'been there and done that'. Seeing how they operate on a personal level, how they treat the people around them and the impact that they can have on individuals has always fascinated me.

When I get to meet these people, I like to just sit and chill out with them, but if I had to ask them just one question then it would be to learn something that would enhance my development as a person. Below I have included the questions I would most like to ask each of the individuals I am yet to meet, when I eventually meet them.

"Great minds discuss ideas; average minds discuss events; small minds discuss people."

~ Eleanor Roosevelt
(First Lady of the United States, 1933 to 1945)

☑ **Meet Sir Alex Ferguson.** *The great man came to the 25th anniversary celebratory dinner of the Sion Mills Manchester United Supporter Club. The dinner was held just a few months after*

Manchester United became the first English club to win the 'Treble' of Champions League, League Championship and F.A. Cup. To make the occasion even better my brother and I had our photograph taken with the European Cup, which later appeared in the clubs official magazine, 'United', which is sold all over the world.

☑ **Attend dinner with the President of Ireland.** *At the time, I was a member of Rotary Club, No.1 Europe and as part of our 100th year celebrations the President of Ireland joined us at dinner. In preparation for the event, I went out and purchased some new shoes. A great night was had by all. It was only in the morning after, when my girlfriend was tidying away my new shoes that she realised that the shoes that I wore to dinner with the President were not a matching pair! They were both from the same manufacturer and the differences were negligible, but it did not stop us from having a good laugh at my expense.*

☑ **Attend lunch with the Taoiseach.** *The Taoiseach is Ireland's Prime Minister and I had planned to ask him "What are your plans for getting the Irish economy back on track and how open are you to following Iceland's structure regarding dealing with the nation's debts?" Mr Kenny was a pleasant enough man, however, within a very short time span, he made a speech, devoured his lunch and fled out the door towards the airport to catch a* *flight to a European Union meeting in Brussels. The poor man was so busy that he never got the chance to meet me.*

☑ **Attend Mass with the Pope.** *This was the World Youth Day 2008 Mass in Sydney, Australia and the abiding memory that I have of this event was the silence. Despite there being 400,000 people in attendance, it was astonishing how little noise there was. There was no rustling, no text messages, no sneezing and no whispering, instead there was a feeling of calmness and it felt as if a 'contentment dust' had been sprinkled over the entire area.*

☑ **Chat with Bono.** *It was a wet and windy Tuesday night in Dublin and I was on my way home from class at around 10:00pm. The only thing on my mind was to get home for a hot cup of tea and some food. The streets were totally empty as I crossed the quays, apart from one man coming towards me.*

On such a night, I normally would not notice the person coming towards me, but this man was different. He was holding his collar and wearing sunglasses! "What is going on here?" I thought. As he got closer, I noticed that it was Bono from the rock group U2. Once I noticed who this strange man was, I mouthed out the word "BONO" and with that, Bono stopped for a chat. Fair play to him. We talked about nothing much for a few minutes, before we shook hands and went on our way. Decent lad.

☑ **Take Miss World out on a date.** *I did meet her once and she agreed to give me a kiss (on the cheek), but not a date. Anyway, I am ticking this one off, because I have my own Miss World now and that is better.*

☐ **Meet motivational speaker Sean Stephenson.** *Can I have a hug?*

☐ **Dance on the streets of Byron Bay with Thomas Franklin.** *What are you listening to?*

☐ **Meet President Michael D. Higgins.** *What was the best mistake you made, that provided you with the greatest learning value?*

☐ **'Chew the fat' with Irish entrepreneur, Seán Quinn.** *What are the indicators you look for in a potential business venture that you believe offer the most information in predicting sustained success?*

☐ **Drink tea with Oprah Winfrey.** *After the many people that you have helped, is there anything that I can do to help you?*

☐ **Chill out with Nick Vujicic.** *What has scared you the most?*

☐ **Wander with Annie Leibovitz.** *What cannot be captured in a photograph?*

☐ **Comb the beach with 'Sand Dancer', Peter Donnelly.** *What is your favourite part of the day: walking up to virgin sand or* *walking away from your art as the tide sweeps in?*

☐ **Wash the feet of Mātā Amrtānandamayī Devī, "The Hugging Saint."** *Who was it that filled you up with so much love?*

☐ **Attend yoga with Russell Brand.** *Which would you prefer: 1) to be humped by a donkey, with no one ever finding out, or 2) not be humped by a donkey, but everyone believed you had?*

(I read a version of this question in a football magazine a few years ago and I thought to myself, "What a bizarre and interesting question". Obviously not a question that you could just ask to anyone – I think Russell could handle it though).

☐ **Wave to the traffic in Hamilton, Bermuda with 'Mr. Happy Man', Johnny Barnes.** *What is your last thought each night?*

☐ **Have tea with Anthony Robbins.** *What single person has had the greatest impact on you?*

☐ **Shake hands with President Nelson Mandela.** *When imprisoned on Robben Island where did that inner strength come from when, forced to complete hard labour, not only did you finish your own work, but also you helped your fellow prisoners to finish theirs?*

☐ **Chill out with Sir Richard Branson.** *Fold or scrunch?*

☐ **Meet His Holiness the Dalai Lama.** *Why do poor people seem happier than the rich do?*

Indigenous People

As a general rule of thumb, the more detached a people are from Western civilisation, the more interest I have in meeting with them and learning about their ways.

"When white man found the land, Indians were running it with no taxes, no debt, plenty buffalo, plenty beaver. Women did all the work, medicine man free. Indian man spend all day hunting and fishing, all night making love to the women. White man dumb enough to think he could improve system like that?"*

~ Old Cherokee Chief

☑ **Maasai Tribe, Kenya.**
"It is impossible to find a man who has everything, but it is possible to find one who enjoys the things he has."

~ Maasai Proverb

☑ **Berbers, Morocco.**
"Knowledge is better than wealth: you have to look after wealth, knowledge looks after you."

~ Berber Proverb

Maasai Warriors

seven as a holy day, because to him all the days are God's days."

~ Ohiyesa, Charles Alexander Eastman (Santee Sioux)

☑ **Sami, Scandinavia.**
"Time is a ship that never casts anchor."

~ Sami Proverb

☑ **Australian Aborigines.**
"We cultivated our land, but in a way different from the white man. We endeavoured to live with the land; they seemed to live off it."

~ Tom Dystra (Aboriginal man)

☑ **The Uru People, Lake Titicaca.**
"Frogs do not drink up the pond in which they live."

~ Incan Proverb

☑ **Pygmies, Uganda.**
"Happiness can grow from only a little contentment."

~ Pygmy Proverb

☑ **Māori, New Zealand.**
"Turn your face to the sun and the shadows fall behind you."

~ Māori Proverb

☑ **The Orthodox Jews, Jerusalem.**
"A bird that you set free may be caught again, but a word that escapes your lips will not return."

~ Jewish Proverb

☐ **The Amish, USA.** *Not indigenous by definition, but certainly a group that I would like to spend some time with due to their reluctance to use modern technology.*

"Bibles that are coming apart usually belong to people who are not."

~ Amish Proverb

☑ **The Himba, Namibia.**
"Don't start your farming with cattle, start it with people."

~ Himba Proverb

☑ **The Navajo Indians, USA.**
"Whenever, the course of a daily hunt, the hunter comes upon a scene that is strikingly beautiful, or sublime; a black thundercloud with the rainbow's glowing arch above the mountain, a white waterfall in the heart of a green gorge, a vast prairie tinged with the blood-red of the sunset; he pauses for an instant in the attitude of worship. He sees no need for setting apart one day in

Patrick Hamilton Walsh

People Watch

It is like bird watching except it is with people, as you observe how they act, dress and relate to the immediate environment. It is not like voyeurism, it is simply the act of observing people and their interactions, to get a feel for the essence and rhythm of the surrounding community. The more crowded the area and the more friends that you are people watching with, then the more interesting it is. It is a really fascinating and fun way to spend a few hours whilst chilling out. For me it usually consists of ordering a nice cup of tea and sitting back to watch the show.

"People travel to faraway places to watch, in fascination, the kind of people they ignore at home."
~ Dagobert D. Runes (Philosopher and author)

☑ **Santa Monica boardwalk, Los Angeles, USA.** *From Hollywood babes and surfer dudes to lost hippies and muscle men, this is one of the great people watching locations on the planet. With an average of 340 days of sunshine a year, this is a guaranteed freak-fest, as the people of Los Angeles gravitate towards the beach on a daily basis to escape the heat of the city. I personally enjoy sitting back and counting the many different inventions that the locals use to propel themselves along the boardwalk.*

☑ **The French Concession, Shanghai, China.** *'New money' does its thing as it attempts to be as 'Western' as possible.*

☑ **Ipanema Beach, Rio de Janeiro, Brazil.** *Ipanema is the cool and trendy area of this thriving city, offering a chilled out atmosphere, great restaurants and a busy nightlife. In addition to this, the legendary Ipanema beach, immortalized in many songs and films, offers good surf and an assortment of people. The coastline is split into areas known as Postos, with Ipanema nestled in between Arpoador Beach at Posto 7 and Leblon Beach at Posto 12.*

The different sections of society will gather around a particular Posto. The

Yoyogi Park, Tokyo

beautiful people hang around Posto 7, gays and lesbians have their own beach spot at Posto 8, with 'potheads' at Posto 9. I honestly cannot remember the societal groups that 'own' the other Postos, but after spending a few minutes on the beach, it will soon become obvious to you when you visit.

☑ **Nevsky Prospekt, St Petersburg, Russia.** *Old Russian men struggle to get out of the best cars that money can buy as their beautiful young lady friends, in high heels and short skirts, scamper off into the designer stores to spend their money. This is 'new money' at its worst and it is great to watch.*

☑ **Yoyogi Park, Tokyo, Japan.** *If there was ever a 'People Watching*

World Championship', this is where it would be held. Yoyogi Park is a gathering place in Tokyo for people to play music, practice martial arts and walk their decorated dogs, amongst many other activities. Outside the entrance to the park, there are the Gothic Lolita girls whose dress emphasizes Victorian-style girl's clothing in order to imitate the look of Victorian porcelain dolls. Hanging around the gates of the park, I found the Sweet Lolita girls wearing more childish pastel-coloured clothes, with lots of lace, bows and ribbons attached to their dresses.

As I entered the park gates, I was confronted with the rockabilly groups performing their 1950s dance moves. Think Japanese men and women

dressed up in an exaggerated form of clothing from the movie Grease. Next, there are dudes doing tricks on BMX and to the right of them, on the grass, there are sword wielding Samurai Warriors (do not ask to touch their sword). Then there are the famous Harajuku girls who take their inspiration from Gwen Stefani music videos. Or is it the other way around?

Throughout the park there are people dressed in many fashion styles including Decora, Kogal, Ganguro, Wamono, Second-Hand Fashion, Cyber Fashion and Avant-garde, to name but a few. Each will be more extravagant than the next. I could attempt to explain them all, but I could never do these people justice. The most unique of all are those in Anime Fashion. This group choose to dress like a character from their favourite animated cartoon. Think human-size Pokémon standing with "Free Hugs" signs in their... em... paws! If you are ever fortunate enough to be in Tokyo on a Sunday morning then be sure to visit Yoyogi Park. You will not regret it.

☑ **Manly Beach, Sydney, Australia.** *Situated in Sydney's Northern Beaches, Manly is arrived at after taking a ferry from the city's famous Circular Quay. Bondi is the beach where the tourists gravitate towards, but Manly is the beach where the beautiful people of Sydney pout, pose and strut. The waves are not too bad either.*

☑ **Fifth Avenue, New York, USA.** *This major passageway in the centre of Manhattan is lined with prestigious shops and is consistently ranked among the most expensive shopping streets in the world. In turn, it attracts some of the wealthiest people on the planet into the area and who does not like to watch the habits of the rich and famous up close?*

☐ **South Beach, Miami, Florida, USA.**

☐ **Dubrovnik, Croatia.**

☐ **Camden, London, England.**

VIII

To Dream is
to create new worlds

T o dream is to live in a world of wonder. Take a minute to sit back and put yourself in this position: You have a bank account and every single day at midnight that account is credited with €86,400. At the end of each day, at one minute to midnight, all the unspent money in that account is wiped away by the bank, so that it can re-credit the account with another €86,400.

It is a 'use it or lose it' agreement. Whatever you do not spend wisely you lose forever. So, what would you do? Would you sit back and just stare at your account and let the money go unspent? It is my guess that you would withdraw every single penny and go out and fill the day with new experiences that make you happy and leave you fulfilled.

Now imagine that this was not just another daydream and that this bank was real. In fact, this bank is real. It is called the *'Life Time Bank'*. Every midnight we are credited with 86,400 seconds and at the end of each day, whatever time we have wasted is written-off forever. No balance is carried over, no overdraft is provided and no interest is earned. Every second is precious.

Charles Richards understood the value of making the full use of time when he stated, *"Don't be fooled by the calendar. There are only as many days in the year as you make use of. One man gets only a week's value out of a year while another man gets a full year's value out of a week."* He was right. Not every hour is created equally. Nor is every day, week, month or year. It is up to us to make the most of our time and to fit in to our lives all the great experiences that we desire.

We must live in the now, based on the time lodged into our account for today. We must invest each second in the things that really matter. We are encouraged to invest in happiness, as a day filled with hearty laughs is a day well spent. It is advisable to spend our seconds on love; otherwise, we will have no one to share our time with. If we do not spend time on our health, then we may not receive any credit to use tomorrow.

The clock is always ticking. With each passing second, we are closer to running out of credit. All that we can do is make the most of today, have a smile on our faces, make a difference and spend each second living the life of our dreams. We all dream to experience the best of everything that this world has to offer and I am no different. I want to spend my seconds travelling in luxury and staying in the best accommodation so I can sample the finest foods as I overlook the world's fabulous locations.

To dream is to create wonderful new worlds in which we can live, in the hope that our dreams may one day become a reality. However, it is vital that we treasure each of the 86,400 seconds that we are credited with every day and spend them doing something special. Therefore, make today special enough to be worthy of our precious time. Bear in mind that time waits for no one. Yesterday is gone. Tomorrow may never come. Today is our greatest gift... I suppose that is why we named it *the present*.

H i g h   L i v i n g

"As long as you're going to be thinking anyway, think big!"
~ Donald Trump (Entrepreneur)

☑ **Own season tickets at Old Trafford.** *When I sat down at the age of sixteen to consider my dream life, this was the first thing that popped into my head. Having my own seat at Old Trafford and being able to go and watch my team at any time was my ultimate dream at that time. Although it is not what many would consider 'high living', for me this was a dream that I just had to achieve. I realised pretty early in life that I was never going to play for Manchester United, so to watch them live every week at Old Trafford was the next best thing. It was a great time to be a Manchester United fan, as they won everything possible during that time including; Club World Cup, Champions League, League Championship, F.A. Cup, League Cup and the Community Shield.*

☑ **Own a Porsche before I am 30.** *When I set this objective at the age of sixteen, I had never even seen a Porsche, apart from on the television and in books. Yet, I believed that this objective would be within my grasp when I got to the top of my three-step Ladder.*

Once I had the money gathered up to purchase the Porsche, I flew to England with my father to collect it. When the money was paid and all the paper work was complete, I put the key in the ignition and as the engine behind me roared into life, I felt massive satisfaction. I had achieved a goal that few others would even set, but what made it even better was that I knew that my father, in the passenger seat beside me, was so proud as we drove that car out onto the highways of England.

The reason that I wanted to own a Porsche whilst I was still in my twenties was that I wanted to be young and fresh as I drove around in it, as it always seemed to be older men in Porsches. In order to obtain the funds to buy my dream car, I was quite lucky that a few investments that I had made had all came good around the same time. Although, I was quite lucky when I sold it also, as I made a nice little profit on it. There are not too many people that make a profit on the sale of a car, but that just goes to show how nice of a car it really was.

Despite the sense of satisfaction that derived from owning a Porsche at that time in my life, once I had completed all my Professional exams and training, I had no hesitation in putting it up for sale. It was time for me to go and explore the world as a backpacker – I did not need stuff anymore, no matter how nice it was. The bizarre thing about this was that people around me could not believe that I would "give up my nice stuff" for a life of wanderlust.

In fact, I was more than happy to sell up and live free, because what

I noticed about owning much-sought-after material items is that you do not actually own them at all – they own you. The more stuff we have, the more trapped we are. Too many of us are addicted to the 'stuff' we own. The most popular excuse I hear from people who want to travel the world, but think that they cannot, is that they have to wait until they have paid off their car/house/laptop or whatever. I am proud of the fact that I was able to sell up and walk away from my stuff.

☑ **Take an around the world multi-continent flight.** *In 2008, I had the pleasure of flying around the world along the following route: Australia – North America – Europe – Asia – Australia. My next around the world multi-continent flight will hopefully include South America and Africa as well.*

☑ **Fly First Class.** *On a flight to Bangkok, I was fortunate enough to be awarded a free upgrade to fly First Class on Thai Airways, simply because I was cheeky enough to ask for it. As I sat in First Class making the most of the fabulous service on offer, all I could do was smile. Everything I was offered I accepted. Everything. However, the next time I travelled by air following that, I was back sitting in the economy seats, which prior to that I always enjoyed. Now it almost felt like I could have been on a 'chicken bus' travelling through Guatemala. If I hadn't seen such riches, I could live with being poor.*

☐ **Have a bespoke suit made for me at Saville Row, London.**

☐ **Own an Aston Martin before I turn 40.** *In a total contradiction to what I have just written above, about our 'stuff' trapping us, I have to admit that I do believe that many of us are addicted to our 'stuff' and I see evidence of it everywhere. However, I do not plan to live the rest of my life sitting on the back of a horse and cart, dressed in an old sack. I do like nice things and given the choice between shopping in a luxury store or in the bargain basement, I would choose the luxury items.*

As I mature, I have an increasing appreciation for the finer things in life. At the moment I do not own any car, never mind an Aston Martin, but I look forward to repeating the feeling of satisfaction that I got when I first drove my Porsche out on to that highway. However, like the Porsche I will ensure that I do not grow too attached to the Aston Martin or any of the other 'stuff'.

☐ **Sail around the world on the cruise ship 'The World of Residensea'.**

☐ **Charter a private jet.**

☐ **Own a house by the beach in a warm climate.** *I really love the thought of being able to walk around in bare feet all the time and the biggest clothing issue I have is the colour of the t-shirt I will wear if I have to go into town. Only people that live in locations where it rains all the time will appreciate this small luxury.*

Dine

The earliest memory I have of eating out was the celebration meal that I shared with my wider family following my First Holy Communion service. I got to sit at the top of the table and for dessert I was allowed to order as much ice cream and jelly as my stomach could handle. Overall I managed to wolf down six portions of ice cream. I really do not know how, as a seven year old, my stomach could handle so much food, considering that the dessert menu is something that, as a fully grown man, I am now forced to pass on whilst out dining.

Ever since that day, I have always thoroughly enjoyed eating out. I really appreciate the good food and great service that is to be found in the restaurants that have turned one of life's most basic requirements of survival into an art form. It is thanks to these passionate men and women that good food and good wine, shared with good friends in good surroundings, equates to a good time.

"One cannot think well, love well, sleep well, if one has not dined well."

~ Virginia Woolf
(Modernist writer)

☑ **Guillaume at Bennelong, Sydney, Australia.** *From the day I learned that there was a restaurant nestled under the iconic sails of the Sydney Opera House, this was the restaurant that I had been most looking forward to eating in. However, the best thing about the evening was the commanding views on offer of Sydney Harbour. I felt a little bit let down by the cuisine and the service.*

☑ **Gordon Ramsay restaurant at The Ritz-Carlton Powerscourt, Co. Wicklow, Ireland.** *Gordon Ramsay has been awarded 13 Michelin stars to date (he holds twelve at the time of writing) and after dining in his restaurant at The Ritz-Carlton Powerscourt, I finally got to experience for myself what all the fuss was about. Great food, friendly knowledgeable staff and fair prices in a wonderful setting, combine to offer a magnificent dining experience. This restaurant has not received a Michelin star yet, but it may be the one that brings Mr. Ramsay back up to 13.*

☑ **El Avion, Manuel Antonio, Costa Rica.** *This restaurant is unique as it is set around the old Fairchild C-123 cargo plane that was a part of one of the biggest scandals of President Reagan's Administration. In the 1980s a bizarre network of arms sales to Iran was set up, designed to win the release of US hostages held in Lebanon and raise money to fund the Nicaraguan "Contras." With the help of the CIA, the Contras* purchased several items, including two C-123 cargo planes, which would set off from a secret airstrip on an American-owned ranch in northwest Costa Rica.

In October 1986, a US C-123 cargo plane was shot down over Nicaragua, which set in motion an incredible chain of cover-ups and lies that mushroomed into one of the biggest scandals in American political history, the Iran-Contra Affair. As a result of this, the cargo operation was suspended and one of the C-123s purchased by the Contras has been retired to less risqué endeavours.

Now sitting on a cliff overlooking the sea and serving as a restaurant and bar, I had the privilege of eating wonderful food under its wings at sunset before retiring to the fuselage pub for drinks. This restaurant may not have any Michelin stars but this is an experience that I am not likely to forget in a hurry.

☐ **Chapter One, Dublin, Ireland.** I lived 100 metres from one of the world's finest restaurants and I have never been over for dinner. I really need to make a booking and sample some of the great food that this restaurant has on offer.

☐ **Restaurant Patrick Guilbaud, Dublin, Ireland.** This internationally acclaimed Irish restaurant has been a centre of fine dining in Dublin since 1981 and holds the prestigious title of being Ireland's only two star Michelin restaurant.

☐ **Al Muntaha restaurant, Burj Al Arab, Dubai.** The name Al Muntaha is Arabic for 'The Ultimate' or 'The Top'. It certainly lives up to its name, as it rests 200 metres above sea level on top of the world famous Burj Al Arab hotel. In addition to the fabulous surroundings within the hotel, it offers unparalleled views of 'The Palm' and 'The World' man-made Islands below as you enjoy your dinner.

☐ **Al Mahara restaurant, Burj Al Arab, Dubai.** Just getting to this restaurant is a truly memorable experience as a three-minute submarine voyage from the hotel lobby is required. It is these types of locations that fit perfectly within this section of the book, because someone had a dream in relation to this, which ultimately became a reality.

Taste

One of the things that I have noticed about travelling around the world and sampling as many varieties of food as possible is that meats, fruits and vegetables do not like to travel. It appears that, just like people, food gets jet-lagged and seasick. If you want to sample food and drink at its best then go to the source, I say.

"Seize the moment. Remember all those women on the 'Titanic' who waved off the dessert cart."
~ Erma Bombeck (Journalist and columnist)

☑ **Sushi in Tokyo, Japan.** *I got to experience eating sushi right off the boats down at the docks in Tokyo. The surroundings may not be perfect but this is the best sushi on the planet. Do not take my word for it, go and check it out when you visit this great city. After sampling sushi in Tokyo, it just does not seem to measure up anywhere else.*

☑ **Cajun Chicken in New Orleans, USA.** *Trust me, nobody makes better Cajun Chicken than the Cajun people deep in the swamps of Louisiana. No real surprise there.*

☑ **Steak in Argentina.** *It was as good as people say it should be, but if I am honest, the best steak I have ever had was in Kathmandu, Nepal.*

☑ **Haggis in Scotland.** *Most people are aware of Haggis as the national dish of Scotland, but I am always surprised by how few people know what it actually consists of. Haggis is a kind of savoury pudding containing sheep's pluck. The pluck is a nice way of describing the sheep's heart, liver and lungs, which are traditionally encased within the sheep's stomach. Then after adding some oatmeal, spices, suet and onion the mixture is left to simmer for up to three hours before being served up. Decide for yourself if you are still interested.*

☑ **Fried insects in Thailand.** *Do not make the same mistake as I did and think that they cannot be that bad. They are.*

☑ **Airag in Mongolia.** *Airag is the traditional national beverage of Mongolia, made from fermented mare's milk. The most important animal to the Mongols is the horse, with the mare's milk maintaining a special status in the country.*

☑ **Guinea pig in Peru.** *Known as "Cuy," guinea pig is a national delicacy in Peru, but not a dish I would recommend. When I felt the eyes of the Guinea Pig pop in my mouth, I knew I had gone too far.*

☑ **Pizza in New York, USA.** *Massive slices of pizza that I could eat on the go, which tasted delicious, filled me up and were really cheap. It is the perfect NYC food.*

☑ **Fufu in Zimbabwe.** *Fufu looks like mashed potatoes, but is actually* a thick paste that not only serves as a food but also as a utensil. It is made by boiling the roots of starchy vegetables, before pounding and grinding the boiled roots in a bucket until the required consistency is reached. As I sat down to dinner with a local family in Zimbabwe, I was instructed to wash my hands before taking a scoop of fufu no bigger than a ping-pong ball with my right hand.

I was then shown how to make an indentation in the fufu, to use it as a spoon and scoop up the accompanying stew before finally swallowing the fufu itself. I made the mistake of trying to chew on the fufu, which the family frowned upon. It did not taste so good, so I was more than happy to wash it back. I was given quite a small portion that I assumed would work as a starter. In fact, fufu is so filling, I was struggling to finish the portion I was given.

☑ **Hákarl in Iceland.** *Kæstur hákarl, to give it its full name, is Icelandic for "fermented shark" which is a nice way of saying "rotten shark". There is a reason why they probably do not sell this in your local supermarket or restaurant and that reason is simply because it does not taste very good.*

☑ **Pasta in Milan, Italy.** *Unfortunately, the worst Italian food that I have ever tasted was when I was travelling through Italy. I obviously was going to the wrong restaurants... every single time!*

So much for my 'go to the source' theory.

☑ **Natural ice cream in New Zealand.** *The freshest fruit plucked straight from the trees combined with dairy cream from cows that graze on organic pastures, frozen, rolled into a ball, put on top of a cone and sold with a smile so that my mouth could have a party on that hot day.*

☑ **Reindeer in the ICEHOTEL, Sweden.** *This was a really delicious dinner, which was helped significantly by the restaurant and the setting. I just know that somehow this dinner would not taste as good anywhere else.*

☐ **Dog in Vietnam.** *I have grown to have great affection for dogs over the past few years, so when I witnessed a table full of dogs being chopped up by a really angry woman, I decided that I just could not go through with this.*

Dog for dinner in Vietnam

S t a y

"Of course great hotels have always been social ideas, flawless mirrors to the particular societies they service."
~ Joan Didion (Author)

☑ **Capsule Hotel, Tokyo, Japan.** My hotel room measured one metre x one metre x two metres and was made of reinforced plastic, with the capsules being stacked three deep. You may think that this is what it would be like to sleep inside a refrigerator in a white goods scrap yard. However, these capsules are really comfortable. Inside the sleeping capsule is every amenity you could possibly require; adjustable lighting, television, radio, alarm clock, privacy shutter and even a panic button. Not only was it was an intriguing experience but I also had a great nights sleep.

☑ **Hotel de Sal, Salar de Uyuni, Bolivia.** Salar de Uyuni is famous as the world's largest salt flat standing 3,656 metres above sea level and covering an area of 10,582 kilometres^2. It is an expanse of white for as far as the eye can see and somewhere in the middle of it is one of this planet's most unique, if not most resourceful hotels; Hotel de Sal, or in English, The Salt Hotel. The clue is in the name here.

This is the only hotel on the planet made entirely from salt. The walls, roof, beds, tables, chairs, bar and everything else is made entirely of salt. Well everything apart from the one and only toilet. Whilst staying there I had a great time, despite the whole setting seeming more like the place where the 'baddie' hangs out in a James Bond movie scene than something you find in one of the most desolate locations in the poorest country in South America.

☑ **The Ritz-Carlton, Powerscourt, County Wicklow, Ireland.** This is the perfect hotel experience. From the friendly doorman welcoming us through the doors, to the cheery reception staff thanking us for choosing their hotel as we left. The suite we were allocated was incredible. We were provided with a free upgrade and despite the room being large enough to host a dinner party, it was cosy enough to feel homely (this is coming from a man that has in the past asked to be downgraded due to the room being too big and unwelcoming).

However, as fantastic as the suites and service are, they are not the best part of this hotel. We were afforded a glimpse of what sets this hotel apart from the others when we stepped out onto the balcony that ran for 25 metres around our suite. Within clear view of the iconic Sugarloaf Mountain, the Ritz-Carlton, Powerscourt is situated amidst one of the most scenic and historic estates in Ireland. Located in the mountains of Wicklow on four kilometres^2, the resort's tranquil countryside location traces its origins back to the 12th century, falling into the possession of the le

Poer (Power) family, from which the estate takes its name.

It was the le Poer family who built a castle here in the year 1300. As it did then, the estate still offers the ideal opportunity to explore the great outdoors and pursue many of the activities favoured by the country gentry such as horse riding, fishing and shooting. However, just to wander through the trees and sit by the river was sufficient to keep a look of contentment on my face. The Ritz-Carlton, Powerscourt seem to have achieved the perfect balance when it comes to getting away for a few days of rest and respite.

☑ **ICEHOTEL, Jukkasjärvi, Sweden.** As ICEHOTEL is rebuilt every year (for obvious reasons), it would be more informative to explain that I stayed in ICEHOTEL 21. It was an experience utterly unlike any other and one that I would highly recommend. The one question that everyone has asked me ever since has been, "Is everything made

of ice?" Yes, absolutely everything is made from ice.

All the rooms and suites are made from solid blocks of carved ice, every piece of furniture in the hotel is made from ice, the IceBar (including the drinking glasses) are all made of ice and even the bed I slept on was a massive slab of ice. As the temperature in my room was hovering at around minus five degrees Celsius, I was provided with furs to lay my ICEHOTEL sleeping bag on and all night I was as snug as a bug in a rug. It was an enthralling experience and one that I would most definitely recommend.

☑ **Matchbox: The Concept Hostel, Singapore.** 'Flashpacking' is the hottest word in the travel lexicon and nowhere matches this description better than this 'Concept Hostel'. With its pod-style bed cabins and designer touches splattered in bright colours throughout the building, Matchbox delivers above and beyond the usual promises. As

Arktikas Suite by AnnaSofia Mååg @ ICEHOTEL

soon as we entered the building, we were greeted by big smiles from Cass and Mag, the dynamic owners, and that feeling of warmth and welcome was evident throughout. Situated in the middle of the chic Ann Siang Hill heritage district of Chinatown, this hostel has raised the bar for hostels all around the world. This place is way too cool for me to list its great offerings here. That would only spoil the surprise.

☐ **Hotel Imperial, Vienna, Austria.** I have always wanted to spend a weekend in a historic and storied hotel. I would fly into a great European city, book a suite and not leave the confines of the building during my entire stay; I would just hang around the hotel, enjoying the facilities on offer and open myself to the experience of a few nights of classic atmosphere. With such a chequered past, I believe that the exclusive five-star Hotel Imperial in the heart of Vienna would be the perfect place to experience this.

☐ **Burj Al Arab, Dubai.** Standing on a custom made artificial island and designed to mimic the sail of a ship I present to you "the world's only seven-star hotel." This hotel is all about luxury. When I visited (I didn't stay), I was told that everything that looks gold is solid gold. Despite the Burj Al Arab being the world's second tallest hotel, it holds only 28 double-story floors that accommodate 202 bedroom suites. The smallest suite occupies an area of 169 metres^2 with the largest covering a massive 780

metres^2. Apparently room prices range from approximately €950 to €25,000 per night.

☐ **The Library Hotel, New York, USA.** I really like the thought of this unique hotel and I am delighted that people were willing to invest to allow such a great idea to become a reality. The Library Hotel is aimed at travellers with a passion for culture and individual expression. There are ten floors at the hotel, with each being dedicated to one of the ten major categories of the Dewey Decimal System: The Arts and Religion, General Knowledge, History, Languages, Literature, Math & Science, Philosophy, Social Sciences and Technology. If I had the choice, I would stay on the Philosophy floor. What floor would you choose?

☐ **Utter Inn, Västerås, Sweden.** What looks like a typical Swedish red house floating on the surface of Lake Mälaren is actually the entrance to this underwater accommodation. It apparently provides amazing views of the underwater world. I suppose that the success of this experience will depend on the transparency of the water at the time of the stay, otherwise it may be like staying in a low-laying hotel room that has a think fog outside the window.

☐ **V8 Hotel, Stuttgart, Germany.** This is the ultimate theme hotel for car-lover's and mechanics, with the design inspired by the world of automobiles. The hotel is located within Böblingen's Meilenwerk, an exclusive car museum in the centre of Germanys international hub for car dealers. The luxurious rooms are fitted out with everything that you would find in an enthusiasts garage with guests given the opportunity to sleep in everything from a Mercedes to a Morris Minor.

☐ **Bellagio, Las Vegas, USA.** Inspired by the villages of Europe, Bellagio is the ultimate Las Vegas hotel experience. Located in the heart of 'the strip', this hotel overlooks an eight-acre Mediterranean-blue lake in which fountains perform a magnificent ballet choreographed to music and lights. The outdoor pool area resembles a Mediterranean villa for those that like to lounge in the desert sun. Combine this with its in-house world-class art gallery, Cirque du Soleil performances and great nightclubs and it offers an all in one experience. I think that covers it... oh yeah, it also has a decent casino downstairs.

☐ **Quinta Real Zacatecas, San Pedro, Mexico.** One of the world's most unusual settings for a hotel, Quinta Real Zacatecas is built into the restored grandstand of the San Pedro bullfighting ring, which was inaugurated in 1866 and conserves much of its original, colonial architecture. This unique hotel preserves the character and beauty of the original structure so ingeniously that the restoration project received the International Architectural Award just after it opened. Rooms are set around the

bullring, which has been converted into a beautiful patio, paved with cobblestones and landscaped with an abundance of flowers. Not to worry; the San Pedro witnessed its last bullfight here in 1975.

☐ **La Montana Magica Lodge, Huilo Huilo, Chile.** When it comes to designing a hotel, it takes a pretty special mind to conceive the idea of a hotel built within a man-made volcano covered in rainforest moss and vines, that spews water instead of lava. Then to locate this hotel within a Biological Reserve that consists of 600 kilometres^2 of lush, teeming flora and fauna and make it accessible only via a Monkey Bridge, is really special. Now that is the kind of hotel where I want to rest my head, as I drift off to the sound of the waterfall rushing down over my window.

☐ **Hotel Kakslauttanen, Saariselkä, Finland.** Deep in the vast wilderness of Finnish Lapland, surrounded by towering pines is where you can find 20 futuristic domed, thermal glass "igloos." It is a simple matter of clearing the snow from the entrance, climbing in to the snug yet spacious 'room' and allowing the spirit of the arctic winter to do its thing. With the northern lights becoming more prevalent until this cycle's peak in 2015, there cannot be a better place for me to witness this great spectacle than from this almost surreal setting.

IX

Exploring the Weird and Wonderful is vital to expanding our minds

Some people appear to achieve success relatively easy, whilst others must work very hard to reach their ambitions. Then there are those that never fulfil their desires. Why is that? It obviously has nothing to do with physical characteristics; otherwise, the most physically perfect people would also be the most successful. The reason, therefore, has to be the mind.

Increasing numbers of people are of the belief that it is the thoughts in our mind that determine the lives we live. It is our thoughts that create our reality. Thoughts become things.

Based on this, I realised a few years ago that my current position in life was a result of all my past thoughts. Likewise, my future position would be the result of my current thoughts. Thus, I understood that I had to change my thoughts so that they would reflect the future that I wished for myself and I summed it up with this little saying; *if I always think what I have always thought, then I will always get what I have always got.*

I have many desires in life that I wish to obtain and I know that my old way of thinking will have to change in order for me to achieve them. Every day I now make a conscious effort to be flexible in my thoughts and not to stand rigid to any set of beliefs. I feel, at this stage of my life, that it is most beneficial if I am open to all new information and practices that come my way. I can then ponder on them.

Then, each day I will conclude whether this new information or way of doing things is beneficial to me and if it is I will make it part of my life for the foreseeable future. Alternatively, I will discard it and move on. The worst thing I could do, would be to build barriers around me and live in a bubble of strict beliefs, filtering everything that does not agree with those particular beliefs.

Following this approach, over the past few years, I have got involved with many activities that previously I had considered 'weird'. Of course, I use this approach throughout all areas of my life, but I am now more willing to open up to new practices and trains of thought that I otherwise would have avoided. Maybe there is something to be learned from ancient cultures and past practices. This is equally true of innovative new ways and approaches. Unless, I give it a go, I will never know.

Consider this: whom would you rather spend an evening with; a person that regards them self as 'normal' and always follows the crowd and has 'tunnel vision', or someone that has lived a life of vast experiences and has an expansive and open mind? Personally, I would much rather spend time with the latter. It may be a wonderful thing to be regarded as 'weird'. I certainly do not wish to be 'normal'.

The Weird and Wonderful

"The most beautiful thing we can experience is the mysterious. It is the source of all true art and all science. He to whom this emotion is a stranger, who can no longer pause to wonder and stand rapt in awe, is as good as dead: his eyes are closed."
~ Albert Einstein (Theoretical physicist)

☑ **Learn to interpret body language.** *Body language is a form of mental and physical non-verbal communication. It is estimated that as little as seven percent of communication is verbal. Non-verbal communication consists of facial expressions, eye movements, body posture, touch and gestures, which humans submit and translate almost entirely subconsciously. It is said that the body never lies.*

☑ **Get hypnotised for a reason that will lead to my greater good.** *I was lucky enough to attend a talk by Tom Ryan at a Conscience Living meet-up in Dublin, when he talked about how hypnosis can help with the Buteyko approach to breathing and in turn cure the 'problem' of Asthma. Within a week, I was lying back on a chair with Tom talking sweetly to me – I never thought I would say that.*

☑ **Have a vortex cleansing performed.** *Over time, our Chakras can get clogged up to such an extent that energy no longer flows smoothly through them. They are just like a drainage pipe that fills up with mud and litter, preventing water from seeping through as effectively as it once did. When the Chakras get into this state then, as you would do with a clogged pipe, you should go and get it cleansed. After my friend Shaughna Whelan had performed this cleansing, I felt as if a massive weight had been lifted from my shoulders. In fact, I felt so good that I could have tapped danced in wellington boots.*

☑ **Have my aura read.** *An aura is the electro-magnetic energy field that is believed to surround every living thing, including plants and animals. They contain information about what is going on within the living being at a deeper level, for instance, communication, truthfulness, emotions, et cetera. These skills have developed so far that it is now possible to have an aura captured by a special camera and have a reading performed from that.*

☑ **Search for UFO's around Roswell, New Mexico, USA.** *It was a great experience to spend some time in that UFO obsessed town, but unfortunately, I did not get to see any Unidentified Flying Objects on my visit to the area. Nevertheless, just hanging around the downtown was pretty cool, as everything has a UFO theme to it, including the local Wal-Mart and McDonalds. They also have very interesting streetlights there, with alien-heads being used* as lamps to illuminate the downtown streets.

☑ **Meet a Witch.** *This one came unexpectedly. As we were about to board a Zodiac to take us from our* ship onto the Antarctic continent, I noticed that one of the older women in the group had her life jacket on incorrectly, so I tapped her on the shoulder with an offer to help. As I tapped her she jumped like a bolt of

*Roswell, New Mexico
– near Area 51*

lightening had just went through her. I did not know what had just happened. Thankfully, she had a big smile on her face as she turned around to face me.

Later, when we were back onboard the ship she came over and told me she was a Witch from Cuba (as you do) and proceeded to inform me about what she had learned about me from the tap on the shoulder. Some of the information she offered was very accurate and she went on to provide me with some advice about my future. She was a very interesting woman indeed.

☑ **Research numerology.** This is the study of numbers to help determine and reflect a persons talents, characteristics, motivations and path in life, with experts able to determine the dates of key events in people lives. From research, I have learned that I am a 'Four'. The characteristics of 'Fours' are productivity, punctuality, dependability and obedience. They believe in effort and are goal-oriented, but their goals are simple and down to earth. As a result, they can be the perfect employees, but they do not tend to excel in social environments.

Therefore, it would appear that a 'Four' is the stereotypical accountant, based on this. After learning this I wonder if it is possible to change number, because when I look back over my life I would say that I used to be all of these things, but I would be the first to admit that in my development, I have lost some of these characteristics. After reading down this page, would anyone say that my goals are still 'simple and down to earth'?

☐ **Have a past life regression performed.** This is a technique used to recover memories of past lives or incarnations, typically undertaken in pursuit of a spiritual experience. Most people have this regression performed to examine the experiences that form the roots of their current fears and phobias in order for those fears to disappear. It is becoming increasingly popular with it even being featured on the Oprah Winfrey Show.

☐ **Have a psychic look into my future.** Throughout history, kings, queens and leaders valued the counsel of the wise and requested their expertise often. These great people knew of the existence of the "X factor," that something invisible that can be used to promote or restrain growth and success in the future. The people that they confided in are what we know today as psychics.

A psychic is a person with the ability to perceive information that others cannot, through using extrasensory perception. Times have changed and today these skills seem to be automatically frowned upon and the facilitators cast off as frauds and con-people. However, as I move through life I believe that there are many people with these abilities, yet because they do not want to be deemed 'weird' they keep their gift suppressed. I think that being able to look into the future is a skill that is worth having for many reasons.

☐ **Have a palm reading.** This is something that we always used to mess around with as kids, pretending to read each other's palms, but I would love to come across someone that claims to be proficient in this.

☐ **Have an Akashic Record Reading.** Akashic Records are energetic records of all the events, thoughts, feelings and beliefs that have ever occurred and contain all possibilities yet to happen. The term Akasha derives from Sanskrit and means "hidden library" referring to a secret hall of records (the Akashic Records) with each soul's "Book of Life" stored there.

☐ **Have my astrological chart made up.** There is more to this than the twelve little boxes spewing generic information in the daily newspapers under the word 'horoscope', which are usually not accurate and just for fun. Astrology is an ancient art form, which is said to be very mathematical and precise in its original and complete form, with Star Signs making up only one aspect of astrology. For a complete reading, the exact time and place of birth is required and it is believed to provide very accurate information into the essence of the person.

☐ **Develop my intuition.** Intuition is the language that the Universe uses to guide us. To develop intuition we must simply learn to listen out for this guidance. In the beginning, intuition will develop out of feeling and knowledge and will occur in the context of relationships. However, as we tune in to its presence, even in the subtlest of ways, we will bring it to the foreground. I call it, 'listening to my heart'. I have been intentionally developing my intuition and listening to my heart for a few years now, but as this will be a continuous development process. I still have quite a way to go.

☐ **Stand in the middle of a crop circle.** Also referred to as crop formations, because they are not always circular in shape, they were first reported as appearing in the 1970s in the south of England. Documented cases have substantially increased from the 1970s with over ten thousand crop circles being reported in 26 countries since then. 90 percent of crop circles have been found in southern England with many appearing near ancient monuments, such as Stonehenge. One study found that, close to half of all circles found in the UK in 2003 were located within a 15 kilometre radius of Avebury, with them all appearing during the summer months.

Thanatourism Locations

Thanatourism has always existed because people have always had an interest in the pain and suffering of others. The people of Rome derived great pleasure in coming to watch the Gladiators fight, as did the people of England when the Village Witch was being burned alive. Today we will stand up on a bus and crane our necks as we drive slowly past the scene of a deadly accident.

Derived from the Greek word 'Thanatos', meaning death, Thanatourism has developed into a very lucrative travel niche. By its very definition, Thanatourism is slightly sadistic as it ultimately consists of spending holiday time travelling to locations associated with death, pain, suffering and torture. The suffering may be due to natural or manmade disasters and from what I have noticed the results are usually still evident on the faces of the people living in the area.

Looking over the list that follows, I was slightly shocked that I have been attracted to so many Thanatourism locations across the planet. I admit that I probably would never have gone across to Rwanda to visit Kigali if it had not been for the terrible genocide that happened there so recently.

In spite of this, I always find that the people that live in the Thanatourism destinations I have visited benefit from the pain that has been generated from the darkness of the past. Tourism to the area can be vastly increased, thus creating the prospect of earning a living from the results of such atrocities.

As the tourist money trickles down through the local communities the people are provided with a greater chance of earning an income. However, it would be difficult to admit that they are ultimately better off. From the tourist's perspective, one must ask what benefit is to be derived from opening sites such as The Exclusion Zone in Chernobyl or The Killing Fields in Cambodia? Can they provide a responsible educational function, or do they serve as evidence to the shortcomings of human beings?

I would love to tell you that travelling to the sites of tragedy that have been opened to tourism serve as a means of learning from the past. I would love to say that opening these sites will ensure that we never allow such atrocities to ever happen again. However, we all know that somewhere in the world right now a massacre is being carried out. We do not learn from these atrocities. Sadly, we open these Thanatourism locations because we can profit from them.

"The first time it was reported that our friends were being butchered

there was a cry of horror. Then a hundred were butchered. But when a thousand were butchered and there was no end to the butchery, a blanket of silence spread. When evil doing comes like falling rain, nobody calls out 'stop!'

"When crimes begin to pile up they become invisible. When sufferings become unendurable, the cries are no longer heard. The cries, too, fall like rain in summer."

~ Bertolt Brecht (Poet and playwright)

☑ **Tuol Sleng, Security Prison 21, Phnom Penh, Cambodia.** *The site is a former high school, which the Khmer Rouge converted into a prison and interrogation centre, later known as Security Prison 21 (S-21). Between 1975 and 1979, it is estimated that up to 20,000 people were imprisoned at Tuol Sleng (meaning "Hill of the Poisonous Trees"), with a maximum of 1,500 prisoners being held at any one time. Most never left the prison alive.*

Upon arrival at S-21, each prisoner was photographed and forced to provide detailed life stories, beginning with their childhood and ending with their arrest. They were then forced to strip to their underwear and taken to their cells were they were shackled to the walls or the concrete floor. Inmates were then repeatedly tortured and coerced into naming family members and associates, who were

in turn arrested, tortured and killed.

☑ **Killing Fields and Genocide Museum, Phnom Penh, Cambodia.** *As I wandered around the grounds of the Genocide Museum in the heavy rain, I noticed something strange below my feet. As the rain washed away the top level of the soil, bits of bone and many teeth rose to the surface. It was a few seconds before the realisation of what I was standing on hit me. I was standing on a mass grave!*

This is one of the many sites where good people were tortured and executed by the ruthless Khmer Rouge regime. Today, this site is a very popular Thanatourism destination and a prime example of how pain and suffering can be turned into a lucrative tourist attraction. The sick part about these locations in Cambodia is that the people that are responsible for the creation of these terrible sites are apparently the same people that are profiting from them today.

☑ **Cu Chi Tunnels, Ho Chi Minh City, Vietnam.** *It was from the Cu Chi Tunnels that the Viet Cong launched its Tet Offensive, which ultimately forced a humiliating withdrawal of US troops from Vietnam. Despite their place in history today, the tunnels offered appalling conditions for those forced to operate within them. In addition to offering minimal space with unbearable humidity, many of the passages were wired with*

The Killing Fields of Cambodia

booby traps. This is not to mention the deadly spiders and wandering scorpions that the young foot soldiers were forced to share the space with.

☑ **The mass graves of the Great Famine, Co. Cork, Ireland.** *To get an understanding of the level of devastation that the Great Famine had on Ireland, consider for a moment that a census taken in 1841 revealed a population of slightly over eight million, with the country expected to reach a population of nine million by 1851.*

However, due to the Great Famine, the years 1845 to 1852 was a period of mass starvation, disease and emigration, with a census in 1851 counting only 6,552,385 people. The Great Famine ravished the country and its impact was felt long after, with the census of 1911 stating Ireland's population at only 4.4 million. This is about the same as the population in 1800 and similar to the number counted in the year 2000

census, with the country still only recording half of its peak population.

☑ **The Kigali Genocide Memorial Centre, Rwanda.** *Through the media, this genocide was sold to the world as a tribal conflict between the tall, educated, upper class Tutsi and the uneducated, stocky Hutu peasants. A simple civil war they said. They were wrong. This was not a chaotic tribal war, but a deliberately planned and premeditated genocide. It was on 6 April 1994 that President Habyarimana was assassinated. This was the day that hell came to earth for all Rwandans. Within hours of the Presidents death, roadblocks had been set up around Kigali, manned by Hutu militia. Everyone was interrogated at these roadblocks in order to determine the Tutsis from Hutus.*

Once separated, Tutsis were then hacked to death with machetes at the roadside. Even Hutus that were suspected of being Tutsi for any reason, such as being tall, were also murdered. People were forced from their homes and assembled at predetermined places of massacre in a methodical manner. Here they were murdered. The slaughter was relentless and it was allowed to continue for three months without restriction, quickly spreading to the countryside.

"Doing murder with a machete is exhausting, so the militias were organized to work in shifts. At the day's end, the Achilles tendons of unprocessed victims were sometimes cut before the murderers retired to rest, to feast on the victims' cattle and to drink. Victims who could afford to pay often chose to die from a bullet." *(Wrage, "Genocide in Rwanda: Draft Case Study for Teaching Ethics and International Affairs," unpublished paper, 2000.)*

How could this be allowed to happen? How could the governments of the world not know about this? Well, in fact, they did. "Arms, from machetes to rocket launchers, were supplied by France, South Africa, Egypt and China. In the year in which the genocide was planned, Rwanda, a country the size of Wales, became the third largest importer of weapons in Africa." *(Zed Books, "A People Betrayed: The Role of the West in Rwanda's Genocide" By Linda Melvern, 2000.)*

Out of a population of 7.4 million people, the official figures published by the Rwandan government estimated the number of victims of the genocide at 1,174,000. In three months, nearly 17 percent of the population was murdered by other members of their community – an average of eight people hacked and beaten to death every minute during the period from 6 April to mid-July. Before the genocide, Rwanda was described by many as "a tropical Switzerland in the heart of Africa." No one says that anymore.

Walking around the streets of the capital Kigali provided me with an eerie feeling. There were many people going about their daily duties that had very visible scars, inflicted by their machete-wielding neighbours. This left a sickening question in my mind: Are the people without the scars the ones that wielded the machetes? There are thousands of widows, many of whom were subjected to mutilation and rape and as a result are now HIV-positive. Then there is estimated to be about 400,000 orphans, some who are still teenagers and have lived their entire lives without a single person to call their family. These are the survivors of the Rwandan Genocide of 1994. Are they the lucky ones?

☑ **Trảng Bàng, Vietnam.** *You know the iconic Vietnam War Pulitzer Prize winning photograph of a nine-year-old girl running naked along a road after being severely burned by a napalm attack? Well this is the location of that photograph. I was informed that it was the bomb that had blown her flimsy clothing off, but* here I learned that the girl, Phan Thị Kim Phúc, had torn off the burning clothes herself to survive the attack. That terrified little girl is still alive today and has grown into a great woman, with these words to say:

"Forgiveness made me free from hatred. I still have many scars on my body and severe pain most days but my heart is cleansed. Napalm is very powerful, but faith, forgiveness, and love are much more powerful. We would not have war at all if everyone could learn how to live with true love, hope and forgiveness. If that little girl in the picture can do it, ask yourself: Can you?"

~ *Phan Thị Kim Phúc, 2008*

☑ **Robben Island, South Africa.** *From the 17th to the 20th century, this island has served as a place of isolation, banishment and imprisonment. It was a place of much suffering for many people. The island was a leper colony as well as a jail, housing people right up to the end of Apartheid, with Nelson Mandela being the most famous inmate.*

☑ **The Plaza de las Tres Culturas, Mexico City.** *Did you know that the Mexican government massacred up to 1,000 students, civilian protesters and onlookers on the night of 2 October 1968? No? Well not to worry, not many did. The summer of 1968 was a time of great hope, with the entire country seemingly on the verge of transformation. Students without a central leader were out in the streets calling for change. A nonviolent revolution similar to the recent 'Arab Spring' was unfolding, driven by anticipation and expectancy, fuelled by passion.*

With the eyes of the world about to be cast upon the city, the powers-that-be in Mexico did not like this coming together of the people. Something needed to be done to clean up the streets to prevent these protestors from 'embarrassing' them in front of the watching world. Just ten days before the opening ceremony for the Olympic games, the government stepped into action.

Around 10,000 students had congregated in the Plaza de las Tres Culturas in Tlatelolco to listen peacefully to speeches regarding the unlawfulness of recent governmental actions. It was reported that at around 6:30pm 'the Olympic Battalion', composing of 5,000 soldiers, police officers and federal security agents surrounded the plaza with up to 200 tanks and police vehicles.

Flares were shot from a helicopter as a signal to the Olympic Battalion to seal off the two entrances to the Plaza to prevent anyone from entering or leaving. In her book "Massacre in Mexico" (University of Missouri, 1991), Elena Poniatowska reports that "Flares suddenly appeared in the sky overhead and everyone automatically looked up. The first shots were heard then." *The massacre had begun... and the killing continued throughout the night. Witnesses claimed that* initially the bodies were removed in ambulances and later officials stacked the bodies into military trucks. They did not stop to determine whether the victims were dead or injured.

By the next morning, the government-controlled media obediently reported the Mexican government's version of the events. Newspapers reported that demonstrators fired the first shots and that approximately 25 people had been killed, with hundreds wounded and many more detained. However, it is only thanks to determined researchers that the truth of this tragedy has unfolded. The one thing about the truth is that it is similar to a football held under the water; it always rises to the surface eventually. The truth does not fear investigation.

☑ **Auschwitz-Birkenau Concentration Camp, Poland.** Oswiecim, as it is known in Poland, was the largest of all Nazi concentration camps. It is believed to have served as an extermination camp for more than one million people, most of which were local Polish people and Jewry from around Europe.

Similar to most German concentration camps, Auschwitz-Birkenau was constructed to serve three purposes: 1) to imprison indefinitely the enemies of the Nazi regime and the German occupation authorities in Poland; 2) to maintain a supply of forced labour to work in SS-owned construction-related projects including weaponry; and 3) to serve as a location to eliminate targeted groups whose death was deemed essential to ensuring the security of Nazi Germany.

Like most other concentration camps, Auschwitz-Birkenau contained a gas chamber and crematorium. Trains frequently arrived at Auschwitz-Birkenau with transports of Jews and other targeted groups from almost every country in Europe occupied by or allied to Germany. These 'trains of death' arrived from 1942 to the end of summer 1944. It was upon arrival at Auschwitz-Birkenau that the people underwent selection with the SS staff separating those that they deemed fit for the forced labour from those that were not. The majority of people were deemed unfit for forced labour and were sent immediately to the gas chambers, which were disguised as shower installations.

The soldiers responsible for the crimes committed in Auschwitz-Birkenau argued during their trials that they were "only following orders." Thankfully, this defence did not work for them, nor has it worked in hundreds of cases since.

"When all this is over, people will try to blame the Germans alone, and the Germans will try to blame the Nazis alone, and the Nazis will try to blame Hitler alone. They will make him bear the sins of the world. But it's not true. You suspected what was happening, and so did I."

~ Iain Pears, The Dream of Scipio, Vintage Books, 2002

Individually, we must ensure that we are aware of our actions on an individual basis and do not blindly 'follow orders'. Evil can only transform when good people say nothing and allow themselves to be 'charmed' by men and women in positions of power. We know when something does not feel right so we must think for ourselves and ensure that we are not a generation that allows a tragedy like this to ever happen again.

☑ **Rocinha Favela, Rio de Janeiro, Brazil.** *The crimes that this city has become notorious for are usually committed between rival drug gangs. These drug gangs have long infested the great favelas of Rio de Janeiro, home to 20 percent of the city's seven million residents. These gangs are so powerful that they have seized total control of entire favela neighbourhoods, with law-enforcement unable to suppress them, and the statistics do not enhance the cities reputation.*

"Between December of 1987 and November 2001, violent death claimed 3,937 Cariocas *(favela residents)* under 18 years of age. By comparison, during the same period, 467 minors died in and around the West Bank between Jordan and Israel, which is considered a war zone by the international community" *('Drug Lords and Young Soldiers' by Sam Logan)*. This urban warfare also involves police fighting against the gangs. When I was there in 2007, it is estimated that the police had killed 1,330 people in the state of Rio de Janeiro that year. This compares to 347 people killed by the trigger-happy police throughout the United States of America during 2006.

Rocinha, which means "Little Farm" in Portuguese, is the largest favela in Rio de Janeiro and has seen its fair share of disturbance. Built into a steep hillside overlooking the city, there is estimated to be up to 200,000 inhabitants in this urbanised slum made from concrete and brick. However, this is not like the shantytowns or slums found in India or Africa. Rocinha has developed an infrastructure that houses hundreds of businesses, including banks, supermarkets, pharmacies and Bob's, a major Brazilian fast food chain. Therefore, lets hope that things start to turn around for the residents, as Brazil gets closer to hosting the World Cup and the Olympic games in the coming years.

☑ **Ground Zero, New York City, USA.** *Right in the heart of this 'city that never sleeps' is a location where a pocket of silent reverence remains, incongruous to the otherwise manic effervescence of the Big Apple. A terrible tragedy happened here on 11 September 2001, the full story of which remains to be told. I can only imagine how terrifying the conditions were inside the towers that so many people decided on an individual level that they would* rather jump than wait to see if they would be rescued.

☑ **The Berlin Wall, Germany.** I visited the city during the mid 1990s and at that stage; much of the wall was still in its original state. At that time, the local people still considered the wall an eyesore and did not have much love for it. During this period, the entire city was a massive construction site with development taking place everywhere; people were very much focused on the future.

Along the streets, vendors were selling large chunks of the wall for little more than a few cents. I wanted a souvenir of the wall to take home with me, but I wanted to make sure it was original. So, I picked up an iron bar that was laying close by and started hammering chunks off the wall as the locals wandered past with that 'stupid tourist' look on their faces. Unfortunately, I have not been back in Berlin since then, but my guess is that such actions would be frowned upon these days.

☑ **The Cerro Rico Mine, Potosi, Bolivia.** This is the silver mine that bankrolled Spain's colonial empire for centuries. There is a saying here that with the silver dug out from Potosi, one could build a bridge from Bolivia all the way to Madrid. However, another story the Spanish are less willing to repeat says, that with the bones of those who died in the mine they could build two such bridges to Madrid.

Cerro Rico was known as the "mountain that eats men" due to the number of miners who perished within its confines. It is believed that as many as eight million people died in the mines of Potosi, most of them slaves. They were trapped underground for six months at a time and forced to work 20 hours a day. Some died from disease, some were killed in accidents, but many were worked to death, dying from exhaustion. In addition to this, a huge number of suicides went unrecorded. Potosi is a site of an unknown, forgotten and hushed up genocide. Maybe it is the site of the largest genocide in the history of mankind? However, I am sure there is a lot that we have not been told.

☑ **The Exclusion Zone, Chernobyl, Ukraine.** *Toxic. Eerie. Forgotten. Unnerving. The silence here is deafening. Everything I brought*

into the Exclusion Zone stayed there – including my shoes. The shorts and t-shirt that made it out with me were put in the bin before I jumped into the shower. I will not be revisiting this site. Now I pray for the people of Japan.

☑ **Sniper Alley, Sarajevo, Bosnia and Herzegovina.** *Meša Selimovića Boulevard is a route that runs through the heart of Sarajevo, the capital city. This road serves as a link between the industrial region of the city to the west and the Old Town's cultural and historic sites to the east. This wide boulevard also divides the city into northern and southern sections, making it an important landmark within Sarajevo. "Sniper Alley" was the name given to the street during the Bosnian War.*

Snipers' had taken up posts within many of high-rise buildings in the area as it afforded them extensive fields of fire on their primary target: the civilians of Sarajevo. The people of the city were required to move about within the area in order to survive, despite the constant Serbian shelling from the surrounding mountains. Unfortunately, the only source of clean water in the city was located on the Boulevard. So despite the city being under constant Serbian bombardment the people still had to venture into the city in order to survive, thus routinely risking their lives.

Signs reading "Pazi – Snajper!" (Beware – Sniper!) became common. As people scuttled across the streets, from corner to corner to obtain the basics for the survival of their families, the snipers would unload. According to data gathered in 1995, the snipers shot 1,525 people, killing 225. Of the total dead, 60 were children.

Fairground Chernobyl

Throughout Sarajevo the battle scars of the urban warfare the city experienced during the Bosnian War are highly evident, but nothing is more glaring than the Sarajevo Rose. I had never known of the Sarajevo Rose until I visited the city and came to ask a passerby what the arrangements on the ground signified. I was told in very harsh tones that the infamous Sarajevo Rose is a lasting reminder of a mortar shell fired from the Bosnian Serb forces on the hills.

When the mortars exploded on the concrete, they created a unique fragmentation pattern that looks almost floral in arrangement. This floral pattern is further enhanced throughout the city where explosion marks have been filled with red resin to mark the area where a mortar explosion resulted in the deaths of one or more Bosnian civilians. The Bosnian Book of the Dead reveals 97,207 names of Bosnia and Herzegovina's citizens killed and missing as a result of the 1992-1995 war.

☑ **Leper Colony, India.** Throughout its history, leprosy has been feared and misunderstood. Today many leper colonies remain across the globe, with India alone having more than 1,000 colonies. Leprosy is common in many countries worldwide, with two to three million people estimated to be permanently disabled because of disease. The disease is most prominent in temperate, tropical and subtropical climates, with India

recording the greatest number of cases, with Brazil second and Burma third. Even the United States of America is liable to this disease with approximately 100 cases per year being diagnosed.

India reports over 50 percent of the world's leprosy cases with more than 130,000 people officially diagnosed every year. Given the number of new cases, it came as a great surprise when I learned that India had announced in 2005 that it had eliminated leprosy. Based on the official target set by the World Health Organisation, a country can announce the 'elimination' of leprosy when the number of cases falls below one case for every 10,000 people.

Contrary to folklore, leprosy does not cause body parts to fall off. The disease attacks nerve endings, destroying the patients' ability to feel pain and injury, leaving them susceptible to infections and ulcers. Over time, these infections can result in tissue loss, so fingers and toes become shortened and deformed as the cartilage is absorbed into the body resulting in the 'clawing' of hands and feet. If infections are neglected and not treated properly this may lead to the loss of fingers, hands, toes and feet due to repeated injury resulting from lack of sensation and cause blindness and facial disfigurement

The stigma that haunts the disease derives from the widespread fear that leprosy is highly contagious. The reality is that 99 percent of humans are naturally immune to this biblical ailment, which has resulted in campaigners naming it the world's "least contagious communicable disease." Science is still unsure exactly how leprosy is spread due to the long incubation period, with the disease residing in the body long before symptoms appear, making it difficult to determine where or when the disease was contracted.

My clearest memory of the time I went to a Leper Colony in Northern India, is not what went on inside, but the cries of a baby boy standing outside, whose mother had abandoned him at the gate. As flies crawled all over his face, I gave him some biscuits in the hope that he would stop crying. He accepted the biscuits, but as he held them tight in his little hand, he continued to scream out for his mother in a manner that will forever haunt me.

☑ **Pont de lama Road Tunnel, Paris, France.** This is the location where Princess Diana of Wales died on 31 August 1997, along with her boyfriend Dodi Al-Fayed and their driver Henri Paul. Quite bizarrely, a Flame of Liberty, which is said to be an exact replica of the Statue of Liberty's flame, sits above the entrance to the tunnel to mark the spot. For a great woman known throughout the world as "The People's Princess", it is not quite the memorial that one would expect.

☐ **The River Kwai Bridge, Thailand.** During World War II, much of South East Asia was firmly under Japanese occupation. With this, the Japanese laid plans to further the expansion and invade India. The Japanese forced a quarter of a million people, both Asians and allied prisoners of war, to construct a railway to aid this expansion. During construction of the 416 kilometre long Siam – Burma railway an estimated 100,000 workers died, of which approximately 13,000 were prisoners of war. Their bodies were buried alongside the tracks wherever they had dropped. The track is today unofficially known as the "Death Railway."

☐ **Dharavi Slum, Mumbai, India.** This is not only the largest slum in India, but also the largest slum in all of Asia, being home to almost one million people. Immortalised by Hollywood in the Oscar winning movie; Slumdog Millionaire, Dharavi Slum greets visitors with endless displays of destitution, disease, disorder and living conditions beyond comprehension.

☐ **The World's great Graveyards.** I find graveyards to be fascinating places to visit. When I am in a new city, in a new country I will often go in search of the grandiose graveyard that every city seems to have. One of the attractions is that burial customs are different all over the world. Visiting graveyards is not as strange as it sounds, because in the 1800s, before the dawn of the public park, graveyards doubled as places of leisure. Graveyards were utilised as locations where families and lovers could spend a few hours relaxing over a picnic in a landscaped area. They would spend their free time in the graveyard for the serenity it offered as well as the elegance of the place.

Today the public park has become the 'go-to' destination for outdoor activities, but the ambience of a graveyard is still very tempting to many. Appealing to art lovers and weirdo's alike (guilty on both accounts), these silent cities of the dead are steeped in the history and folklore of the region. Nowhere else can provide such a unique blend of art and nature within a walled garden. They are also the resting place of the rich and famous, as well as the infamous. Walking through the grandiose graveyards of big cities can offer more people of fame and fortune than an Academy Awards ceremony.

Graveyards such as the old St. Louis Cemetery No.1 in New Orleans, Glasnevin Cemetery in Dublin and Colon Cemetery in Havana are quite fascinating and could keep you occupied for days on end. However, most backpackers seem to enjoy the wonders of Paris' Pere Lachaise as a tourist destination. This 445,000 metre^2 graveyard with its famous inhabitants of Richard Wright, Jim Morrison and Oscar Wilde certainly is worth a look.

Although, out of them all, I think that it is La Recoleta Cemetery in Buenos Aires that must be seen to be believed.

People go to Buenos Aires just to visit this graveyard. Most go to see just one grave—that of Eva Peron—but it is the entire setting that entices them to return. The entrance to the graveyard is through marvellous neo-classical gates adorned with soaring Greek columns. The great unfolding passageways of marble tombs, statues and mausoleums in La Recoleta are truly sublime. The workmanship and attention to detail is unrivalled.

The entire cemetery is laid out in a grid pattern, reminiscent of city blocks, as grand tree-lined central walkways branch out into mausoleum filled pathways. Would it be wrong to describe a graveyard as being glamorous? Considering that La Recoleta Cemetery in Buenos Aires is located in the hippest part of town, glamorous may not be too strong a word. After all, it is the pride of the city's residents, both living and dead.

The Chakra Points of the Earth

"Those who dwell among the beauties and mysteries of the Earth are never alone or weary of life."
~ Rachel Carson (Biologist and writer)

The word "Chakra" derives from the Sanskrit word for "wheel." The concept originated in the Hindu tradition and refers to spiral-like vortices that are believed to exist on the surface of the body of all living beings. The Earth, as a living organism, is included in this, thus, scattered around the globe are powerful vortices that make up the Earth's Chakra system.

Within the Chakras, energy and consciousness can move from one frequency to another in spiralling fashion. The Chakras are said to be focal points for the reception and transmission of energies, which permeate with rotating vortices of subtle matter.

Until recently, many discarded these vortices and energy grids as pure fantasy, but modern science is revealing that these points on the Earth do exist. In fact, they are now able to confirm what the great healers in the East have been preaching for millennia. Consequently, there is now a degree of common consensus that the following are the locations of the Earth's seven major Chakra points:

☐ **Base: North America: Mount Shasta, California, USA.**

Mount Shasta, located at the southern end of the Cascade Range, is the first Chakra of the Earth, known as the base Chakra or the Muladhara. This corresponds to the Chakra of the hips, legs and lower back on the human body. Mount Shasta is regarded as a sacred location by many Native American tribes. The energy that derives from Mount Shasta is said to spring like a geyser, with a massive surge of life energy exploding from the Earth at irregular intervals.

☑ **Sacral: South America: Lake Titicaca, Bolivia.**

Situated high in the Andes between Peru and Bolivia, on the Island of the Sun, is found the Titicaca Stone, which is the geometrical centre for the second Earth Chakra. Also known as Svadhisthana, this Chakra correlates to the sexual area in the human body. This is the world centre for the creation of new species and significant evolutionary advances within existing species. This Chakra governs all species, taking a special interest in positive mutations and evolutionary advancements.

☑ **Solar plexus: Australia: Uluru and Kata Tjuta, Northern Territory.**

These two sites in the centre of this vast island make up the third Chakra of the Earth, known as Manipura.

This corresponds to the solar plexus Chakra of the human body and is said to be the primary Chakra for the maintenance of global health and vitality. Like an iceberg, this formation is just the visible tip of an enormous slab of rock that extends as far as six kilometres into 'Mother Earth'. It is alleged to be very bad luck to take away any stone or any part of Uluru. There are many reported cases of people who have gone to great lengths to return items that they once 'borrowed'.

Uluru and Kata Tjuta are part of creation legend, held as sacred locations by the Aborigines of Australia. In their ancient creation legends of "Dreamtime," they tell of a great ritual that has yet to be completed at Uluru. The performance of this ritual will complete the great plan of the Earth Spirit, which will allow perfection to spread throughout the world. The event will be symbolised by a great pole, or cosmic umbilical cord, which is destined to unite heaven with Earth. It is predicted that this cord begins to function at the time of the rare Saturn-Pluto conjunction. The next time that this conjunction is due is in 2020.

☑ Heart: Europe: Glastonbury, Somerset and Shaftesbury, England.

As this is the forth Chakra, the area is recognised as the heart of the Earth. Known as Anahata, this region of middle England is associated with the Legends of the Holy Grail. This chakra is connected with the heart, lungs and circulatory system in the human body. Anyone that doubts the existence of Chakra points only has to spend a few days in this beautiful part of the world to get a feel for the wonderful energy that permeates from every hill, street and person.

☑ Throat: Africa: Great Pyramids of Giza and Mount Sinai, Egypt.

The Earth's fifth Chakra, known as Vishuddha, is connected to the throat Chakra of the human body. These locations have ties to Christianity, Judaism and Islam. Personally, I did not feel the great energy that runs through the famous Pyramids either of the times I visited. The Great Pyramids of Giza are so iconic around the world

that they have become a victim of their own success. The majority of the time on the site is spent politely saying 'no' to the locals selling postcards and miniature Pyramid/Sphinx combos. However, I have to admit that sitting on top of Mount Sinai throughout the night and into sunrise was quite a magical experience.

☑ **Third eye: No fixed location: Currently at Glastonbury, England.**

The sixth Chakra of the Earth is associated with the third eye on the forehead of the human body and is known as the Ajna. Many believe that this Chakra is in a perpetual state of motion, moving with the Earth's rotations. It is currently based in Glastonbury, England, but it is believed that when the Age of Capricorn begins in two millennia, it will then move to a location in Brazil.

☐ **Crown: Asia: Mount Kailash, Tibet.**

Corresponding with the crown Chakra of the human body, the seventh Chakra, known as Sahasrara, is located high in the Himalayas at Mount Kailash in Tibet. Buddhists, Bon, Hindus, Jain and the faithful of many other religions hold this great mountain sacred. To climb Mount Kailash is considered desecration and there are no known reports of it ever happening despite the efforts of many. The indigenous people believe it to be so sacred that an attempt to climb the mountain would be considered a slight to the Gods, with the inevitable result being death.

Glastonbury, England

The Mysterious Alignment of Ancient Wonders

It is a little known fact that many of the mystery locations and sites of great ancient construction on this planet run along a single line within a distance of less than one tenth of one degree of latitude. For example, did you know that the Great Pyramids of Giza are aligned around the Earth with the Lost City of Petra, Machu Picchu and Easter Island? Here is the full list of the sites that I wish to visit, in the order that they sit along this line, running from east to west.

"A day spent without the sight or sound of beauty, the contemplation of mystery, or the search of truth or perfection is a poverty-stricken day; and a succession of such days is fatal to human life."

~ Lewis Mumford (Sociologist, philosopher and historian)

☑ **The Great Pyramids of Giza, Egypt.** *It is believed that the Great Pyramid was built around 2560 BC and for over 3,800 years, it was the tallest man-made structure on the planet, at 146.5 metres. There have been varying theories regarding the building of the Great Pyramid. The accepted theory is the idea that it was built by moving huge stones from a quarry and dragging and lifting them into place. However*

there are an increasing number of people that believe that an early form of concrete was created using a mixture of clay, limestone, lime and water, creating building blocks as and when they were needed. The one thing that we do know is that the blocks are so perfectly matched that not even a human hair can be inserted between them.

☐ **The oracular temple of Ammon-Ra at Siwa, Egypt.**

☐ **The paintings and engravings at Tassili n'Ajjer, Algeria.**

☐ **Dogon Country, Mali.**

☐ **The Pyramids of Paratoari, Peru.**

☐ **Temple Hill, Ollantaytambo, Peru.**

☐ **Sacsayhuamán, the capital of the Incan Empire, Peru.**

☑ **Machu Picchu, Peru.** *Often referred to as the "Lost City of the Incas," this is perhaps the most familiar icon of the Inca World. What is less well known is that the Incas worshiped many sacred animals, such as the condor, the puma, the caiman, et cetera and built these into their cities. At Machu Picchu, it is believed that the city was built in the shape of a Condor, as it was etched into the mountainside.*

☑ **Cuzco, Peru.** *Cusco was the capital of the Incan Empire from the 13th century to around 1532. It* is unknown how Cuzco was built, or how its stones were quarried, but many believe that the city was planned as an imitation in the shape of a puma, an animal the Inca's held sacred.

☑ **Nazca Lines, Peru.** *The vast size of these, as well as the mystery surrounding them really got me thinking. The Nazca Lines are giant sketches drawn by unknown peoples in the desert of western Peru. The drawings are so large scale that the shapes created can only be discerned from the air, leading to a variety of theories about their purpose. It is only by flying in an airplane that the straight lines and geometric shapes become depictions of animals, humans and plants. The figures include; a condor, hands, hummingbirds, a human figure, a monkey, a spider, a tree and, what bizarrely appears to be, an astronaut. The drawings are estimated to be up to 1,800 years old.*

☑ **The Paracas Drawings, Peru.** *Sketched into the side of the cliff overlooking the sea they are similar to the drawings found on the nearby Nazca plains.*

☐ **The Statues of Easter Island.**

☐ **Aneityum Island, Vanuatu.**

☐ **Preah Vihear Temple, Cambodia.**

☑ **The Angkor Plain Temples, Cambodia.** *For many years, the temples of the Angkor Plain lay totally isolated from the Western*

world, hidden by thick jungle. French colonialists in the area heard whispers from local people about "temples built by giants" but most discarded them as folk tales. It was not until 1860 that the temples were first discovered by French missionaries, who brought them to the attention of the world. Initially, researchers did not believe that Cambodians built the temples. They believed that another race, which had occupied the region 2,000 years prior, had built the temples.

No one can say definitively why Angkor collapsed but a team from the University of Sydney have been using the latest technology to painstakingly compile a detailed map of the area. What they have found is that Angkor was once the largest pre-industrial urban settlement known to man. It spanned a vast area and was certainly bigger than current day Los Angeles. Their findings suggest that Angkor was a completely artificial landscape, totally dependent on an elaborate irrigation scheme.

The area was stripped bare of forest cover and totally remodelled to suit their needs, to the extent that they even moved entire rivers. It was due to these sophisticated techniques that Angkor Wat managed to survive for so long, with its preservation being due in part to the fact that the moat that surrounded it also provided protection from encroachment by the jungle.

☐ **Sukhothai, Thailand.**

☐ **Pyay Pagodas, Burma.**

☐ **The Khajuraho Group of Monuments, Khajuraho, India.**

☐ **Mohenjo-Daro, Province of Sindh, Pakistan.**

☐ **The ceremonial capital of Persepolis, Shiraz, Iran.**

☐ **The ruins of the Great Ziggurat of Ur, Iraq.**

☑ **The Lost City of Petra, Jordan.** *This ancient, mysterious and hauntingly beautiful site is believed to have been inhabited for over 9,000 years. Enclosed by towering rocks and watered by a persistent stream, Petra possessed the advantages of a fortress and the*
funnelling capabilities of a bridge. For these reasons it was identified as the capital of the Nabataeans and the centre of their caravan trade. Its location allowed them to control the main commercial routes that passed through the city, as traders made their way to the Mediterranean Sea, the Red Sea and the Persian Gulf.

In Arab tradition, Petra is the location where Moses struck a rock with his staff and water came forth. This ancient city was forbidden to foreigners and thus it drained from the memory of people in Europe, forgotten for 600 years. The splendour of this great location was revealed once again in 1812, when Swiss explorer Johann Ludwig Burckhardt, disguised as a Bedouin

"rediscovered it" and revealed its magnificence to the world. Despite the enormous size of Petra, it is believed that we have uncovered just 15 percent of the city, with the vast majority still underground and untouched.

Along this line, you will find the birthplace of all modern religion as well as the location of the first written languages of the world. This mysterious line also crosses over the mouth of the great rivers of this world, including the River Nile, the Tigris-Euphrates River, the Indus River and the Bay of Bengal nearby the mouth of the Ganges. In addition, this mysterious line crosses over both the source and the mouth of the Amazon River.

You can easily observe the alignment of these sites on a globe of the Earth if you line up any two sites on the horizon ring. Alternatively, just by lodging the names of each of the locations into Google Maps you will soon notice a wave like pattern around the planet, as would be expected when a three dimensional object is flattened out into two dimensions.

The Angkor Plain Temples

X

Personal Development is
part of life's journey

U p until this point, all of the goals and objectives that I have listed relate to things that I want to *'do'*. Today's world is all about *doing, doing, doing*. We are always on the move, striving to reach the next milestone. Yet, what meaning do such milestones comprise if we never stop to take stock of our achievements and just *'be'*? After all, we are human *beings*, not human *doings*!

I now realise that it is vital that I take the time to just *be*. Be in the moment—I must not always be thinking ahead to the next adventure. Be with my friends—I must not be talking on the phone to others that are not present. Be in the room—I must not be daydreaming about being some other place. I must be present in the now, showing gratitude and appreciation for what I have in my life at this moment.

The great paradox of life in the 21st century is that we all strive to be human *doings*, when at our very core all we want is to *'be'*. We have somehow become so swept up in all the things that we want to do and have that we rarely sit back and take stock of all the great gifts that we have around us.

We strive for more money, but yet if we were to consider all the gifts that we have in our life that no amount of money could buy, we would realise that we are already rich. We dream of going to far-flung places, that seem more exotic than what we are used to. Yet, when we look around, we see tourists flocking into our region to soak up the wonders that we seem to miss.

Ultimately, my objective is to be a human *being*. To be in the now and appreciate all that I have. When I just be, then I will be able to make a bigger impact on my environs. I will be able to give back to the people around me. I can be a helping hand to those that are down and I can be an inspiration to those that want to go up. I will give more of my time and money to help others to achieve their dreams and I will have more empathy and compassion. Before I can do any of this, I need to just *'be'*.

Inner Development

"When you find peace within yourself, you become the kind of person who can live at peace with others."

~ Anne Frank (Writer)

☑ **Become an early riser.** *I had never related success and accomplishments in life with the time that I wake up. I had always slept in until I had just enough time to get up and do what I had to do before leaving home to be exactly on time for school or work. At the weekends, I would sleep in until I could sleep no more. However, whenever I started to travel I was continuously surrounded by magnificently successful people who would tell me about all the great things that they had done and seen that morning, as I slept.*

In addition, I have never read a quote from any of the worlds most conscious and successful people saying that their accomplishments derived from sleeping in late. Every single successful person that mentions their sleep patterns talk about how waking up early has been a key ingredient in their success. This pattern is simply too obvious to ignore. Rising early provides a supercharge in our lives if we want to be more productive, successful, conscious and live better and healthier lives. Therefore, I changed my sleep patterns to the point that

now I get up earlier than I ever did and greet each wonderful new day with a smile.

If ever I am not feeling that spring in my step in the morning, then I think about the words of the Dalai Lama, who said, "Everyday, think as you wake up, 'today I am fortunate to have woken up, I am alive, I have a precious human life, I am not going to waste it. I am going to use all my energies to develop myself, to expand my heart out to others, to achieve enlightenment for the benefit of all beings, I am going to have kind thoughts towards others, I am not going to get angry or think badly about others, I am going to benefit others as much as I can.'" *Great, isn't it?*

☑ **Practice QiGong.** *This is a philosophy rooted in Chinese martial arts and medicine and involves the alignment of breath and movement in order to balance qi (translated as "intrinsic life energy") through exercise. I first got involved after witnessing people practicing QiGong in a Beijing park. Most people practice this philosophy just after sunrise, so when I was invited to come along, I did and I thoroughly enjoyed the experience.*

A typical QiGong practice session involves rhythmic breathing, coordinated with slow fluid movements, whilst in a calm state of mind. Considered by some practitioners as an exercise and by others as a type of meditation, QiGong is believed to help develop human potential, by awakening our true nature through accessing higher realms of awareness.

☑ **Practice Faun Gong.** *This is a spiritual discipline first introduced to China in 1992. It is a discipline that combines slow-moving exercises with meditation. The three central tenets of the belief are "Truthfulness, Forbearance and Compassion". Together these principles are regarded as the fundamental criteria for differentiating right from wrong. Despite the fact it looks like the participants are not doing very much, it is a total workout and very rewarding.*

Its growth in popularity was astonishing. In fact, it became so popular that the Communist Party of China, launched a campaign to "eradicate" Faun Gong completely on 22 July 1999, less than seven years after its introduction.

☑ **Learn to Meditate.** *How can we take control of our destiny if we do not have control of our minds? It Is only through meditation that we can truly master our minds. Having a clear mind is essential to achieving abundance and wellbeing in every area of our lives. It is important to spend 15 minutes every morning and night in meditation. If you find that you are too busy to do this, then it is advisable to spend 30 minutes in each sitting.*

☑ **Practice yoga.** *Yoga is a physical, mental and spiritual discipline with its origins in ancient India. Yoga*

brings together physical and mental disciplines to achieve strength in body and stillness in mind, providing the perfect combination to allow us to relax and manage stress. I started practicing yoga around the turn of the millennium for reasons that I am not entirely sure. It just seemed to appeal to me on some level. However, at that time it seemed to be a female only exercise, as for years I was the only male partaking in the classes. Since returning from my travels and attending yoga practice sessions, I am pleased to report that every single time I have went to a class recently, about a quarter of the participants where male. Yoga is something that I have always recommended to my male friends, particularly the ones that are involved in competitive team sports.*

☑ **Eliminate the word "hate" from my vocabulary.** *It is such a strong word and its use cannot be justified in any situation or scenario, so why use it?*

☑ **Become a Reiki Master.** *The word Reiki derives from two Japanese words—Rei, meaning "Universal" and Ki, which means "life force." Therefore, Reiki is "universal life force" energy. Reiki is a gentle but powerful healing art administered through the palms of the hands. It is based on the idea that the life force energy that surrounds us is channelled to flow through us to restore balance and harmony to the mind and body. I first learned about Reiki when I was in Africa. I had fallen, hurt* my knee and was having trouble in moving around. Then, Luc Gielis, a Reiki practitioner performed a Reiki treatment directly into my knee and after twenty minutes all pain and discomfort had disappeared.

A Reiki treatment provides a wonderful glowing radiance that flows through and around the person receiving the energy. This is because Reiki treats all aspects of the person including physical body, emotions, mind and spirit.

This creates many beneficial effects that include, relaxation and feelings of peace, security and wellbeing. I was fortunate enough to be tutored through each of the levels by the wonderful Angela Gorman, until I became a Reiki Master. Personally, I feel that many areas of my life have taken an upturn since starting to practice Reiki.

☑ **Learn to let the things that I have no control over to run their course.** *I have come to learn that*

Ghats in Varanasi

everything is always perfect at all times. No matter how good or bad the situation may seem it is still perfect. It is for my greater good. I have faith that everything will work out for the best and everything will run its course. Anyway, my father once told me, "Worrying is like sitting in a rocking chair: it will keep me busy, but it will not get me anywhere".

☑ **Learn to forgive.** *We have all been hurt by someone at one time*

in our lives. When we feel that we have been treated badly then it hurts in our hearts. This pain is a normal reaction, but we must be vigilant not to let the pain linger for too long or this can cause problems throughout our lives, now and in the future, making us reluctant to open up to new experiences and people. The result is that we stop ourselves from enjoying the best of what this wonderful world has to offer. Holding that grudge takes up too much energy so we must learn to let go. The gift of forgiveness will set us free and allow us to move on to discover our lives path.

☑ **Bathe in the Ganges at sunrise, in the holy city of Varanasi, India.** *Aptly called the cultural capital of India, Varanasi has provided the right platform for all cultural activities to flourish, with the city being a pilgrimage site for Jains, Buddhists and Hindus. Varanasi is associated with the promotion of spiritualism, mysticism, Sanskrit, yoga and Hindi language. Knowledge, philosophy, culture, devotion to Gods, Indian arts and crafts have all flourished here for centuries.*

According to the Hindu mythology, anyone who is graced to die in the holy city of Varanasi circumvents reincarnation and hence obtains a permanent place in the Swarg (Heaven). It is the Ghats on the banks of the Ganges at Varanasi that complement the concept of divinity with these being the holiest locations of Varanasi. The city is constantly filled with pilgrims who flock here to take a dip in the holy Ganges, which is believed to have the power to wash away the sins of mortals.

It is believed that people who bathe in the Ganges are cleansed physically, mentally and spiritually. This belief has encouraged the disposal of half-burnt corpses into the river after cremation, so that the individual is cleansed after death. It is at the Ghats that you witness life and death together. The fact that the Ganges ranks among the five most polluted rivers of the world may not make it seem like an ideal place to bathe but, believe me, this is something not to miss. In fact, when I look back to the person that I was and the person that I am now, I believe that the changes that happened in me occurred around the time I bathed in the Ganges that autumn morning.

☑ **Learn to live in the 'now'.** Living in the now is one of the most important things that we can do to enhance our daily lives. Living in the now requires us to slow down and really experience life and the world around us. Therefore, I try to really tune into the areas of my life that I previously considered mundane and what I find is that I am surrounded by beauty and greatness, which has really inspired me.

Instead of constantly worrying about events from the past and looking to the future I try to spend most of my time in the now. To do

this I tend to focus on my thoughts and emotions rather than letting my mind become a flurry of scattered activity. I still have moments where I find myself thinking about the past and daydreaming about the future, but overall I have made incredible progress in slowing down and enjoying what is in my life right now.

☑ **Get 'cured' of Asthma.** If you or any of your family suffers from Asthma then you have to go right now and purchase the book, 'Close your mouth' by Patrick McKeown. It worked for me. Since reading this book and attending Mr. McKeown's seminars, my life has been transformed. My advice to you if you have been suffering from Asthma is to go to the website www.patrickmckeown.net to see if there is a seminar that you can visit in your area, but if this is not possible then the book is the next best thing.

☑ **Thank my parents for everything they have done for me.** I have to admit that prior to writing this book, I had not actually sat my parents down and thanked them for the support, encouragement and love they have showered upon me throughout my life. They have always encouraged to me get educated, to travel, to have my own style and approach to life, but mostly they have always encouraged me to just be myself.

When putting this book together, I knew that out of all the fantastic experiences I have lived through and the dreams I am yet to realise, that thanking my parents was one of the most important goals to have achieved. Life is short. The life that we have with our parents is even shorter. Way too short. Therefore, although I have ticked this off now, after treating my parents to a fantastic day out whilst expressing my gratitude, this is something that I need to do more often.

☐ **Stop eating junk food and become vegetarian.** *Eating the rotting flesh of a tortured dead animal is not the most appetising thing on this abundant planet. Yet, through what can only be described as laziness at times when I am hungry, I will still go and purchase a big greasy burger. This has to end. In fact, I would like to go on and take this a step further and become a raw vegan. This is a diet where I will only eat raw uncooked foods consisting primarily of nuts, fruits and vegetables. It is said to be the secret to perfect health. It does not do the gorillas any harm and look how strong they become.*

☐ **Cleanse and detoxify my body by fasting for three days.** *This will have to be an absolutely nothing-in-my-mouth-but-water fast. It will be tough, but I bet I will feel cleansed and energised after it.*

☐ **Practice Tai Chi.** *Originally developed in ancient China for self-defence, Tai Chi evolved into a graceful form of exercise that is now described as "meditation in motion." To do Tai Chi, you perform a series of flowing postures in a slow, graceful*

manner. Each posture flows into the next without pause, ensuring that the body is in constant motion. Practicing Tai Chi is said to provide a feeling of serenity obtained through the gentle movements that are designed to connect the mind and body and ultimately reduce stress and help with a variety of other health conditions.

I believe that performing mind-body practices such as QiGong and Tai Chi will allow me to sustain and improve the health of my immune system, nervous system and internal organs; as well as reducing stress, which is the cause of many Western diseases and illnesses. To be truly healthy, I hope to further integrate mind-body practices into my daily life.

☐ **Take up a Martial Art.** *The art of self-defence is a really beautiful thing and brings with it an inner confidence. My parents had me attending karate classes for a few years as a child, but as I never really bought into it, I never benefited from it. This is something that I hope to rectify in the future.*

☐ **Join Toastmasters and become a great public speaker.** *I did go to a few Toastmasters meetings last year, but that is not the point. To be a 'great public speaker' is the objective here and I am not there yet. I really need to put aside one evening per week over the next few years and work hard to achieve this vital skill.*

☐ **Develop enhanced persuasion skills.**

☐ **Purchase a plot of land where I can get back to basics and grow my own food.** *How rewarding would it be to be able to bring food from the turf to the table by myself? That is the simplest thing in the world, the basis of our survival, yet how many people do you know that live like this? I do not know anyone that does!*

☐ **Complete all the lessons in Sean M. Kelly's 'Dare to Dream' course.**

☐ **Get back to being a great listener.** *When I was a child, my grandmother complimented me on being a great listener. In all honesty, as a nine-year-old boy, I thought that this was the stupidest thing anyone could say. However, when I got home and told my mother, she informed me that good listeners are the best conversationists. Listening is different from hearing, it is an essential part of communication, it is not just hearing the words people utter.*

I realised a few years ago that I had lost the great gift that my grandmother had complimented me on and I had become more interested in getting my point across. I was listening only for my turn to speak. I soon learned that people like good listeners—who would you rather speak with, someone who was interested in what you were saying or someone who was indifferent and kept interrupting?

In this modern society, listening has become increasingly difficult with us constantly multi-listening to the barrage of noise around us. I now make a point of listening with my eyes. When I am listening to someone, I make sure I keep my eyes focused on him or her. Another skill I am working on is to listen for the message within the message.

By listening intently, I understand that most people are looking for encouragement and maybe answers or insights to the subject matter they are talking about. By listening in this manner, I am able to connect more effectively and in return, I have become a better communicator. In addition, when I listen I am learning. When I am speaking, I am not learning anything new. Maybe that is why we were designed with two ears and only one mouth?

366-Day Challenges

I have met a few people that have been involved in some really interesting 365-Day Challenges. I think this is a really interesting concept and it got me thinking of some things that I would like to do, which would have a positive impact on my life.

Obviously, the challenge is to perform a particular activity every single day for 365 days in a row with the objective of getting into a habit that will have a positive impact on my life and help me to develop. However, I have chosen to take this a day further so to encourage myself to continue on into the next year with these challenges to ensure that they are built into my life going forward and do not end abruptly on the anniversary of when they began.

"Challenges make you discover things about yourself that you never really knew. They're what make the instrument stretch—what make you go beyond the norm."
~ Cicely Tyson (Actress)

☑ **Stretch out my arms, legs, shoulders and back, every morning for a year.** *Stretching is the deliberate lengthening of muscles to facilitate an increase in muscle flexibility and joint range of motion. I have grown into the* habit of performing mild stretches and exercises of my major muscles and joints before breakfast each morning. I feel as if this does wonders for my body, realigning and rebalancing my body and mind and getting my blood pumping again as I start my day. I have noticed a vast improvement in my energy levels since I first started doing this a few years back

☑ **Spend 15 minutes meditating every day for 366 days.** *Put in the simplest of terms, meditation has allowed me to become a better, happier and healthier person. I find that the best time of day to meditate is early in the morning as it is the easiest time to quiet a restless mind. A state of deep mediation is more difficult for me to achieve once the day is in full flow and my mind becomes busy with all the hustle and bustle of daily life.*

☑ **Live without a phone for a year.** *I rarely go anywhere without a Nokia device these days, as I primarily use it as a camera and it provides me with so many other great technologies if I need them. However, it is the actual telephone part that I can easily do without. After spending most of the last few years being non-contactable by phone, I was shocked by what a nuisance it can be when I got back to Ireland.*

Telephones are very intrusive and no matter what someone is doing they will stop to answer the phone, even if they do not know who is calling. It is

Swim in the sea everyday for a year

really all the other technologies that come with mobile phones these days that make them so appealing. I use the 'flight mode' option as much as possible. I highly recommend it.

☑ **Log my thoughts of the day in a journal, every day for a year.** *I did this a few years ago and I have not yet went back and read over my thoughts from that year. It will make for very interesting reading to find out how I was as a person then, what my dreams were for the future, what I have achieved and, most importantly, how I have developed since then.*

☐ **Spend 15 minutes every morning giving gratitude for everything in my life.**

☐ **Save €5 every day for 366 days and at the end of the year spend the resulting €1,830 on one new thing that I should not really spend €1,830 on.**

☐ **Go 366 days without alcohol.** *One of the great things about Ireland is also the single worst thing about Ireland: alcohol. It is at the centre of everything. When a child is born, everyone goes out to get drunk in celebration. When the child is christened, everyone goes out to get drunk in celebration. When the child makes its First Holy Communion, everyone goes out to get drunk in celebration. It continues on like this for confirmations, graduations, engagements, weddings and birthdays and goes on and on as a way of marking every social occasion in a persons life right up until they die, when of course everyone goes out to get drunk in celebration of the persons life.*

This does not even take into consideration the alcohol that is consumed every Friday and Saturday night as well as the odd Thursday and Sunday night. Of course, the pubs and clubs are also packed Monday, Tuesday and Wednesday with students, who eventually go on to get married and have their own babies and so the circle continues. As anyone that has ever been to a big Irish occasion or simply on a night out in a local pub in Ireland will confess, it is great craic and nobody on the planet throws a party like the Irish.

Now, imagine an Irish man living in Ireland that did not drink alcohol—shocking stuff! Now imagine that he give it up, not because he was an alcoholic and 'went off it' but he simply made the choice not to drink anymore. Well that is where I am currently at. On my last birthday, which at the time of writing was just over a month ago, I decided that I was not going to let even a sip of alcohol pass my lips until the day after my next birthday. Already, I am astounded as to how many references there has been to 'going out for a drink' with someone or another and the look of confusion on their faces when I tell them that I am off it for a year.

Not drinking alcohol is the 'Irish Leprosy'. It is probably worse. I half expect to have a bell chained around my neck and for people to shout "Unclean, Unclean" as I walk down the street. I can just imagine the people down the pub talking about me and saying, "well at least a Leper would come into the pub for a pint when offered." Already, peoples reactions to the fact that I will not be drinking alcohol for a year, has made this so much fun and makes me more determined to follow this

through. This is going to be great craic, in itself.

☐ **Swim in the sea every day for a year, no matter how cold it is outside.** *I was reading recently that swimming in cold water boosts the immune system, burns calories, provides an all-natural high, gets the blood pumping and improves sex life. This would not be a bad way to start each day.*

To help you achieve your 'Life is' 366 Day Challenge I have designed the, fantastically named, 'Life is 366 Challenge' sheet especially for you. Each and everyday when you achieve your goal you can tick the sheet, which will allow you to keep track of your progress and maintain your motivation. This will help to spur you on to achieve your goals.

Go to www.theisbook.com and print out your 'Life is 366 Challenge' sheet now.

Contributions

"At the end of our lives, we will not be judged by how many diplomas we have received, how much money we have made or how many great things we have done. We will be judged by 'I was hungry and you gave me to eat. I was naked and you clothed me. I was homeless and you took me in.'"

~ Mother Teresa (Social activist)

☑ **Distribute supplies of food and clothing to the homeless during the winter.** *My parents taught me that I would only get out of life what I am willing to put in. Thus, if I can make a positive impact in the life of someone else, then this will make a positive impact in my life. At the time of writing a recession is strangling the world, with people everywhere suffering as a result. On a daily basis people that once held steady employment are being forced out of their homes to live on the street through no fault of their own. This could be any of us. By helping the homeless, I am doing something that is greater than me, as this act will help another person to feel better and suffer less. This was an extremely rewarding experience and one that I will continue to fulfil.*

☑ **Donate a full wardrobe of clothes to charity.** *This was as liberating for me as it was rewarding for the people that I helped.*

☑ **Break a Guinness World Record for a good cause.** *Longest ride on a fair ground/Theme Park attraction. We rode a Ferris wheel non-stop for 24 hours 30 minutes starting at 10:00am on 22 October 2011 at The Point Village, Dublin, Ireland. The attempt was in aid of the Bone Marrow for Leukaemia Trust. The great people at Nokia sponsored me €2,500 to complete the challenge, which I know was desperately needed and was well spent by the charity.*

☐ **Volunteer at a soup kitchen for the homeless.**

☐ **Volunteer my time at an animal shelter.**

☐ **Sponsor someone from a disadvantaged background to gain the education of his or her dreams.**

☐ **Fly out and help on the ground at a disaster relief effort.**

☐ **Set up the '*is foundation*' and donate €1 million to good causes.**

☐ **Decide that I am satisfied with the money I have and give everything else that comes after to good causes.**

☐ **Do something that can change a person's life for the better.** *In the city centre of Dublin I had walked past this homeless lad a few times until one bitterly cold Sunday morning I finally stopped to talk. I had stopped to talk to many people*

Break a Guinness World Record

that morning as I walked around the city taking phoneographs. It was sympathy combined with it being the first really cold day of the winter that caused me to stop. I asked him about his life and what had happened that he had ended up on the streets begging.

His story was that he was living with his French fiancé in Paris, managing a chain of Irish Pub's and life was perfect. It got even better when they had a beautiful healthy little baby girl. He was living the life of his dreams. However, life took a turn for the worse when his baby daughter was a few months old and he found her dead in her cot one morning. She had suffered from cot death and had died during the night. There was nothing he could do about it.

This pushed his life off the rails. He started drinking heavily and it eventually got to the point that his fiancé called his parents and told them to collect him and bring him back to Ireland, which they did. After some time in a psychiatric hospital, he discharged himself as the drugs they were giving him made him feel like he was losing his mind. After discharging himself against his parents wishes, he eventually found himself sleeping rough on the streets of Dublin. A tragic tale by any standard. After he had told his story, we talked about life in general and as I left to go on my way, I shook his hand and wished him better luck in the future.

About 50 metres up from where he sat there was a shop selling tea and coffee for €1. With it being a really cold morning, I decided to go in and buy each of us a cup of tea to warm us up. Whilst I was in there I noticed that the Euromillions lottery had a jackpot of €30 million for the next draw. It was then that I decided that if this lad, who looked to be still in his twenties, was due a bit of luck then this may be it. I purchased a ticket for each of us and with that went back to where he was with the tea and the lottery tickets.

His eyes lit up when I handed him the tea and he was genuinely grateful. Then I pulled the two lottery tickets out of my back pocket, held them up and told him to choose one. He excitedly choose the one from my left hand and as he looked at the numbers he animatedly stated, "It's got my birthday on it" before hurriedly planting it into the inside pocket of his ripped jacket for safekeeping. I could see in his darting eyes that his mind was elsewhere; maybe imagining the possibilities of what a big win could bring to him. Then with his attention somewhere else, I once again wished him the best of luck in life and went on my way.

On the Wednesday after our meeting I learned that the €30 million jackpot had been won in Ireland. I wondered whether one of the tickets that I had purchased on that cold Sunday morning could be the winning ticket. I checked mine and I found that I had not won anything. So, with that I wondered if the Gods had looked fondly upon *my homeless friend after a testing few years? Later that week I was close to where I had seen this lad hanging around many times before, so with curiosity I ventured over to see if he was there. He was nowhere to be seen!*

About four months have passed since I purchased that Euromillions ticket for him and, despite passing his 'spot' many times in that period, I have never seen him again. Now, I do not know if he won it or not and I am not saying that he has. There are 30 million explanations as to where this guy could be, but maybe... just maybe... he did. Here is hoping!

Seeing Hands

Just Because

There are some experiences available to us in this world that, for no reason in particular, I would just love to accomplish. They are not necessarily life-changing experiences, but for one reason or another they have resonated at my level and I know that they would enhance my life in one way or another.

"Live as if you were to die tomorrow. Learn as if you were to live forever."
~ Mohandas Gandhi
(Political and ideological leader of India)

☑ **Fire walk barefoot over a bed of hot embers.** *Fire walking is the practice of walking barefoot across a bed of burning coals without being burned. I will forever remember the heat on my face as I stood back from the raging fire as the organisers stoked it to get it up to the required heat of 1,234 degrees Celsius—a number I will never forget. I did not know much about the science behind fire walking until I arrived at the event. In the hour before the walk, I learned that fire walking is designed to help transform fear in order to inspire people to achieve goals they did not think they could.*

The single most harmful force preventing people from achieving their dreams is fear. Fear is the great

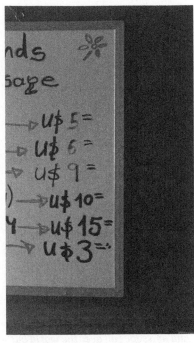

event experiencing a huge mind-shift, but I used this experience to build on other areas of my life were I needed to overcome limiting beliefs.

☑ **Make a rap video.** *This was great fun. As we were driving through Uganda, we pulled out the cameras and re-made 'Jesus Walks' by Kanye West. Check it out on www. theisbook.com/fun-blog if you want to have a few minutes laugh. (For your information, I am the bearded 'rapper').*

☑ **Dump my TV and never buy another.** *The biggest challenge we face in achieving the life of our dreams is overcoming the distractions of life. There is always something to watch on television or a chore we need to complete that is preventing us from discovering who we are. It is relentless. I decided that the first thing I needed to do to make my life better was to dump my television. I knew that the television was the one thing holding me back more than anything else.*

Giving up watching television has been the number one factor in allowing me to tick off the majority of the objectives in this book, achieve so much and live through so many of life's great experiences. Nothing is holding you back more from attracting your dreams than watching television.

☑ **Become a minimalist, whittling my belongings down to 99 items.** *'Stuff' is heavy and tiring. The less 'stuff' we have the*

blockade to success and achievement and it can only be overcome by confronting it. There is no better manner in which to transcend fear than choosing the thing that causes the most fear and then overcoming it. Thus, the reason fire walking is so successful at helping overcome fear is that participants learn that their limitations are not inherent to their nature, but rather the result of self-limiting beliefs.

It certainly worked for me. After walking across red hot embers and coming out the other side with nothing but black ash under my feet I came to the conclusion that there is more to this 'reality' than I previously understood. I am not saying that I came away from the freer we feel. Now, I prefer to spend my money accumulating great experiences that add to me as a person, only purchasing 'stuff' that I deem essential.

☑ **Feature in a Mardi Gras parade.** *Whilst living in Sydney, I was fortunate enough to live on Oxford St., the area were all the gay people of the city come out to party. Incidentally, it was also the starting location of the annual LGBTQI Mardi Gras parade. It was through a friend of a friend that we managed to get on one of the parade floats, dressed as 'Thunder Bags'.*

What this consisted of, was dressing in a blue Thunderbirds costume and dancing inside a massive handbag. We even had a special, very-gay, dance routine that we had to act out as we made our way past thousands of screaming gays over a 1.7 kilometre path through the Sydney CBD and Darlinghurst. A real eye opener, yet an unforgettable experience. Gay for a day!

At the time, I was working as an accountant at a very reputable company and I was sort of hoping that no one from work would notice me. However, when I got home after the parade I had a large number of text messages on my phone reporting that my face was being flashed up on all the major news stations as they reported on the Mardi Gras events in the city. In addition to that, the news report had been put up on Facebook within minutes of it being aired, with me

'tagged' in it. I got some funny looks in work on the Monday morning.

☑ **Have a 'Dr. Fish' pedicure.** *This is when hundreds of small live fish eat the dead skin off your feet, thus giving your feet a pedicure. It is screamingly funny, due to the fish tickling the soles of my feet. I had it done in Cambodia and it cost $1 for 30 minutes and that included a beer and a head and shoulder massage as we sat with our feet in the tank. Bargain of the century.*

☑ **Receive a 'Seeing Hands' massage from blind people.** *Seeing Hands has been set up to provide training and employment opportunities in massage therapy for young blind people in various locations around the world. I have had massages all over the world but for me the Seeing Hands massage was the best. The masseuses are all visually impaired, but are highly trained at their craft with a minimum of 100 hours spent in clinical practice.*

It is hard to explain why their technique is superior, but in my opinion, they just seem to have an instinctive ability to create pressure and apply rhythm in the areas that require it most. The eventual aim of the Seeing Hands projects is to evolve into a self-sustaining social enterprise, run by the blind, for the benefit of the blind.

☑ **Take the mercury fillings out of my teeth.** *Hundreds of studies over the years have shown* a clear link between mercury amalgam fillings ("silver fillings") and disastrous neurological effects in the human body. As a child, I had mercury fillings inserted, as my parents simply trusted the professionals. To this day parents are still told that mercury poses no health threat whatsoever and it is still inserted into the mouths of children. This is despite it being one of the most toxic heavy metals known to modern science.

Quite bizarrely, the history of the term "as mad as a hatter" is linked to 'hatter's' that worked with mercury in the process of curing felt used in some hats. It was very difficult for hatters to avoid inhaling the mercury fumes given off during the hat making process. As a result, the hatter's and others that worked in the mills, died at an early age due to the residual mercury that caused neurological damage, distorted vision and confused speech. As the mercury poisoning progressed to dangerously high levels, sufferers began to experience psychotic symptoms such as hallucinations. It was a result of this that when a person was seen to be acting insane, they were deemed to be "as mad as a hatter."

Mercury has been linked to several neurological disorders including Alzheimer's, autism, multiple sclerosis, Parkinson's disease and others. I have now removed as much of this poison from my mouth as possible.

☑ **Attend Spring Break in Cancun, Mexico.** *Also known as "American kids gone wild". Depending on your age and energy levels this is either your definition of heaven or hell. Families tend to avoid this holiday paradise around this time every year as university students from the USA and Canada flood in to let their hair down... as well as their swim shorts and bikinis. The whole town turns into one big crazy party as the kids try to out-do the antics of their older brothers and sisters in previous years. Everything goes.*

Also, without knowing that it existed I ended up in the middle of the Australian version of 'Spring Break' in Bali. Known as "Schoolies", this is party time for a younger crowd, who are celebrating graduating from school and despite drinking more alcohol than they could handle they were not as wild as those on Spring Break in Mexico.

☐ **Walk barefoot over a path of freshly broken glass.** *For one reason or another people fear the 'glass walk' more than the 'fire walk', which seems strange to me. My approach is that if I can do one then I can do the other. The difference between the two is that the glass walk requires total focus and the steps are taken very slowly and deliberately, whilst the fire walk is based on confidence and is briskly strolled across.*

When we manage to fully concentrate on an experience

and prevent any part of our mind from wandering, then something spectacular can happen, as we can become the experience itself. Walking barefoot on razor-sharp pieces of broken glass may seem as an extreme way in which to reach this 'isness'. However, this zen-esque practice can help us to become completely present in many daily challenges. Focusing our minds on a single moment, allows us to achieve things we once thought impossible. That is the lesson to be learned here.

☐ **Hand out €20 notes to complete strangers on a wet Tuesday morning in January.**

☐ **Learn sign language.**

☐ **Throw a party inviting everyone I know, with the instruction for them to invite everyone they know, with all drinks on me.**

☐ **Experience the sensation of weightlessness.**

☐ **Be an audience member at the 'Late Late Show', Dublin.** *Have you ever wondered what celebrities have to say about the week's hot topic? ... Me neither! Although on this show, the worlds longest running chat show, they do have great giveaways for "everyone in the audience" and I would really like to be apart of that.*

☐ **Watch every movie that has won the Oscar for 'Best Picture'.**

☐ **Learn to sculpt from marble.**

☐ **Represent my country.** *Due to the peculiar circumstances that surround the location of my birth, I have as good a chance of achieving this as most other people on the planet, simply because I qualify to represent three regions: Northern Ireland, the United Kingdom and the Republic of Ireland. It is all due to the messed up politics that provides citizens of Northern Ireland with duel citizenship of both the United Kingdom and the Republic of Ireland. The one time that I have been involved in something that represented one of these regions was when I contributed in a small way to Irelands entrant for the Eurovision song contest in 2013.*

My good friend Wez Devine wrote and produced the song 'Only Love Survives' which was performed by another friend, Ryan Dolan in the competition. My involvement consisted of using my Nokia to record people from around the world making a heart shape with their hands and saying, "Be love" into the camera for the music video. I cannot really take much credit for the success that Wez Devine and Ryan Dolan had with the song but as the video was being played on repeat across Europe during the build up to the competition I have to admit that I did feel a sense of pride for my small contribution. Lets hope that I can make a more significant contribution in the future.

In the End

"Stay true to yourself no matter who or what may try to stop you from doing so. Being you is the greatest gift you can give yourself and others!"

~ Unknown

It is important for me to always be a first-class version of myself, rather than a second-class version of somebody else. I must be true to myself at all times as a day spent trying be liked by another person or 'fit in' to a group is a long and draining day. I know that my true self is good enough for any situation that I find myself in, so I must remain true to that and never attempt to emulate anyone else. I must value everything that I am and the gifts that I have been blessed with so that when the end comes, I can look back and say...

☑ I am happy.

☑ I said what I needed to say.

☑ I know how it feels to give and receive true love.

☑ I forgave those who upset me.

☑ I followed my heart.

☑ I am filled with gratitude for all that I have.

The Backpacker who sold his Supercar

☑ I stood alone when required.

☑ I am proud of the person I am.

☑ I have been truthful with myself.

☑ I have taken full responsibility for my life.

☐ I did what I needed to do.

☐ I made the most of my life.

☐ I became the best version of me.

Continuous Objectives

Living a long and happy life is something that we all wish for. Up until recently, it was believed that those that lived to be more than 100 years old did so due to their genetics. However, we now know that this is not the case. Research in a population of adults aged between 95 and 107 by the Albert Einstein College of Medicine, New York has found that two personality traits held the key to a long and happy life:

- a positive attitude (optimistic, easygoing, happy, outgoing) and;

- emotional expression (not bottling up emotions but expressing them openly).

Before learning this, I had not connected a long life to being happy, but now it seems almost commonsensical. Of course, being positive and sharing our emotions will contribute to a happy and healthy life. So why do we not do it? Well it all comes down to vigilance. To live a long life that is filled with health and happiness requires us to ensure that we are constantly on the look out for opportunities that make us feel good whilst allowing us to express who we truly are.

As a result, I have come up with a number of opportunities that I am constantly on the look out for. In a way, they are goals that I attempt to reach on a daily basis. These are goals that encourage me to be vigilant of ways in which I can be of assistance to those around me when I am out in public.

Due to the ongoing nature of these goals, I will never be able to tick

I stood alone when required

them off, as every new day I will have the opportunity to be of assistance once again. Through showing a positive attitude to others, we can develop our emotional expression and go on to live long and happy lives. Through helping others, we help ourselves.

Kindness

"Compassion and tolerance are not a sign of weakness, but a sign of strength."
~ Dalai Lama (Tibetan Buddhist)

☐ Give up my seat to someone on the bus or tram at every opportunity.

☐ Over-deliver on promises and obligations.

☐ When I hear someone say something nice about a person I know, be sure to pass it on to him or her.

☐ Share my umbrella on a rainy day.

☐ Pay for the person behind me in a shop at least once a week.

☐ Give without expecting to get back.

☐ Send a text message, letter or email at random times when I know people will appreciate it most.

☐ Go out of my way to wish people a happy birthday.

☐ Help the shopper in front of me that needs an extra few cents to avoid breaking a large note.

☐ Remember that *"If I admire somebody then I should go ahead and tell them, because people rarely get the flowers when they can still smell them."*

☐ Donate 10 percent of my monthly income to good causes and great efforts.

☐ When groups of friends or a loving couple are taking a photograph, offer to take the picture for them.

☐ Give someone a copy of a book that helped me, if I think it may help him or her.

☐ Become a mentor for students having difficulties with accounting exams.

Mindfulness

"Mindfulness is simply being aware of what is happening right now without wishing it were different; enjoying the pleasant without holding on when it changes (which it will); being with the unpleasant without fearing it will always be this way (which it won't)."

~ James Baraz (Author and Buddhist teacher)

☐ Make an effort to remember people's names and mention it when I talk to them.

☐ Appreciate people the way they are.

☐ Think, speak and act in a loving manner.

☐ Say "Please" and "Thank you" (in the person's native tongue when possible).

☐ Forgive people. No matter what.

☐ Listen intently to people's stories, maintain eye contact and not try to fix everything.

☐ Stand-alone and be separate from the crowd when needs be.

☐ Never gossip. Ever.

☐ Observe everyone without judgment.

Eleanor

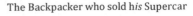

☐ **Replace what I have used.**

☐ **Accept people just the way they are.**

☐ **Be more like Eleanor.** *Whilst staying in a hostel in the Norwegian Arctic I was organising my towel and shorts to complete my dream of going for a swim in the Arctic Ocean. As I was just about to leave, an elderly woman entered the dorm and with a massive smile on her face she bounded up to me and said, "Hi, I am Eleanor." We got talking about the usual backpacker topics such as where we had been and what we planned to do that day. I told her "I am just about to leave to go swim in the Arctic waters." With this, she excitedly responded, "Would you*

mind if I came with you? I have my swim suit with me!"

As we walked to the seaside Eleanor regaled me with tales of her late husband and her adult children and what they had brought to her life. She also told me that she was 83 years old. As she continued to talk, all I could think was, "How many 83 year old women do I know that would take the train to the Arctic and bring a swimsuit with them 'just in case' they fancied a swim?"

Upon reaching the water, she stripped off behind her towel, got into her swimsuit and made her way to the water straight away. The cold water was no barrier to her enjoying her swim. Her willingness was such that after our first swim in they icy waters, she encouraged me to go back in for a second swim, as "it would not be as cold the second time."

This woman had such a zest for life and an energy and enthusiasm for everything that this world had to offer. She would stop to smell any flower we came across and she would "OOhhh" and "AAhhh" at the wonderful nature around us. Being in her presence, I was alarmed at how much I had taken the beauty of this world for granted. As I ate my dinner that night, I vowed that I would become more like Eleanor.

Next day I was to leave Norway by train, heading towards Singapore, with my first stop being in northern

Sweden. Just as the train was about to depart, Eleanor boarded without a care in the world and with that same big smile on her face. I noticed that she had a small bag with her as she sat down across from me. After some pleasantries, she told me how she had noticed some beautiful fjords as she studied her map of the region that morning. The fjords were deep in the Arctic Mountains and after some research, she learned that she would not have sufficient time to explore the fjords and make the last train back. So, she decided that she would bring what she needed for the night and just stay up there, sleeping rough, getting the train back the following day.

As the train crept towards her destination Eleanor told me about her life and experiences. She would often stop midsentence to point out the scenery or a bird or something of beauty that had caught her eye. It was usually something that I had taken for granted. Soon there were eight people sitting and standing around her, listening without saying a word, as she talked. She was the embodiment of the fact that 'active is attractive'. What she said was simple, yet it was full of knowledge and insights. As she talked her gaze remained fixed on the beauty unfurling outside the window.

In a very isolated area close to the Swedish border, the train came to a halt and the conductor came in and informed Eleanor that this was her stop. With this, she bounded over and grabbed her bag. Without a word, she enthusiastically ran to the door of the train and walked back up to where the train had just come from and out of sight. I went to the door of the train and watched her as she walked. She never looked back. I do not think she ever did.

This wonderful 83 year old German woman has a zest for life and an enthusiasm for all that this beautiful world offers. The traditional barriers and boundaries do not come into it; she focuses on the objective and the fun she will have achieving that objective. She maintains a deep appreciation for all that is in her life and she lives with an energy and enthusiasm that I have never before been witness to. I want to be more like Eleanor.

Self-Awareness

"If your emotional abilities aren't in hand, if you don't have self-awareness, if you are not able to manage your distressing emotions, if you can't have empathy and have effective relationships, then no matter how smart you are, you are not going to get very far."
~ Daniel Goleman (Author and psychologist)

☐ Greed, anger and ignorance: avoid all three at all times.

☐ Stand up for what I believe in without forcing my beliefs on others.

☐ Listen to my heart and blank out the chatter in my head.

☐ Say the words *"This is the life"* at least once a day.

☐ Increase my levels of empathy and compassion for other people.

☐ Use all the manners that my parents taught me as a child.

☐ Speak the truth. Avoid even white lies, no matter the situation.

☐ Remember that non-judgment, gratitude and forgiveness are the secret to a prosperous life.

☐ Understand that attachment is at the root of unhappiness.

☐ Think well of myself and believe in myself with all of my heart.

☐ Cry when I feel like it. Both tears of joy and tears of sorrow.

☐ Never use age as an excuse.

☐ Spend so much time improving myself that I have no time remaining to criticise others.

☐ Cultivate a mantra that strengthens and empowers me.

The word mantra is derived from two words: man, which is the Sanskrit for "mind"; and tra, meaning "instrument". Thus, a mantra is an "instrument of the mind", which produces a powerful vibration or sound. This instrument gets its power through a series of words containing certain energy that are repeated over and over. The more a mantra is repeated, the more powerful it becomes. The mantra that I have developed and built into my life is as follows:

"I am whole. I am perfect. I am strong. I am powerful. I am loving. I am harmonious. I am happy. I am perfectly healthy. I am abundantly wealthy. I am filled with love."

I have developed this mantra from many different sources, taking parts from other mantras and blending them into my own. I say my mantra first thing in the morning, last thing at night and every time I am walking up and down steps. In all honesty, when I started this mantra I did not really believe that I was 'powerful, 'filled with love' et cetera, but within a few months I truly did. A mantra is a powerful tool that we can all easily carry and something that I would highly recommend developing.

Community Spirit

"Too often we underestimate the power of a touch, a smile, a kind word, a listening ear, an honest compliment, or the smallest act of caring, all of which have the potential to turn a life around."
~ Leo Buscaglia (Author and motivational speaker)

☐ **Park my car further from the entrance, walking the extra distance to help free up the closer spots for people who may need them more.**

☐ **Never pass by a person standing looking at a map without offering directions.**

☐ **Ask people for their opinion or advice.**

☐ **Be courteous when driving by letting people merge in front of me.**

☐ **Donate blood.**

☐ **Let a person with only a few items cut the line at the supermarket.**

☐ **Wave to neighbours and check up on them if they look lonely.**

☐ **Smile when making eye contact with strangers and be approachable to all.**

☐ Introduce myself to one new person every day and talk to strangers as much as possible.

☐ Stand up for and lend a voice to the neglected and the powerless in this world.

☐ Support independent local artists by purchasing books, albums and artwork that has not yet made it to the mainstream.

☐ Hold the door open for the person behind me.

☐ Send e-mails of appreciation to business owners.

☐ Stop to help when someone has pulled over with a flat tyre, or is in need of some assistance.

☐ Compliment strangers on their appearance to boost their morale.

Positivity

"Keep your thoughts positive because your thoughts become your words. Keep your words positive because your words become your behaviour. Keep your behaviour positive because your behaviour becomes your habits. Keep your habits positive because your habits become your values. Keep your values positive because your values become your destiny."

~ Mohandas Gandhi
(Political and ideological leader of India)

☐ Encourage people to follow their dream, no matter how big, small or crazy it is.

☐ Wear a cheerful expression at all times.

☐ Encourage health, happiness and prosperity in every person I meet.

☐ Live each moment with enthusiasm and be enthusiastic about all successes.

☐ Contribute time, ideas and a listening ear to other people's passions.

☐ Expect and accept only the best that life has to offer.

☐ Forget mistakes and push on towards greater achievements in the future.

☐ Be optimistic and look at the sunny side of everything.

☐ See the world as I wish it to be.

☐ Treat every small interaction with other people as an opportunity to make a positive impact in both our lives.

☐ Maintain such strength that nothing can disturb my sense of wellbeing.

☐ Live in the belief that the universe will always be on my side as long as I follow my heart.

☐ Set a positive example and only spread good news.

☐ Keep dreaming.

☐ Make a difference.

☑ **Be myself.**

Concluding Thoughts

"I would like to say to the diligent reader of my writings and to others who are interested in them that I am not at all concerned with appearing to be consistent. In my search after Truth I have discarded many ideas and learnt many new things . . . What I am concerned with is my readiness to obey the call of Truth, my God, from moment to moment, and therefore, when anybody finds any inconsistency between any two writings of mine, if he still has any faith in my sanity, he would do well to choose the later of the two on the same subject."

~ Mohandas Gandhi
(Political and ideological leader of India)

We often ask ourselves, "What is life all about?" By reading through this book you will have gained an understanding of what my life is all about and where my focus is. As you look back over the objectives that I have completed and all the experiences that I have lived through it may seem like a lot, but it really all unfolded as part of the flow of life. It all derived from a simple choice that I made as a sixteen year old and it gained momentum.

I was a dreamer and I wanted to live the life of my dreams. I find myself in some great company because every great leader and innovator, from the dawn of civilisation until today, was a dreamer. The world has always cried out for pragmatic dreamers who can put the wheels in motion to see their dreams come to fruition. Dreamers always have and always will be the shapers of our world.

The recession that is now gripping the world as a result of the 'credit crunch' brings with it an opportunity we have not seen in this modern world. Gone are the levels of self-indulgence, greed and arrogance, replaced by patience, humility and community spirit. This, combined with the global village that we are now part of, provides us all with the opportunity to go where we want to go, be who we want to be, experience all we desire and live the life of our dreams. The dreams of dreamers have never been more accessible.

Henry David Thoreau said it best when he declared, *"Do not lose hold of your dreams or aspirations. For if you do, you may still exist but you have ceased to live."* Therefore, if you believe in your dreams and they feel right, then go ahead and follow them. Kindle in your mind the fire of courage, hope and trust that you need to realise your dreams. Write them on a piece of paper, declare them on Facebook, scream them from the rooftops if you must, but do not let anyone dump on your dreams.

Discouragement will come, I can assure you of that. You will also be faced with temporary defeat on the way to achieving your dreams. That is a certainty, but ignore your *'I-told-you-so'* 'frenemies' for they have not yet come to know that in every failure is the seed of an equivalent success.

When I look back on my life so far, I liken it to sitting on a boat in the middle of the ocean just drifting with the tide, not really going anywhere. I made a choice to go in a certain direction and by doing this, I raised my sails and the winds carried me towards my dreams. No doubt, I have come across a number of tidal waves along the way and a few storms are still to come, but with my sail up, I have come a long way and I am still moving in the right direction. Once I came to understand that persistence is the enemy of failure, I started to see results.

What I hope that you will take away from this book is that your life, your success, what you become and where you ultimately end up are all under your control if you can raise your own sail. Our current circumstances are the result of our past decisions and whether they are good, bad or ugly, we are individually responsible, no one else.

Maria Robinson said it best when she declared, *"Nobody can go back and start a new beginning, but anyone can start today and make a new ending."* Everything that I have achieved began with *The Carrot, The Ladder* and *The Pencil* and my decision to aim for my dream life. I made that choice and I now hope that you will make a similar choice using the same method I did.

I used *The Carrot* to clarify in my mind what my dreams were, giving me something to aim for. *The Ladder* provided me with the means to lift myself out from the life I had, into a better way of living. *The Pencil* helped provide clarity and focus, through writing down my objectives, thus making it easier for me to maintain motivation and self-discipline.

When I had my goals written down, it gave me something to work towards, knowing that the benefits would all accrue to me. No longer did I complete my homework because the teacher said that I had to. No longer did I put in that extra bit of effort in work just to impress my manager. I did it because I knew that all the energy and effort I spent on even the most simple of tasks was for my benefit and advancement. It was all for *my* greater good.

Patrick Hamilton Walsh

What Really Matters

As I write the concluding paragraphs to this book, seventeen years after it all started, I have enhanced clarity regarding what really matters to me. Out of all the items that I have mentioned in this book, I now realise that the first and last objectives that I listed are the only ones that really matter: *'Find true love'* and *'Be myself'*.

It was John Lennon and The Beatles that gave us the best advice in the simplest of terms when they said, *"All you need is love."* Love is easily life's greatest experience. No force is greater. Indeed, no force is a greater motivator than love and its pursuit. This is as true today as it was with the primitive people of prehistoric times, when the hunter would go off in search of animals for food and warmth in order to impress his woman. In turn, she would prepare what he had brought home to the best of her ability to impress him.

Today it is not skins or animals that we desire to bring home, but large salaries, prestigious cars and designer clothes. Love is the primary motivator behind all great deeds. People that have attained great fame, accumulated large fortunes and achieved immense power have done so, primarily, to fulfil their desire for love. If this sounds like nonsense, then consider what all of our achievements would be worth if we had no loved-ones with whom to share them with?

In order to find true love, the most important thing for me was to just *be myself*. It was so important that I let the world see the true me and I had to stand strong in the belief that the best of what was in me was good enough. I need to be who I am and what I am, staying true to the essence of my very being. It was only through being myself that I found the woman of my dreams on the other side of the world.

However, the paradox of obtaining our dreams is that what we want from life is progression. No matter what we have achieved we all want to move forward. We are programmed to create and progress from one circumstance to the next. Once we achieve something or overcome a challenge, we will bask in the glory of it for a short time before something else captures our imagination.

This is why being alive today is so good. There is so much to do and achieve and aim for. Progression is a great thing, it is healthy for the mind and for the body as it gives us a reason to get up in the morning, to push our boundaries and attempt new things. Our world is pregnant with the desire to advance.

To have found that special person in my life makes it all the better. Love is the foundation upon which all obstacles can be overcome. Aim for this as your main objective and give up caring what other people think about you. Do what you need to do to get back to being yourself and from that basis build the life of your dreams.

Recognise whom it is that makes you feel happy and spend more time around those people. Decide what activities bring you joy and spend more time doing them. Living the life of our dreams is based on the decisions we make and is ultimately just a state of mind. It is simply being at ease with who we are and understanding that, despite our progress, where we are now is exactly where we need to be.

Thus, being myself is simply the satisfying blend of loving myself, loving where I am, loving what I do and loving whom I am with. Because when my thoughts, my words and my actions are all in harmony then that is when I am truly being myself and I can then use this as the springboard to go on and live the life of my dreams.

That is the *isness* of life.

For more information check out my websites:
>www.PatrickHamiltonWalsh.com
>www.theisbook.com
>www.thephoneographer.org

Twitter:
>*Follow me*
>@theISbook
>@PatrickHWalsh
>@ThePhoneographr

Facebook:
>*Subscribe to me*
>– Patrick Hamilton Walsh

>*Like my pages*
>– Patrick Hamilton Walsh
>– The Backpacker who sold his Supercar
>– Life is
>– IS book
>– The Phoneographer
>– Active is Attractive

>*Join my groups*
>– is: Nothing but a Nokia
>– is: The Phenomenon of the Facebook Status

Couchsurf:
>– Patrick Hamilton Walsh

Vimeo:
>– www.vimeo.com/ThePhoneographer

YouTube:
>*Subscribe*
>– www.YouTube.com/PatrickHamiltonWalsh
>– www.YouTube.com/ThePhoneographer

Also, if you wish to tell me about any great experiences that you have had or any that you think I would be interested in, then please get in touch, as I would love to hear your stories, interests and feedback. If you wish to contact me for any reason then please mail me at:

patrick@theisbook.com

Through looking into the experiences that I have lived and the achievements I dream of for my future, you will have built up a picture as to the type of person I am. You will also realise that one mans treasure is another mans trash. The wonderful thing about this world is that we all desire different experiences. We are all on very different paths through life and we all have very different dreams and ambitions.

I have achieved everything that I have simply because I have taken the time to look within. I asked myself two very simple questions and the answers that I received have lead me to achieving nearly everything that I have ever dreamed of and more. By answering those two simple questions I got to find out who I was and got to know myself better.

I attribute the simple action of looking within as being the solid foundation from which I could go on to build the life that I dreamed of. Knowing myself has been the foundation of my wisdom. Pushing myself has been the foundation of my success. Being myself has been the foundation of my happiness.

Now I invite you to take *The Carrot, The Ladder* and *The Pencil* approach to your own life. It is never too late to make changes, no matter the current situation. To help with this I have released the follow up book '*My Life is*' to enable you to live the life of your dreams.

For those interested in following an approach similar to mine, '*My Life is*' is an incredibly powerful tool that you can use to aim towards achieving the life experiences that you wish to live, using a similar structure to mine. In addition, I have filled it with insights and quotes to enable you to stay motivated as you move towards living the life of your dreams.

*"Life is an opportunity – benefit from it.
Life is beauty – admire it.
Life is a dream – realise it.
Life is a challenge – meet it.
Life is a duty – complete it.
Life is a game – play it.
Life is a promise – fulfil it.
Life is sorrow – overcome it.
Life is a song – sing it.
Life is a struggle – accept it.
Life is a tragedy – confront it.
Life is an adventure – dare it.
Life is luck – make it.
Life is too precious – do not destroy it.
Life is life – fight for it."*

~ Mother Teresa of Calcutta

The full colour 8" x 8" version of this book
is now available for purchase
under the title, *'Life is'*.

Also available on eBook

To all the people that have accompanied me on this journey, made me laugh, told me their story and helped me out, I am humbled by your generosity of spirit and grateful for your wisdom. There are many thousands of people that I owe the contents of this book to and I want to say a massive thank you to each and every one of you, including:

Adam So, Adam Wilson, Adeola Obasa, Adolfo Luna, Aimee Harcos, Alan Kelly, Alan McGregor, Alanna & Michelle Major, Almery Tessarolo, Amy Frith, Amy & Ella Nibbs, Andreas Dahlgren, Andrew Armitage, Andy Giefer, Anthony Peake, Avegail & Matt Pitman, The Bandgren Family, Barry & Kelly O'Connor, Barry Wade, Blaize & Leanne Montgomery, Ben Jakobi, Betsy Hirsch, Bo Hoefs, Bobby Williamson, Brendan Bolles, Brendan Byrne, Brian & Sonja Pinnell, Bridget Molloy, Cam McFarlane, Camille Tuutti, Catherine Szulyk, Christian Greene, Christine Deneau, Christine DeLeon, Christine Grasso, Chris Feld, Chris Loftin, Chris & Lyndsey Warren, Ciaran Butler, Cody Land, Coffee Johnson, Colm Mackin, Conor McCauley, Dale Derrick, Dan & Charlene Patton, Daniel Dotterer, Daniel McClymont, Danilo Miravite, David McNulty, Dennis Lindberg Laursen, Dom & Luke Marrone, Dominika Wojciechowska, Duncan Jones, Edwin Surijah, Elina Strode, Elliot Gould, Emily Hogan, Emma Kearney, Emmett O'Neill, Ezequiel Peralta, Felicity Dalzell, Fred Richards, Gabriela Roa, Gaby Selby, Gary Halpin, Gary Maguire, Gemma Booth, Ghislain Denyse, Gielis Luc, Gordon Johnsen, Grace O'Malley, Graham Keogh, Grainne O'Kane, Gregg Burgess-Salisbury, The Hamilton Family, Iain Sheils, Inia James, James Piek, Janelle Connor, Jasmin Seiberth, Jean Taylor, Jeff & Lila Nagy, Jessica Stewart, Jimmy Jansson, Jo Reason, Joakim Jarpell, Johanna Bandgren, Joel Lahera, John & Melissa Tschohl, John Quinn, Johnny & Paddy Lalor, Jonas & Ole Bramserud, Jonathan Cowley, Jonathan Doyle, Jason Christison, Justin Caldwell, Karen & Brad Thomson, Karen Whelehan, Kayleigh Hinton, Keith Walsh, Kelvin Hotbaatar Mawer, Khalid Waseem, Kim Toland, Leighton James, Liz Cullen, Louis Rials, Louisa Dean, Luke Richmond, Marek Fuchs, Margaret-Anne Murphy, Mark Hucks, Marianne Van Der Heijden, Mark McCloskey, Mark Mungovan, Marloes Van Daatselaar, Mat Dry, Matthew Tanner, Max Leone, Maxime de Bruin, Mette Duelund Hedtoft, Micah Rivetti, Misha Teasdale, Morten Jensen, Natalie McLaren, Nelsy Batista, Niamh Walsh, Nicolas Gerardo, Olivier Guglielmi, Owen Fox, Patrick & Niamh O'Callaghan, Patrick Strake, Paul Walsh, Peter Rowley, Rachel Quigley, Richie Lambe, Rod Manalo, Robbie Andrews, Rose Soria, Rowan Pybus, Roxana Popescu, Salma Shamel, Samuel Oliveira, Sandra Egan McKenna, Scott Jennings, Seok-Min Song, Shaughna Whelan, Shawn Mansoff, Simon Cox, Simon Long, Spencer Healy, Stephen Vd Merwe, Stewart Pearce, Summer Wallbank, Susan Clince, Tal Neder, Tariq Batanoni, Taylor Pierce, Terry McGonigle, Tessandra Gabiniewicz, Tessa Ost, Therese Clarke, Tony & Shirley Lane, Tony Pikus, Tracey Walsh, Virgil Schaken, The Walsh Family, Wezley Devine, Yancy Davis, Yu Yen Huang, Zuzana Botkova…

…and You

The Beginning.

CPSIA information can be obtained at www.ICGtesting.com
Printed in the USA
LVOW04s1617161214

419118LV00018B/741/P

9 781490 717791